Service Design with Applications to Health Care Institutions

Service Design with Applications to Health Care Institutions

Óscar Barros

BEP BUSINESS EXPERT PRESS

Service Design with Applications to Health Care Institutions

Copyright © Business Expert Press, LLC, 2017.

First published in 2017 by
Business Expert Press, LLC
222 East 46th Street, New York, NY 10017
www.businessexpertpress.com

ISBN-13: 978-1-63157-570-9 (paperback)
ISBN-13: 978-1-63157-571-6 (e-book)

Business Expert Press Service Systems and Innovations in Business and Society Collection

Collection ISSN: 2326-2664 (print)
Collection ISSN: 2326-2699 (electronic)

Cover and interior design by Exeter Premedia Services Private Ltd., Chennai, India

First edition: 2017

10 9 8 7 6 5 4 3 2 1

Printed in the United States of America.

Abstract

This work presents an innovative approach to business design, known as Business Engineering, and its application to service offerings design in general and health services in particular. Such an approach is characterized by:

- Integrating many disciplines—Ontology, Strategy, Business Models, Modularization, Platform Design, Case Management, Business Processes, Business Intelligence, Information Systems, and IT—in generating detailed Enterprise Architecture designs for services, which are aligned with and make operational stakeholders' interests.
- Providing a hierarchical design methodology that allows managing the complexity of full enterprise design by starting with overall aggregated designs, which are then detailed by hierarchical decomposition.
- Basing designs on Business, Architecture, and Process Patterns that abstract and formalize the knowledge and experience generated from hundreds of business design cases in which the approach has been applied.
- Introducing advanced Analytics—for example, predictive and prescriptive data-based models, optimization techniques, and simulation—to support business development, by using models to generate new or improved service designs, and management by embedding models in operating process design; this allows generating truly Business Intelligence that optimize service performance.
- Using formal constructs to model patterns and designs based on the Business Process Management Notation (BPMN) notation, allowing simulation and eventual execution of the designs using Business Process Management Suits (BPMS) and Service Oriented Architecture (SOA) technology.

The book is a sequel to *Business Engineering and Service Design*, published by this editorial, which provides the foundations of Business

Engineering, reviews the several disciplines integrated within its methodology and presents plentiful evidence of its power by giving detailed real application cases, including very impressive results in private and public situations. This volume is dedicated to health care, presenting our view of the foundations for the design of institutions that provide such service, general architectures for making designs operative, and many real cases that show how to do formal design and the benefits to be obtained.

Keywords

Analytics, BPMN, BPMS, Business Design, Business Design Patterns, Business Engineering, Business Intelligence, Business Process Patterns, Enterprise Architecture Design, Health Care Architectures, Health Care Services Design, Service Design, Service Engineering, Service Processes Design

Contents

Acknowledgments

I want to recognize the continuous support I have received during my academic career at the Department of Industrial Engineering of the University of Chile. I have found a very good environment for my creative efforts in this academic unit, including the ideas of Business Engineering, theme of this book, and the Master in Business Engineering that I designed and implemented here.

I also wants to deeply thank the hundreds of students that have worked in my academic projects, several of them identified in the text when their work has been cited, in trying to put to test my ideas in the real world, which is what any engineering discipline should do. They have had a very positive disposition to test innovative proposals, providing the laboratory I needed to prove that they work. This testing would have been not possible without the collaboration of several private and public health care organizations that have been willing to act as research subjects; many thanks to all of them.

Prologue

For almost 20 years I have been working on the development of the foundations of what I call Business Engineering, with the aim of providing tools, as other engineering disciplines have, for the design of businesses. This effort has been directed to show that enterprises can be formally designed and that their architectures, including processes, personnel organization, information systems, IT infrastructure, and interactions with customers and suppliers should be considered in a systemic way in such design. This Enterprise Design is not a one-time effort, but, in the dynamic environment we face, organizations have to have the capability to continuously evaluate opportunities to improve their designs. Other researchers have recognized this need, as the ones who have worked under the idea of Enterprise Architecture (EA), but they have mostly concentrated on the technological architecture and just touched on the business design issues. Our work resulted, in 2003, in a graduate program of study, the Master in Business Engineering at the University of Chile,[1] which has been taken up by several hundreds of professionals. Such Master has been the laboratory where many of the ideas we propose have been tested and many new ones generated as generalization of the knowledge and experience generated by hundreds of projects developed in the theses required by this program.

I have published books (in Spanish and English) and papers (in English), all detailed in the references, that touch on different topics of my proposal. In this work I give a compact summary and show how my proposal can be applied to health care, based on work we have been doing in this domain for at least 15 years, where we have carried out research and development efforts by adapting our approach to provide working solutions for a large number of Chilean health institutions. These solutions are already implemented and showing that large increases in quality of service and efficiency in the use of resources can be attained.

Our approach includes the integrated design of a business, its service configuration (architectures) and capacity planning, the resource management processes, and the operating processes. Such an approach is based on general patterns that define service design options and analytical methods that make possible resource optimization to meet demand. This is complemented with technology that allows process execution with Business Process Management Notation (BPMN) and Business Process Management Suites (BPMS) tools and web services over a System Oriented Architecture (SOA). In summary, we integrate our business design approach with Analytics and supporting IT tools in giving a sound basis for service design.

General patterns provide reference models and general process structures, in given domains, as a starting point to design the processes for a particular case. The key idea is to formalize successful design knowledge and experience in these models, reuse such knowledge when designing, and avoid reinventing the wheel. Patterns are normative in that they include what it is recommended as best practices and the ones we have found that work in practice in hundreds of projects, as it has been remarked before. So they contain specific guidelines on how a process should be designed, allowing reuse of such patterns, thus avoiding to start from very expensive "as is" process documentation, proposed by methodologies such as Business Process Management (BPM).[2] It is our experience that "as is" documentation is very expensive, running into the millions of dollars for large organizations, and there is a low to medium probability that the effort ends in failure, because of killing of the project without any result whatsoever. This has been the case of two large government agencies in Chile, which spent more than one million dollars each on "as is" studies and eventually decided to terminate the projects because of lack of results, and two large private banks and one of the leading holdings companies of the country, which have had similar experiences.

There are two key concepts that characterize our proposal for Business Engineering: Ingenuity and Form. We posit that good engineering requires Ingenuity to design the innovative solutions businesses require in the extreme competitive environment that organizations currently face. Thus our emphasis on systemic, integrated, and innovative business design explicitly oriented to make an organization more competitive in the private case and more effective and efficient in the public case. On the other hand, the design has to materialize in a Form, in the traditional architecture sense proposed by Alexander,[3] which can follow certain patterns based on existent knowledge that provides a starting point for such design. Software engineers took their pattern ideas[4] from Alexander and this is also the inspiration for our patterns proposal.

One particular characteristics of this book is that it illustrates all its ideas and proposals with many real cases, coming from projects that have been implemented in practice and provided very impressive results, which are detailed in the text. The cases show how the same design guidelines we will present successfully provide good results in very different situations and environments.

As Spohrer and Demirkan propose in the presentation of the series in "Service Systems and Innovation in Business and Society," of which this book is part, I embrace the idea of integrating scientific, engineering, and management disciplines to innovate in the services that organizations perform to create value for customers and shareholders that could not be achieved through disciplines in isolation. The integration developed in this book can be located in the Spohrer and Demirkan's System-Discipline Matrix, included in the following, as centered on "Systems that support people's activities" that are designed with the participation of most of the disciplines defined in the matrix. Thus, for example, as it will be presented in this book, quantitative marketing—with the tools of Data Mining—is used to model customers needs and options; Management Science allows characterizing providers' logistic; Economics theory permit to model competitors' behavior; knowledge management and change management define people roles in service change; Industrial Engineering and Information Sciences provide the tools for information analysis and supporting tools definition; and all these disciplines plus Strategic Planning, other Analytics—as Optimization Models and Business Analytics—process modeling and design, project management, and others serve as a basis to generate ideas to produce and implement a design that realizes the value for the customers and stakeholders.

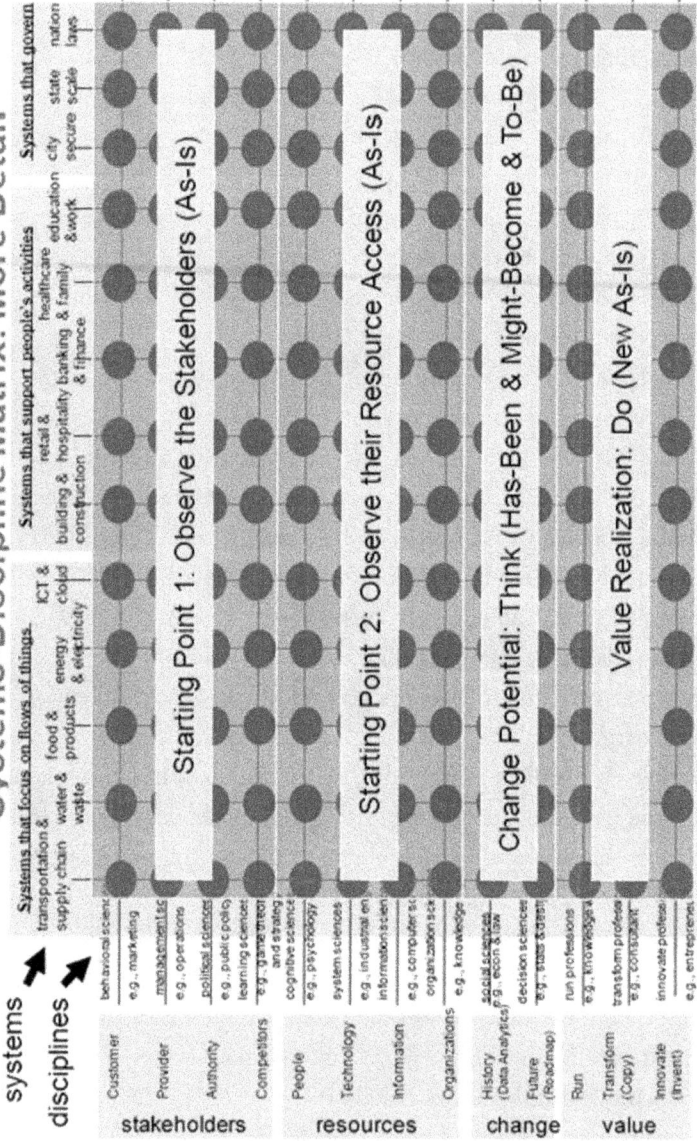

Systems-Discipline Matrix: More Detail

Hence, this book is completely aligned with the purpose of this series and its contribution is to provide an original Business Engineering approach that emphasizes service design and derives an integral and systemic solution that starts with Strategy and Business Model definition, follows with business design, processes design, and information system design, and finished with well-planned implementation.

This is a revision of a previous book with Business Expert Press, *Business Engineering and Service Design with Applications for Health Care Institutions*, which is being published in two volumes: *Business Engineering and Service Design* and the one we are presenting now. In this revision we restructure the original chapters dedicated to health services, creating four new ones dedicated to present cases for the different design level we propose in our hierarchical approach: Business Design that defines the new Capabilities a health service requires to be more competitive; Configuration and Capacity Design that provides the EA and its components with the required resources to make operative the health Business Design; Resource Management Process Design dealing with the resource levels that are necessary to process demand according to given Service Level Agreements (SLA) in the routine operation of a health service; and Operating Management Process Design which determines the practices, with proper IT support, and the flows that should be followed in running the health service. These chapters include new real cases that show how these design ideas are implemented in practice and the results they provide. The original chapter "Foundations For Health Care Institutions' Design" is maintained but complemented with several new ideas: "Health Network Architectures," a proposal for patterns that can guide the design of complex multilevel structures of health services is presented; a design methodology for the design of health services is also included; and to make this book more self contained, several topics detailed in the previous volume *Business Engineering and Service Design* are summarized here, including "Summary of Relevant Disciplines," "Intelligence Structures and Business Patterns," "General Architectures," "Hospital Architecture," and "Health Network Architecture."

CHAPTER 1

Introduction

Ever since the idea of Service Science was proposed,[1] several lines of work in what is now called Service Science, Management, and Engineering (SSME) have been put forward.[2] In the Prologue, we linked our work to a framework related to SSME, developed by Spohrer and Demirkan, for "Service Systems and Innovation in Business and Society" and concluded that our proposed approach is congruent with their ideas.

This book reports our research and development work in the engineering part of SSME and, in particular, the design of the components of health service systems. As stated in the Prologue, our main source of inspiration is Business Engineering, which not only shares the ideas and principles of SSME, but also tries to cover a larger domain including any type of business; its emphasis is on how to design any business—including Strategy, Business Model, Capabilities involved, processes, and IT support.[3] Our experience with the design of many different businesses, such as manufacturing, distribution, bank services, retail, and hospitals,[4] has enabled us to propose the conceptual model (Ontology) in Figure 1.1. According to this model, designs are based on the **Strategy** and the **Business Model** that an organization wants to put into practice. We found that Porter's ideas[5] for Competitive Strategy, complemented with the Delta model[6] for strategic positioning, are useful in providing options for business innovation. In particular the Delta model defines the following positioning strategies: (a) **best product** that means developing unique attributes for a business' products that attract clients' preferences; (b) **integral solution to clients** that implies understanding their needs in such a way that customized solutions can be offered, its final aim being for the offering organization to get placed into the Value Chain of the client; and (c) **systemic lock-in** that attempts to create conditions that makes it very expensive and almost impossible for a client to make do without the services of an offering organization (lock-in), by creating an

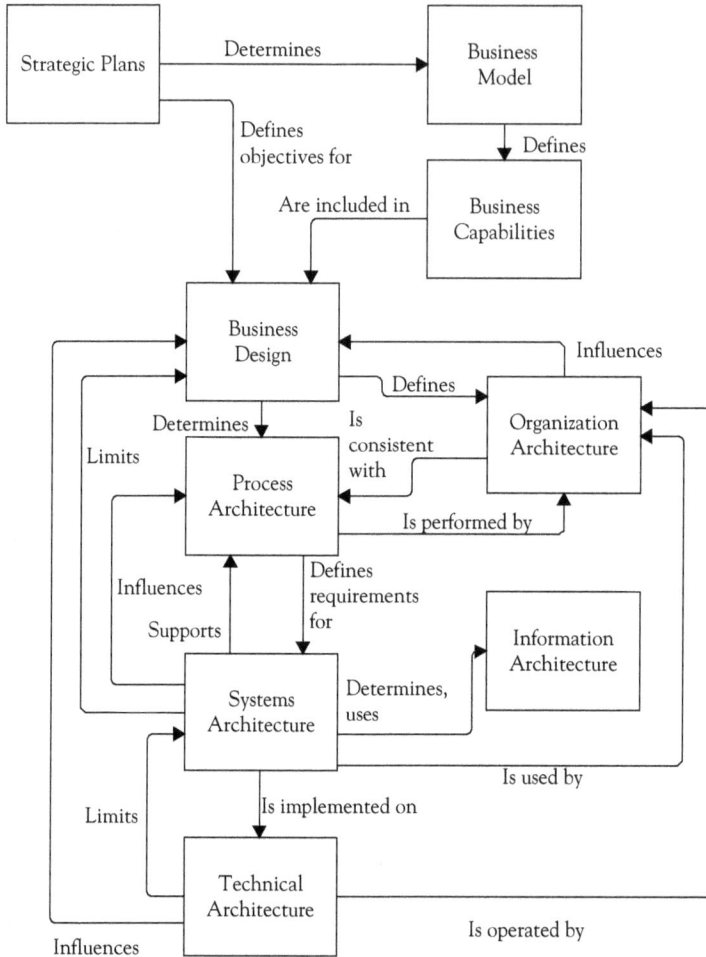

Figure 1.1 Ontology for Business Design

extended company that includes all the clients and the complementors, who develop value-add products and a portfolio of services they offer to the clients. Also the ideas of Johnson, Christensen, and Kageman[7] and the Business Model Canvas[8] are adequate to define precisely the value that innovations would provide to clients. Other ideas, such as innovation portfolio,[9] can be useful in complementing value creation definition. All these concepts are reviewed in more detail in Chapter 2.

But no Strategy or Business Model specifies **how** the positioning and the value will be actually delivered in operational terms. This is what a **Business Design** will detail, starting with **Business Capabilities** necessary according to the Strategy and Business Model. This must be complemented with the design of processes, systems, organizational and IT support that make the Business Capabilities fully operational, giving rise to the other architectures included in Figure 2.1 that are described as follows:

1. **Process Architecture**, which establishes the processes necessary to implement the Capabilities and Business Design, the relationships that coordinate the processes, the business logic—algorithms, heuristics, rules, and, in general, procedures—that automate or guide such processes and their connection to IT support.

2. **Organization Architecture**, which is related to the common organizational charts and defines how work will be structured—who will do what—and the relationships among them—who will respond and relates to whom. Such architecture is much related to the Process Architecture, as we will detail and exemplify in Chapters 3 and 4, process design determines, in many cases, peoples' roles.

3. **Systems Architecture**, which defines the Information Systems that exists in an organization, their relationship, and the support they give to processes. Again there is a close relationship between this architecture and Process Architecture, since the system support should be, according to our proposal, explicitly defined in process' design, which can be given with current, modified, or new systems that change the architecture.

4. **Information Architecture**, which shows the structure of the Information Systems' data and, for the same reasons as in (3), is also related to processes.

5. **Technical Architecture**, or the contents and structure or the hardware and nonapplication software on which data resides and systems are run, which are obviously related to all the aforementioned architectures.

As a much-simplified example of the application of Ontology, consider a private hospital that has defined a strategy of providing the most advanced services in its market in terms of medical practices and supporting technology. The Business Model then is to provide high-value services to patients, which increases the probability of patients' well-being and for which they are willing to pay premium prices. Then the hospital needs Capabilities and a Business Design that are able to generate such services. The Capabilities are, in this case, the abilities necessary to innovate in medical practices and the knowledge of new technology that supports such practices; the Business Design is a structure of components that delivers the Capabilities. In this case, a new component that performs a new service development, another that is able to put the new services into practice and one that can do associated marketing and selling. Since the hospital does not have these components, new processes that enhance the current architecture to make such components operational should be designed. Among others, a process for a new service development should include the definition of actors' role in the process, which can be a new group created for this purpose or a group comprising the existing people in hospital operations that, with adequate support, form an innovation team that produces new medical procedures. Clearly, there are different organizational structures for the aforementioned alternatives and this shows the relationship between process and organization design. Then process design will determine system support, for example, for new service development planning and tracking, and data, software, and hardware needs related to the other architectures, as illustrated in Figure 1.1.

These general ideas of Business Engineering are applicable to services design in any domain, as we showed in the previous volume cited in the Prologue, and in particular, to health services, which is dealt with in Chapters 3 to 6.

This work poses and intends to prove that, in performing the aforementioned designs, **patterns** can facilitate a task. First, **Business Patterns** that are derived or abstracted from vast experience and knowledge generated in service design, including our own and from literature, are proposed; these emphasize the different structures, components, and relationships a business may adopt in providing services to its clients.

Further, it will be shown that business service designs can be made operational by **Business Architecture and Processes Patterns** that detail how such designs can be implemented, including the technology support needed for their execution; these process patterns will be summarized in Chapter 2 and are documented in other publications;[10] they have been widely used in real projects.[11]

From experience on service design, with an emphasis on business and process design, and taking into account the model defined in Figure 1.1, the following types of design problems can be abstracted, which are exemplified with health situations, the application domain in this book.

i. **Business Design** delivers the structure of components—production, management, supporting, and others–and their relationships, and the interaction with the environment that generates a Business Capability, which provides a service with value for customers in accordance with the Strategy and Business Model. It represents **what a business should do** and does not map to organizational units, area, or product. A case of this type is the design of a hospital with the different service lines it offers—urgency, ambulatory, hospitalization, and others—the degree of management independence of the lines, the interaction among lines by interchanging and sharing of internal services, and the degree of use of outsourced services.

ii. **Business configuration and capacity design** includes the determination of the processes that should be present to assure that the service defined in (i) is provided in an effective and efficient way. In addition, what capacity should each process provide to be able to meet the demand according to the desired Service Agreement Levels (SLA). For example, hospitals' urgency services may have different configurations in terms of its processes, among others: (a) use of a Triage (patient routing), (b) a fast-track line, and (c) several different lines of service. Once the components are determined, capacity for each of them making possible to process demand must be determined to have a desired patient average waiting time. This problem is relevant only when demand behavior changes or there are possible innovations in service technology and it is usually related to strategic investment issues.

iii. **Resource management process design** is the management of people, equipment, and supplies that are necessary to provide the capacity established in (ii). For example, in hospitals, several doctors of different specialties work in each shift. This requires well-designed processes—based on forecasted demand—which plan and assign resources such that capacity is provided at a minimum cost. Such processes are executed with regular frequency depending on demand dynamics.

iv. **Operating management processes design** provides processes necessary for day-to-day scheduling of demand over the resources in order to assure the required level of service and optimize their use. For example, in public hospitals, where there are usually waiting lists of surgery patients, a well-designed process is needed to schedule them in operating rooms in such a way that priorities associated with the severity of patients' illnesses are met and use of facilities is maximized.

We have developed an innovative design approach to solve the aforementioned problems in an integrated and systemic way. Such an approach is based on explicit and formal general business and process models, called Business Patterns (BPs) and Business Process Patterns (BPPs), which enable the definition of service design options and analytical methods that allow customer characterization and resource optimization in designing the service. Analytics, which will be reviewed in Chapter 2, is an important component of the designs we propose, since they allow to embed business logic in the execution of the processes that detect the need to act over the service delivery, determines options for such action, and automate or recommend action taking; for example, monitoring critical hospitalized patients, determining risky situations by means of analytical models, and advising nurses and doctors on possible actions. This is complemented with modeling of the processes with Business Process Management Notation (BPMN)[12] and a technology that facilitates the process execution with Business Process Management Suits (BPMS) tools and web services over Service Oriented Architecture (SOA).[13] This technology is reviewed in Chapter 2 and we show a case of its use in Chapter 6. In summary, we integrate a business and process design approach with Analytics and supporting IT tools in the following chapters.

We propose health services as the application domains for the outlined approach, where there are ongoing research and development projects from which general solutions have been derived. Such solutions cover in an integrated, systemic manner the whole array of design problems faced in health systems, including: (a) centralized governance structures for public health that, among other things, assign resources to promote good service and efficiency; (b) public health network configuration design, including primary services and hospitals of several complexity levels; (c) hospital configuration and capacity design; (d) hospital medical and management processes design; and (e) supporting Information Systems design. The general solutions for these design problems have been tested and very successfully implemented in the Chilean health sector, including 10 hospitals, providing better service and making optimal use of resources, for which analytical techniques have been embedded in such solutions. Some of the solutions and results obtained by their application are presented in Chapters 3 to 6. We are now working on their implementation in other hospitals and they may be eventually used by over a hundred health facilities.

The next chapter presents the foundations we propose for health care institutions design. Then, in Chapters 3 to 6, the design approach proposed and the role of Analytics in the context of design are explained with several health services cases, at different design levels, validating our proposal, including the results generated. Finally conclusions are summarized.

CHAPTER 2

Foundations for Health Care Institutions' Design

This chapter is dedicated to present the ideas of leading authors on how to solve the problems the health system has all over the world, summarized in the second section of this chapter, and our proposal to design health services in trying to solve such problems, which was introduced in Chapter 1. Our approach is based on the ideas of Business Engineering, which emphasize competitiveness; so we start by reviewing the basis for making health services more competitive that various authors have proposed; then our proposal is presented.

Summary of Relevant Disciplines

As already mentioned, there are several disciplines that provide a foundation for the design methodology we propose. We present a brief review of the most relevant ones here.

Strategy

The work of Porter[1] and Hax and Wilde[2] on Strategy provides the starting point for Business Design, as shown in Figure 1.1. The key ideas adopted are:

1. Porter's concept of *Competitive Advantage* is the key for obtaining a position that differentiates a business. He proposes to choose—in our terminology design—a set, or architecture, of different activities— in our terminology processes—that gives a unique mixture of value to the client. It relates to Business Design to perform its activities in a different form or to develop different activities other than the competitors'. For example, the way in which eBay offered auctions over the Internet differentiated it from its competitors.

2. Hax and Wilde's proposal that defines three basic positioning strategies for a business to generate customer bonding and hence Competitive Advantage:

   (a) *Best product* means developing unique attributes for a business' products that attract clients' preferences, such as the unique features Apple intends to provide for them, or good quality at a low price as Walmart does for theirs; another good example of this strategy is by Zara, the second world-level manufacturer and distributor of fashionable clothes, which bases its positioning on novel products at reasonable cost and their fast renovation, together with one of the best logistics in the industry that allows the fast launching to the market and replenishment of products.[3]

   (b) *Integral solution to clients* implies understanding their needs in such a way that customized solutions can be offered; its final aim is for the offering organization to get placed into the *Value Chain* of the client, taking activities from such a chain for which it has top competences, as FedEx does for the complete delivery logistics for some of its clients[4] and Amazon that provides full Internet selling solutions for their business clients.

   (c) *Systemic lock-in* is based on the economic theory of switching costs and network externalities. It attempts to create conditions that make it very expensive and almost impossible for a client to make do without the services of an offering organization (lock-in), by creating an extended company that includes all the clients and the complementors, who develop value-add products and a portfolio of services they offer to the clients. The emblematic case of systemic lock-in is Microsoft, which has positioned Windows as a *de facto* standard, incorporating a great number of complementors to the system that produce a large offering of software that run only on this operating system. Candidates of the same status are Google and Apple iTunes.

After choosing a strategic positioning, among the options presented, we propose that an organization should design its Business Model, processes, and supporting IT applications in such a way that they materialize and make operational the Strategy. Without a disciplined design, like the one we propose in Businesses Engineering, it is difficult to be able to guarantee the success of a Strategy, which means a significant change in the way a business is performed.

Business Model

Also relevant are the ideas of Business Model proposed by several authors[5] that provide key inputs for Business Design. The basic concept of having a good strategy is not sufficient; it is necessary to design a Business Model, as stated earlier, which put strategy into practice and the processes that make it operative. This is how FedEx changed its positioning strategy from package mover to supplier of logistic solutions, which meant a substantial change in its Business Model, offering to its clients the possibility of handling an important part of their distribution logistics, using its own processes and IT applications.[6]

To make the concept of Business Model more precise, the ideas of Johnson et al.[7] are adopted, which define it as a logical history that explains who the clients of an organization are, what they value, and how a positive economic result will be generated through providing such value.

The idea is to materialize a strategic approach in a plausible Business Model. Such a model should include solid foundation assumptions with respect to the customers and what they value, resulting in economic outcomes provided with an adequate justification. These should be reflected in a rigorous economic evaluation.

An example of a good Business Model is eBay, a company that started with the assumption that there were numerous customers who wanted to obtain goods by means of auctions, but did not have access to them or it was inefficient for them to resort to such type of service offering. Such clients would prefer to be users of a simple system at low cost, running fully on Internet, which would allow them to bid for goods of any type following the auction model. These clients would value, in addition to the transaction possibilities, avoiding to physically moving, assuring the payment to the seller, simple procedures of participation and a low cost. They would be willing to pay a percentage of the value of the transaction, generating the income that makes the business viable. In addition, the costs would be low, since the Business Model of eBay did not imply getting directly involved neither in the physical handling of the goods nor in the associate financial handling, which could be handled by a courier and available means of payments. Therefore, the Business Model not only seemed attractive, but also economically sustainable; this has been actually demonstrated with the great success of this company. Notice that the Business Model determines the required processes and structure.

A case similar to eBay is Google, which discovered a value associated with the searches on Internet and a great mass of clients who required it. Google assumed correctly that the users, in this case, were not willing to pay for the service and that the key was to create a great community from which this company could extract value with other products. One of these products was advertising, which, in varied forms, provides income to Google, which has turned it into one of the most successful companies of the world, besides generating a lock-in effect.

Another interesting example of Business Model is of Grupo Multiasistencia, which operates in Spain, France, and Portugal. This organization offers services that allow coordinating repairs of houses, including the ones that occur from events covered with insurance policies. Multiasistencia allows that several companies, in particular insurance organizations, and individuals who need this type of service, sign up by means of the Internet to its network. Subsequently the demand for services of repair work is processed and assigned to a set of outsourced professionals who execute the repairs. Furthermore, their services coordinate the successful execution and the invoicing of the repairs, payment collection, and the fees to the professionals.[8]

One impressive Business Model at the moment is of Apple that, for example, made the downloading of music by means of Internet easy and convenient; it combines hardware, software, and a 24-hour service that are implemented with the collaboration of the music suppliers. With the iPad, the model has become generalized to provide all types of applications developed by complementors. This has made Apple one of the companies of highest market value in the world and put it on the road to systemic lock-in.

A Business Model, according to Johnson et al.[9] besides specifying value for clients, should establish the other factors that are briefly described as follows.

The *Value Proposal* to the objective clients is related to the work needed to solve an important problem or to satisfy a key necessity of such clients; this determines an offer that solves the problem or satisfies the necessity. This is determined not only for what it is sold but also for how it is sold.

The *Profit Formula* relates to: (a) the model of income, that is, how much money can be earned, which is determined by size of market, frequency of purchase, and others; (b) the cost structure that is determined by how the costs are assigned, including costs of key assets, direct costs, indirect costs, and economies of scale; (c) the margin model or the difference between income and cost of each transaction so as to arrive at the desired level of profits; and (d) the rate of use of resources, or how rapidly the resources are used to obtain the desired volume, which includes times of delivery, speed of production, rotation of inventory, use of assets, and similar.

The *Key Resources* are the ones necessary to profitably give the client the value proposal; they may include human resources, technology, equipment, information, channels, partnerships, alliances brands, and licenses.

The *Key Processes* include metrics, rules, and norms that make the delivery of the value proposal profitable and, also, repeatable and scalable. It may include: (a) processes such as product design, development, supplying, manufacture, marketing, hiring and training, and IT; (b) rules and metrics, such as requirements for return for investments, credit rules, times of delivery, and conditions for suppliers; and (c) norms, that is, policies for the channels and clients.

Osterwalder and Pigneur proposed another methodology for Business Model development,[10] which shares many characteristics with the Johnson et al. proposal. The main difference is that it provides a canvas or table that summarizes all the variables that define a Business Model. It can be used as a design tool by systematically assigning characteristics to the variables in the canvas, thus defining the way the Business Model is to be structured. Osterwalder and Pigneur and Johnson et al. concur on most of the variables that define a Business Model and only differ on how to structure and present them. We conclude that they are equivalent and, in what follows, we opt for the proposal of Johnson et al., as it is more easy to use.

Business Intelligence

Business Intelligence (BI) is, in our approach, the application of Analytics, which is defined later, to business design and management. Davenport is the champion of the idea of using Analytics in better managing businesses: As early as 2005, he and others[11] proposed a "new form of competition based on the extensive use of Analytics, data, and fact-based decision making. The Analytics—quantitative or statistical models to analyze business problems—may be applied to a variety of situations, including customer management, supply chains, and financial performance." In a follow-up paper in *HBR* and a book,[12] he elaborated on the subject; in summary, he stated that well-known companies base their success on the use of Analytics and this is a good practice to be followed. He distinguishes the following types of Analytics in order from moderately complex to very complex:

1. Statistical analysis, such as regression and factorial analysis
2. Forecasting/Extrapolation, such as times series models and Neural Networks
3. Predictive models, such as Data and Web-Mining models
4. Optimization models, such as Discrete Linear Programming (LP) and Stochastic models

These analytical techniques are to be clearly distinguished from the more basic, so-called BI tools, which essentially consist of facilities for access and reporting from data by means of information dashboards.[13] Advanced Analytics provides truly BI that generates insights on the state of the business and predictive or prescriptive Capabilities to support optimal or close to optimal actions. For example, Walmart uses online data from all the sales points to feed predictive models that forecast demand for each of such points, which are used by optimization models that determine actions over the supply chain logistics to assure product availability at minimum distribution cost; currently, they are also using social media data to predict shoppers' purchases and act on that basis to plan logistics.

In this work, we consider Analytics of two types: *data based*, oriented to predictive models, which includes traditional Statistics and Econometrics, Data Mining, Web Mining, and Process Mining[14] and *Operations*

Research and Management Science, which make possible prescriptive models, with techniques such as optimization models, both linear and discrete, heuristics, probabilistic models, simulation models, knowledge extraction and characterization models, and many others. These types of Analytics can be further classified as follows:[15]

- *Analytics 1.0* based on assembling internal data oriented to reporting, which can be enhanced by visualization tools. Emphasis in this level is on integrating, structuring, and using the data to generate information on the state of the processes to allow fact-based, improved, and fast decision making. Front-end tools, such as visualization software based on dashboard reporting, are used; also integration tools that allow data preparation, built-in querying on an analytical database and descriptive Analytics—complex graphical analysis—are options.
- *Analytics 2.0* ads, in relation to the previous level, big data. This is fast moving, external, large, and unstructured data coming from external sources, including social media, which is stored and processed rapidly using new technology like parallel servers and Hadoop. Visual Analytics, a form of descriptive Analytics, is introduced. Emphasis is on real-time operations analytic solutions to make organizations more agile and proactive. Main idea is that there is a wealth of data that, adequately used, can generate great value for them. For example, McKinsey[16] has calculated in 60 percent the potential increase in retailers' operating margin by better using big data. It has also estimated in $300 thousand millions the potential value for the U.S. health care by the right use of patients' data. As to impact on the bottom line, McAffe and Brynjollfson[17] have found that companies in the top third of their industries in the use of data-driven decision making are, on the average, 5 percent more productive and 6 percent more profitable than their competitors. As an example of these possibilities we have the case of Ommeo, a division of Siemens that delivers millions of electronic devices and other products throughout

the world, which has developed a solution for supply chain product data management, including data from suppliers, equipment, field service, and repair operations.[18] With this solution they provide suppliers, Ommeo operations and customers with an end-to-end, fast, holistic view of supply chain data. Using such solution, one customer has been able to to search 1.5 thousands million records in less than three second.

- *Analytics 3.0* complements the previous levels by incorporating predictive and prescriptive models in routine service production and management processes, which are based and operate on the internal and external big data. Aim is not only to drive operational and strategic decisions but also the creation of new product and services. Here true BI, as defined earlier, is performed to advise, recommend, and, in some cases, automate decisions and actions or both using the full range of analytical tools: Data Mining, optimization, Machine Learning, and the like. The example of Walmart given before is a good instance of this idea. Other real case examples are to use diabetes patients' data, available in the whole health system, to develop predictive models to allow detecting probable crisis for a specific patient, before it occurs, to prevent serious health problems for him and high emergency treatment costs, a case to be presented in Chapter 6; and monitoring and collecting data on line for mining trucks, using available sensors, by a service company that sells them and also offers maintenance services, in order to develop models that predict failures just in time, allowing to take corrective actions that minimize downtime and maintenance costs.[19] Also dynamic predictive models that use common company data and big data can help discovering new business possibilities with improved or new services and also allow designing and operating them as follows.

These types of Analytics will be included in different BI architectures that will be presented in a following section. The use of Analytics in our design proposal relates to providing business logic that supports *intelligent* business decision making and operations and also business development using well-founded designs. The central idea is that, in executing services delivery and related processes, business logic is necessary to formalize certain routines that use models to assure that certain objectives are attained. For example, one may want to assure that the right services are offered to clients in order to maximize sales, for which a customer behavior's predictive model is needed. Or one may need to assure satisfaction of a certain service level to clients but trying to minimize costs, where a mathematical prescriptive model is required to optimally assign requests to facilities that process them. In both examples, the analytical tool—predictive model or prescriptive model—will be embedded in a business logic that specifies in a formal way how the process should be executed. In some cases, this logic will be fully automated as Amazon does for the logic that makes recommendations for clients or the logic that Walmart uses to optimize its logistics. In others, the logic will make recommendations to the person who operates the process and he will have the authority to follow them or not, as, for example, in prescriptive models that recommend medical actions on patients that we will present later. Also business development, improving current services and designing new ones, is possible by the right use of Analytics. A case we have developed, which exemplifies this possibility, is a distributor of heavy machinery to the mining industry, mentioned before, which, besides the current business of just selling equipment, wants to be able to offer added value services for equipment maintenance by means of a new Value Stream. These are based on online equipment monitoring, by means of remote sensors mounted in them, which feed state data to the service company systems allowing to generate corrective actions just in time, by means of predictive maintenance models; this case is similar to a General Electric business that offers the same services for the equipment it sells.[20] Another case is a children's hospital which has chronic patients with respiratory problems that need permanent monitoring, spending most of their time at the hospital using beads, which is a very scarce resource. So the challenge was to design a new service, with a new Value Stream, that provides a solution for keeping the children at their home with the proper attention that assures their well being, including online monitoring of medical variables—such as temperature, cardiac frequency, and respiratory frequency—and a diagnosis data-based analytical model to determine when the patient is in crisis and needs medical attention to advise care professionals; this case will be revisited in Chapters 3 and 6. These new Value Streams, when they execute externalized customers' processes, produce a lock-in effect that makes it difficult for them to terminate the service. Different streams may execute different Business Models. For example, the hospital case has one Value Stream that executes a traditional hospitalization care, and another Value Stream that gives a proactive service to patients, which generates a high value for them.

We summarize some of the relevant Analytics for this book, which will be specifically used in some of the cases in Chapters 3 to 6, for the more technical reader who wants to get a feeling on how Analytics gets implemented. If one does not want to get into technical details, he can skip the rest of this section without loss of understanding of the cases.

Data-Based Analytics

The first type of model, which corresponds to some of the examples we gave previously in this section, is based on the *model for Knowledge Discovery and Data Mining (KDD)*. A recent version of this model is Cross-Industry Standard Process for Data Mining (CRISP-DM).

One particular Data Mining modeling tool that will be used in one diabetes case we will present later is the clustering algorithm *k-Means*, which works as follows.

A clustering or *Segmentation* algorithm consists of finding groups between a set of individuals. The segmentation technique k-Means, which is a well-known algorithm for clustering and a simple and effective application, follows a procedure of classification of a set of objects in a certain given number of k clusters. It represents each one of clusters by the average (or weighted average) of its points or centroid. The representation by means of centroids has the advantage that it has an immediate graphical and statistical meaning. According to Lloyd, it is simple, efficient, and often results in the optimal solution.[21]

The mathematical formulation of the clustering problem is as follows:[22]

Given a set of observations $(x_1, x_2,...,x_n)$, where each observation is a d-dimensional real vector, k-Means clustering aims to partition the n observation into k sets $(k \leq n)$ $S = \{S_1, S_2,..., S_k\}$, so as to minimize the within-cluster sum of squares:

$$\underset{S}{\arg\min} \sum_{i=1}^{k} \sum_{x_j \in S_i} \| x_j - u_i \|^2 \qquad (2.1)$$

where μ_i is the mean of points in S_i^n.

Based on this formulation, the algorithm for clustering a set of objects (defined by a vector of observed data) $D_n = (x_1, x_2, ..., x_n)$ is as follows:

Stage 1: Choose k initial objects at random and assign each of them to one of the k clusters. For each cluster k, the initial value of the centroid is x_j, the only object in it.

Stage 2: Reassign the objects of a cluster. For each object x_j, assign it to the cluster that is closest to the object, according to a distance measurement (usually the Euclidian distance).

Stage 3: Once all the objects are placed in a cluster, recalculate the centroids of the k clusters.

Stage 4: Repeat Stages 2 and 3 until no more reassignments can be done.

Although the aforementioned algorithm always finishes, there is no guarantee of obtaining the optimal solution. In effect, the algorithm is very sensible to the random election of the k initial centers. Therefore, the k-Means algorithm is used numerous times on a same data set to try to diminish this effect, knowing that the most spaced initial centers give better results.

A clustering method is usually complemented with the technique of Decision Trees, in the particular version of *Binary Decision Trees*, which is considered a *Classification* method. The idea is to know which individuals within a segment have a similar behavior defined using known data on several variables that may explain such behavior. For a particular segment, the Decision Tree technique looks for "twins"; that is, clients who have a similar behavior defined by a variable that clearly generates groups that minimize the difference in the values of the variable for the clients inside a group. The technique of Binary Decision Trees uses division in two groups; so at the start, two branches are generated, one for each group. Then for each of these groups, two subgroups are defined using the same idea of minimizing differences for the values of another variable for clients within a subgroup, creating branches at a second level. And so on, each subgroup is again divided until all the variables for which data is available are included in the analysis. Clearly, this is a very simplified description; important aspects of the technique, such as how to select the order in which variables generates groups and to select the "best branches" to obtain better results, will be avoided.[23] The important thing is that once a tree is built, rules that define clients' behavior can be derived.

k-Means and binary Decision Trees are well-established techniques and are much used, which has been facilitated by its inclusion in popular analytical software packages such as SSSP,[24] Rapid Miner,[25] and Weka.[26]

A variant of data-based Analytics is what is called *Process Intelligence*.[27] Its emphasis is in knowing the state of service production and establishing the performance of the overall flow for action generation to correct and improve the service. For this, data is systematically collected to analyze the individual steps within a production process or operational workflow and evaluate performance, such as:

i. Process compliance for well defined processes, which consists of verifying if process'steps comply with given sequence and times and informing nonconformities; for example, in credit processing inform that risk evaluation is taking more time than a desired level. Business Process Management Suits (BPMS) software[28] allows to do this.

ii. Process flow analysis to discover if there are avoidable delays, frequent avoidable repetition and bottlenecks that can be eliminated. Also overloaded paths and. exception paths, can be found to that need to be improved. These analyses can be done online and information provided to the process operator, based on a business logic that recommends actions such as, for example, avoid dangerous delays in a hospital's emergency.

We will treat this type of Analytic as a particular case of Intelligence Structures that we will propose in the next section. A particular variant of this idea is *Process Mining*[29] that does similar analysis as (ii) earlier, but with a different purpose, which is to discover opportunities for process redesign; it is based on complex algorithms, special software and requires historical data, so it is adequate for such purpose but it is not appropriate for online use.

Machine Learning[30] is a generalization of the predictive methods in this section which has its roots in Artificial Intelligence, having media exposure with success cases as IBM's Watson that has defeated the chess world champion and also the Jeopardy champion.[31] It has also been increasingly incorporated in software products of common use that offers intelligent options such as predictive text, speech recognition, translation, and the like. Currently, it is becoming more available through products in the cloud, such as Microsoft's Azure, IBM's Watson Analytics, and Amazon's Machine Learning. Some of these products include the common predictive Analytics—Classification, clustering, and regression—but also incorporate other methods such as text and social network analyses that discover sentiments, emotions, key words, entities, and high-level concepts; cognitive applications that understand content and context within text and images; personality insights discovery from transactional and social media data to identify psychological traits; and deep-learning Neural Networks.[32] The common characteristic of these more advanced methods is that as much computational capability you give them, the better the result becomes because the results of previous Machine Learning exercises can be fed back into the algorithms. This means that each layer becomes a foundation for the next layer of Machine Learning, and the whole thing scales in a multiplicative way as time goes by. So there is continuous learning and results get even better.

Another class of analytical methods has to do with measuring the productivity and efficiency of a business in order to determine corrective actions to improve its performance. A particular, effective, and proven method for businesses that have replicated facilities or units, such as retail, banks, telecommunications, public health services, and the like, is *Data Envelopment Analysis* (DEA). This method is based on the idea that given data vectors of inputs and outputs for all the units, which represent well the value of the service provided and the costs incurred, including historical data about them, it is possible to calculate their comparative efficiency by solving an optimization model that determines their efficiency frontier. This is defined by the units that are comparatively most efficient according to the data. Then the units that are not in the frontier are not efficient and are candidates for improvement. DEA has analytical complements that make possible calculating potential improvements on outputs by manipulating certain inputs in a defined way.[33] There are also techniques that allow establishing other variables, not considered in the efficiency measurements, which are related to efficiency and if adequately manipulated can improve nonefficient units; in particular variables associated to design considerations, such as unit location, size, mix of services, and the like. So this method is also valuable in generating configuration design ideas in some cases and evaluating them in terms of efficiency, thus complementing the methodology we will propose. We have applied this technique to 40 public hospitals and shown in practice that it allows to define in a very precise way how hospital services should change to improve their efficiency and also improvements in the EA of the public organization that manages them;[34] we are also currently calculating the efficiency of academic departments at the Medical School of the University of Chile and finding similar opportunities as in the hospital case. Both cases will be presented in Chapter 3.

The other type of data-based Analytics we use in this book is *forecasting models*. Next we outline two types of models of this type found to be particularly useful: Neural Networks, which are the same as in the deep learning mentioned earlier, and Support Vector Regression (SVR).[35]

The particular type of *Neural Network* we consider is the Multilayer Perceptron (MLP). Its basic units are neurons that are grouped in layers and are connected by means of weighted links between two layers. Each neuron receives inputs from other neurons and generates a result that depends on only the information locally available and which serves as an input to other neurons, conforming a network.

The structure of the network consists of an output layer with one neuron that generates the desired forecast. The input layer contains the variables that we will use to explain demand, which will be determined subsequently. In the hidden layer, a number of neurons between input and output neurons are used; a high number of them will tend to copy the data (over fitting) and a small number will not generate good forecasts.[36] The basic idea is that historical data predicts demand of a given future month. Regarding the network, several architectures can be tested with several parameters, such as the number of epochs to use, the learning rate, and the number of hidden neurons. The output layer contains simply one neuron that generates the forecasted demand in month N.

The hidden layer contains a number of neurons that provides the model an adequate degree of freedom, usually calculated by: (Number of input neurons + Number of output neurons)/2.

We also present SVR^{37} for demand forecasting. This technique performs a linear regression in a high-dimensional feature space generated by a kernel function as described later, using the ε-insensitive loss function proposed by Vapnik.[38] It allows a tolerance degree to errors not greater than ε. The following description is based on the terminology used in Smola and Schölkopf.[39]

We start with a set of observed data $\{(\mathbf{x}_1, y_1), ..., (\mathbf{x}_1, y_1)\}$, where each $\mathbf{x}_i \in \mathbb{R}^n$ belongs to the input space of the sample (data points) and has an associated target value $y_i \in \mathbb{R}$ for $i = 1, ..., l$. We assume l to be the number of available data points to build a regression model. The SVR algorithm applies a function $\mathbf{\Phi}$, transforming the original data points from the initial input space ($\mathbb{R}^n$) to a generally higher-dimensional feature space ($F \subset \mathbb{R}^m$). In this new space, a linear model f is constructed, which represents a nonlinear model in the original space:

$$\boldsymbol{\Phi}: \mathbb{R}^n \rightarrow F \tag{2.2}$$

$$f(x) = \langle \omega, \Phi(x) \rangle + b \text{ with } \omega \in \mathbb{R}^m \text{ and } b \in \mathbb{R} \tag{2.3}$$

In Equation 2.3, $\langle \cdot, \cdot \rangle$ denotes the dot product in $\mathbb{R}^m$. When the identity function is used, that is, $\Phi(x) \rightarrow x$, no transformation is carried out and linear SVR models are obtained. The goal when using the ε-insensitive loss function is to find a function f that fits given training data with a deviation less or equal to ε and, at the same time, is as flat as possible in order to reduce model complexity. This means that one seeks a small weight vector ω. One way to ensure this is by minimizing the norm $\|\omega\|^2$, leading to the following optimization problem:

$$\min_{\omega, b} \frac{1}{2} \|\omega\|^2 \tag{2.4}$$

$$\text{s.t} \begin{cases} y_i - \langle \omega, \Phi(x) \rangle - b \leq \varepsilon \\ \langle \omega, \Phi(x) \rangle - y_i + b \leq \varepsilon \end{cases} \tag{2.5}$$

This problem could be infeasible. Therefore, slack variables $\xi_i, \xi_i^*, i=1,...,l$, are introduced to allow error levels greater than ε, arriving at the formulation in Equations 2.6 to 2.9.

$$\min_{\omega,b} \frac{1}{2}\|\omega\|^2 + C\sum_{i=1}^{l}(\xi_i + \xi_i^*) \qquad (2.6)$$

$$\text{s.t. } y_i - \langle \omega, \Phi(x) \rangle - b \leq \varepsilon + \xi_i^* \qquad (2.7)$$

$$\langle \omega, \Phi(x) \rangle - y_i + b \leq \varepsilon + \xi_i^* \qquad (2.8)$$

$$\xi_i^*, \xi_i \geq 0 \qquad (2.9)$$

This is known as the primal problem of the SVR algorithm. The objective function takes into account the generalization ability and accuracy in the training set, and embodies the structural risk minimization principle.[40] Parameter $C > 0$ determines the trade-off between generalization ability and accuracy in the training data, and the value up to which deviations larger than ε are accepted. The ε-intensive loss function $|\xi|_\varepsilon$ has been defined as in Equation 2.10.

$$|\xi|_\varepsilon = \begin{cases} 0 & if\ |\xi| < \varepsilon \\ |\xi| - \varepsilon & \text{otherwise} \end{cases} \qquad (2.10)$$

It is more convenient to represent the optimization Problems (6) to (9) in its dual form. For this purpose, a Lagrange function is constructed and, once applying saddle point conditions, the dual problem is converted to a quadratic optimization problem that is easier to solve, which is the one that provides the estimation of $f(x)$. The accuracy of the estimation depends on an appropriate setting of parameters C, ε, and others.[41] So the use of grid-search to find good parameters for SVR can be applied to test combinations of such parameters.

SVR has been also integrated in software packages such as Rapid Miner, mentioned earlier.

Assignment Optimization Models

Another popular structure of optimization is the *Assignment problem.* In its simplest form, the objective is to assign n tasks to m agents so that each task has only one assignment and each agent gets only one task, assuming $n = m$, and that the sum of the assignment costs is minimized. We have solved versions of this problem in assigning technicians to customer requests in telecommunication companies, IT specialists to software projects and for the assignment of operating rooms (ORs) to medical specialties in a hospital. The simplest mathematical formulation for this problem is the LP model:

Minimize:

$$\min \sum_{i \in A} \sum_{j \in T} C(i,j) x_{i,j}$$

Subject to the constraints:

$$\sum_{j \in T} x_{i,j} = 1 \text{ for } i \in A,$$

$$\sum_{i \in A} x_{i,j} = 1 \text{ for } j \in T,$$

$$x_{i,j} \geq 0 \text{ for } i, j \in A, T.$$

The variable $x_{i,j}$ represents the assignment of the agent i to task j, taking value 1 if the assignment is done and 0 otherwise. This formulation allows also fractional variable values, but there is always an optimal solution where the variables take integer values, since the first constraint requires that every agent is assigned to exactly one task, and the second constraint requires that every task is assigned exactly one agent. A and T are sets of equal size that contain agents and task. This version can be easily solved with a standard LP algorithm and also very effective heuristics have been proposed as the Hungarian one.[42]

For more realistic versions of this problem, there are complications such as tasks have execution times and several tasks may be assigned to an agent; agents have a defined capacity available; and the cost structure can be more complex, for example, with multiple objectives. In such cases, the model must be discrete to assure that the assignment of tasks is exclusive, and several more constraints, to take care of the complications outlined earlier, may emerge. Besides these complexities, it is our experience that these types of optimization models can be solved with standard software for discrete problems. However, in some cases, heuristics can be applied, such as Tabu search.[43]

The next problem is also very common in practice; this is the *Job Shop Scheduling*, which can be described as follows. Let $M = \{M_1, M_2, ..., M_m\}$ and $J = \{J_1, J_2, ..., J_n\}$ be defined as two finite sets. In an industrial context, the problem is proposed as m machines and n jobs to be scheduled on them. Furthermore, X denotes a set of sequential assignments of jobs to machines, such that each job is done just one time; $x \in X$ can be describe as a $n \times m$ matrix, where a column i shows the jobs that a M_i machine will perform in order, for example:

$$x = \begin{pmatrix} 1 & 2 \\ 2 & 3 \\ 3 & 1 \end{pmatrix}$$

The matrix indicates that the M_1 machine will perform three jobs J_1, J_2, J_3 in the order J_1, J_2, J_3, while the M_2 machine will execute the jobs in the sequence J_2, J_3, J_1. Also, the cost function $C: X \rightarrow [0, +\infty]$ is defined, which is interpreted as the "total cost of processing" and it can be an expression that represents the cost due to the time the machine M_i takes in doing the job J_j. The Job Shop problem corresponds to finding an assignment of jobs $\in$ X, such that $C(x)$ is minimum. It can be solved using several types of algorithms or techniques; the most popular are branching and pruning, Tabu search, genetic algorithms, and search in directed graphs.[44]

A complex version of this problem is the hospital OR scheduling application we will present in Chapter 6, where, among others, jobs (operations on patients) have an execution time, the cost structure is multi objective and there several other constraints.

Process Modeling

The idea behind process modeling is to design an organization with formal graphical models that allow representing the options of business and process structures that put into practice a Strategy and associated Business Model. Moreover, for each process of the structure or architecture (EA), we want to generate models, also formal, that represent the design of the components of such process. For this we use the Business Process Management Notation (BPMN),[45] which is supported as a standard by the Object Management Group (OMG),[46] which allows detailing activities, the flow, and the logic of a process.

In a nutshell, BPMN is a formal notation that provides many constructs to build process models; here we summarize the more basic ones. BPMN has a set of three core elements of the *Flow Objects*, as follows:

1. *Event*, which is represented by a circle; it is something that "happens" during the course of a business process. They affect the flow of the process and usually have a cause (trigger) or an impact (result). Events are circles with open centers to allow internal markers to differentiate different triggers or results. There are three types of Events, based on when they affect the flow—Start, Intermediate, and End, diagramed as follows:

2. *Activity*, which is represented by a rounded-corner rectangle and is a generic term for the work organizations perform. It can be atomic or nonatomic (compound). The types of activities are task and subprocess. The subprocess is distinguished by a small plus sign at the bottom center of the shape, as follows:

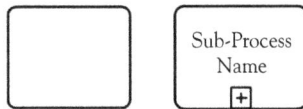

3. *Gateway*, which is represented by a diamond shape and is used to control the divergence and convergence of sequence flow. Thus, it will determine traditional decisions, as well as the forking, merging, and joining of paths. Internal markers will indicate the behavior of the flow of control, as follows:

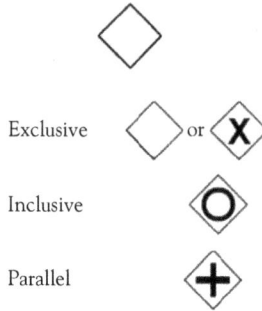

The Flow Objects are connected together in a diagram to create the basic skeletal structure of a business process. There are three *Connecting Objects* that provide this function. These connectors are as follows:

1. *Sequence Flow* is represented by a solid line with a solid arrowhead and is used to show the order (the sequence) in which activities will be performed in a process:

2. *Message Flow* is represented by a dashed line with an open arrowhead and is used to show the flow of messages between two separate process participants (business entities or business roles) that send and receive them. In BPMN, two separate Pools, defined later, in the diagram will represent the two participants. The Message Flow graphical symbol is as follows:

3. *Association* is represented by a dotted line with a line arrowhead and is used to associate data, text, and other artifacts with Flow Objects. Associations are used to show the inputs and outputs of activities and are drawn as follows:

Many process modeling methodologies utilize the concept of "swim lanes" as a mechanism to organize activities into separate visual categories in order to illustrate different functional capabilities or responsibilities. BPMN supports swim lanes with two main constructs. They are as follows:

A *Pool* represents a participant in a process, usually at an aggregated level, such as a company, a division, or a department. It also acts as a container for partitioning the aggregate into smaller components, such as an individual, using lanes. Its representation is as follows:

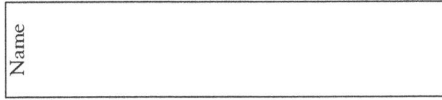

A *Lane* is a subpartition within a Pool and will extend within the entire length of the Pool. Lanes are used to organize and categorize activities.

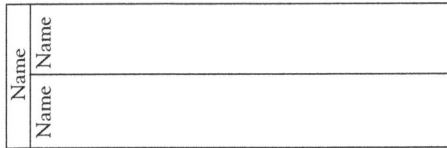

Examples of BPMN modeling that use Pool and Lanes to represent business designs at different detail levels will be presented in this chapter and the following ones.

In the models that will be used to support the design approach we propose, two modeling styles will be used.

The *first style* is a nonprocedural style that follows the ideas of IDEF0,[47] but using a software tool to edit BPMN models.[48] We summarize the conventions of IDEF0 to make this book more self-contained. This technique models processes, subprocesses, or activities by a box (rectangle with rounded corners); defines *Inputs*, which are supplies to them; *Outputs*, which are the product of the transformation that occurs within them; *Controls*, which are policies, rules, restrictions, or any other information that regulates the behavior of such processes, subprocesses, and activities; and *Resources*, which are the necessary elements for their realization. By convention, the inputs are represented by arrows entering from the left to the box; the outputs by arrows leaving to the right; Controls by arrows from above; and resources by arrows at the bottom.

BPMN has many elements of representation, some of which were summarized earlier, and we will use a few of them to implement the first style of process modeling that emphasizes the components involved and their relationships through flows of information. Because BPMN has a clear orientation to the stream and control logic, we must use creatively some of its elements to represent flows of information. So we will use BPMN boxes to represent processes, subprocesses, and activities, and one of the many varieties of arrows, the sequence one, to represent information flows. As stated earlier, a circle with a bold edge and an envelope in its interior represents a flow and associated event that is terminal within the diagram in question, which relates to a given destination in another diagram or outside the company; a similar circle, except for an edge without bold, represents an initial event and associated input flow; a simple circle and associated event initiates or terminates (bold) the process. These elements allow to link diagrams of different degree of detail, such as those generated in the scheme of hierarchical decomposition of IDEF0, which will be demonstrated in this and the following chapters.

At this stage, we will give a very simple use for Pools and Lanes. Pools, which are represented as separate tracks in the diagrams, are used to represent entities or different businesses running self-sufficient processes. Relationships between activities of different Pools are represented in BPMN as a special type of dotted lines called Message Flow. Given these adaptations of BPMN to represent high-level processes in our conception, it is not possible, in general, to directly use simulators or executable code generators, which are discussed later, associated with this language for this level of modeling, since the representation is asynchronous; in other words, there is no strict sequence and many things may be happening simultaneously. But these models can be easily converted to models executable with simulation software as shown by Barros et al. in a case of emergency patients processing in a hospital.[49]

The *second style* of modeling, detailing the first style models by progressive decomposition of higher-level elements (hierarchical decomposition), will be used when we get to the detailed design of processes, including the business logic associated with the computer support; for these we will adopt BPMN conventions in its conception of sequence and control logic, which leads to synchronism. Here we will define two substyles: one that does not intend simulation and implementation of processes by executing them and another allowing for this. The difference between these is the degree of formality of the representation, since, in the second case, strict conventions of BPMN that make feasible the simulation and execution must be respected. The advantage of this second variant is that, under certain conditions, the computing support to the process can be generated automatically, without the need for computational design or writing code. This is feasible because BPMN was designed to make graphic representations, which comply with certain conditions, to be converted to the conventions of software that can generate execution. These types of software, called Business Processes Managements Suites (BPMS), have proprietary complements to BPMN that make the execution feasible and provide the possibility of using web services, which contain logic that cannot be modeled with BPMN that interact with the suite. This type of technology is illustrated in Barros and Quezada[50] and will be illustrated with the case of managing ambulatory patients in Chapter 6.

In summary, depending on the level of design, as defined in Chapter 1, in which we find ourselves within the modeling and design objectives that we pursue, we will use different styles of representation, which can be defined as consistent and complementary. But BPMN does not allow, as stated earlier, to design complex business logic that execute Analytics imbedded in the internal tasks of each activity, particularly those that provide automatic support to complex decisions in the form of algorithm or heuristics. Here, we have the opportunity to integrate the analytical techniques mentioned in the previous section by means of logic, which is encapsulated in computer programs that are called by the activities of the BPMN during the execution of the process by means of a technology such as web services.[51]

The union of the approach of structural design of business processes and analytical methods, made possible by the type of modeling just presented, generates the possibility of a new class of business design, which we will call *intelligent solutions*, to be presented as BI structures in this chapter. The differences in these solutions with the traditional approaches—which only improve the handlings of information in a process, as the Enterprise Resource Planning (ERP) packages typically do, or rationalize the processes, eliminating existing unnecessary activities or improving them with logics based on experience—are to approach thoroughly and rigorously the decisions that exist within a process. To support such decisions, Analytics is used as explained in the previous section. We have important accumulated experience of Analytics embedded within processes that has allowed us to incorporate it in the patterns used for such integration, which will be summarized in this chapter as Business, Architecture, and Process Patterns.

The hierarchical modeling approach based on BPMN allows managing the complexity inherent in integrating very different mental models and tools—problem that was outlined at the beginning of this chapter— since they are progressively introduced, as design goes from structural to detailed. Thus, for example, at the top of the modeling hierarchy, the conceptual models for Strategy determination, Business Model definition, Capabilities determination, and consequent Business Design are the most relevant. Subsequently, Business Design is made operational in Business and Process Architectures, modeled with the first modeling style with BPMN, based on patterns. As this architecture is decomposed with detailed design of its component processes, Analytics provide the tools that allow generating business logic, which assures that the innovations conceived at the structural level really produce the desired results. This results in BPMN designs modeled with the second style that has embedded business logic and appropriate Information System support allowing their execution. This hierarchical modeling approach is detailed later in this chapter and will be present in all the cases reported in Chapters 3 to 6.

Competitive Strategy and Business Model for Health Care Services

We start with the following question: What could be the principles of a Competitive Strategy and Business Model for health care services that provide a foundation for design?

Porter's Proposal

One answer to previous question can be derived from Porter and Teisberg's proposal to concentrate on what Porter calls *Value-Based Health Care Delivery*, which defines the core issue as the value of health delivered or the patient health outcomes per dollar spent.[52] They believe that the fundamental issue in health care is value for patients, not access, volume, convenience, or cost containment, defining value as:

Value = Health outcomes/Costs of delivering the outcomes

Outcomes are the full set of patient health outcomes over the care cycle, and costs are the total costs of care for the patient's condition, not just the cost of a single provider or a single service. Then the challenge is how to design a health care system that dramatically improves patient value. In doing so, several design variables can be manipulated; for example:

- Prevention
- Early detection
- Right diagnosis
- Right treatment to the right patient
- Early and timely treatment
- Treatment earlier in the causal chain of disease
- Rapid cycle time of diagnosis and treatment
- Less invasive treatment methods
- Less care induced illness

The aforementioned ideas imply that people' health should be monitored to determine preventive and effective actions required to avoid people getting seriously ill; by doing so, the need for expensive treatments to correct a situation that could have been avoided is eliminated. In this line of though, we developed a project for a large private medical clinic in Chile, where a Classification model, as in the idea of Data Mining, described in the previous volume, was developed for chronic diabetes patients to predict the risk of complications of their medical conditions. This allowed the definition of rules to generate preventive actions based on the clinical patient information and differentiated medical interventions. The model developed was able to successfully predict the crisis risk of chronic diabetes patients and the use of the model led to 6.4 percent reduction in the annual hospitalization for them,[53] which was also detailed in previous volume.

Other ideas of Porter implicate that, when people get sick, more effective medical methods and processes should be used so that the treatments are the right ones at the right time, minimizing time for the patient and adverse consequences derived from the treatment.

Porter and Teisberg's approach is clearly aligned with a Competitive Strategy of best product[54] in the variant of developing unique attributes for a hospital's services that interpret clients' genuine needs and also partially cover the Strategy of integral solutions to clients, summarized in previous section, since a deeper knowledge of clients will allow to define customized services to them, as shown in the previous example of diabetes patients.

As for a Business Model, the value for clients is its emphasis on services that try to prevent people from falling sick, which means less risk of complications and less cost for society in general, and the value previously defined of minimizing the cost of the health outcomes.

Obviously, the aforementioned approach is not easy to implement since it requires massive and useful data about population health at the individual level. Also, it requires an important change in the medical practices that the profession is reluctant to accept. Hence, it is a model for the most progressive health services, as the one exemplified earlier.

Disruptive Innovation

Another radical proposal for redesigning health services proposed by Christensen et al. is that of Disruptive Innovation, in which the argument states that:[55]

> In any industry, a Disruptive Innovation sneaks in from below. While the dominant players are focused on improving their products or services to the point where the average consumer doesn't even know what she's using (think over engineered computers), they miss simpler, more convenient, and less costly offerings initially designed to appeal to the low end of the market. Over time, the simpler offerings get better—so much better that they meet the needs of the vast majority of users. We've seen this happen recently in the telecommunications industry, where routers— initially dismissed by leading makers of the faster, more reliable circuit switches—came to take over the market.

They posit that this is exactly what is happening in the health services, where its development is geared to developing even more complex solutions for the few illnesses that present more challenges to the medical profession and professionals are trained to treat them. This implies that they are overqualified and too expensive to treat the larger numbers of patients who have much lesser needs, which means excessive costs—a problem that is evident in the health sector of the United States. Hence, their challenge is to develop Disruptive Innovations from below, from the simpler needs up, and give as examples the evolution of treatment of diabetes from complex blood laboratory analysis to present solution where patients pack miniature blood glucose meters with them wherever they go; they are able to manage most aspects of a disease that previously had required much more professional involvement. They also mention angioplasty as another example. Prior to the early 1980s, patients with coronary artery disease were treated through bypass surgery. It required a complex, technologically sophisticated surgical team, as well as multiple specialists in several disciplines, complicated equipment, days in the hospital, and weeks in recovery. The far simpler angioplasty uses a balloon to dilate narrowed arteries and is more effective and much less costly. So they conclude that these types of solutions should be emphasized, but the medical industry, which loses with cost reductions, has so far blocked the popularization of this approach. What solution do they propose? Match the clinicians' skill level to the difficulty of the medical problem, for which they propose a hierarchy of medical problems, from simple to more complex, in the following way:

1. The lowest level of medical problems is the one where diagnostic and treatment can be *rule-based*, as it can be done with many infectious diseases.
2. The middle tier can be approached with diagnosis and treatment based on *pattern recognition*, as Type I diabetes can be detected with a pattern of symptoms and a relatively standardized treatment be applied.
3. The most complex disorders have to be diagnosed and treated with a *problem-solving* approach, which requires collective experience and judgment and implies executing cycles of testing, hypotheses, and experimentation.

Therefore, the conclusion is to orient the investments and efforts to initiatives that focus on the first two levels of the previous hierarchy with an emphasis on simplification as opposed to what occurs worldwide today. We will further pursue this idea on a case presented in the following section.

The Christensen et al. proposal is consistent with the best product positioning, in that it favors the generation of new products that are more adapted to peoples' needs according to the level of complexity of their pathologies and also to operational effectiveness, since it tries to diminish costs for medical problems of complexity levels (1) and (2).

The Business Model behind this approach creates value for patients by providing the medical service that is just right for a given pathology, according to its level of complexity, avoiding overtreatment, with the health risks associated, and unnecessary costs.

Other Proposals

Recently a group of advisors to President Obama has proposed the idea of using Systems Engineering, in solving the U.S. health problem, defined as an interdisciplinary approach to analyze, design, manage, and measure a complex system with efforts to improve its efficiency, productivity, quality, safety, and other factors, including the full suite of tools and methods that can analyze a system, its elements, and connections between elements; assist with the design of policies and processes; and help manage operations to provide better quality and outcomes at lower cost.[56] It is evident the alignment of this idea with the proposals we have made so far in this book, since our approach is not only systemic, using all the disciplines and techniques already presented, but provides a hierarchical design approach that allows managing design complexity.

Another theory that studies the structure of complex layered systems, as public health systems are, is flexibility and complexity.[57] Such theory defines flexibility as the facility to make certain changes in a system, as, for example, changing its function. But flexibility may increase complexity, so the challenge is to design structures that are flexible but not too complex. In analyzing this problem, structure may use typical generic architectures: Tree, layered, and networks. Tree structures are hierarchies more centralized and inflexible than the others and layered are also centralized but more flexible. On the other hand networks are very flexible but complex. Public health is naturally layered, since there is usually a level of complex hospitals, another of intermediate services, and a third of primary care practices. Then an important question is how this layered structure can be managed to maintain flexibility but in a more decentralized way. We will encounter this problem when considering the managing the architecture of the public health system later in this chapter.

In other line, McKinsey has estimated in 300 billion dollars the potential value to the U.S. health system of using big data,[58] using powerful IT and Analytics, in generating better service for patients that will save lives, increase live expectancy and reduce costs. Also a recent report estimates in 3 to 4 trillion dollars, at least a 17 percent of the GNP, the cost of health care in the United States, its efficiency being very low, since its ranks 50 in this item among 55 developed nations.[59] So there a lot of potential of cost reduction by increasing efficiency, which is true for many other countries and, in particular, for Chile.

Our Proposal

On the basis of the experience with many projects in the private and public health sectors in Chile, we propose to concentrate on the following variables that define objectives to be pursued in improving health services:

1. Quality: The treatments must be appropriate to maximize the cure probability and must improve in time to increase such probability, especially for diseases that have a high rate of mortality.
2. Efficiency: Hospitals should maximize their production—measured according to clinical complexity, for example Diagnosis-Related Groups (DRG)[60]—using their resources in the best possible way.
3. Fairness: The patients must be taken care of according to their needs and, in the case of the Public Sector where the resources are always limited, in an order related to the associated risk of life of the pathology that affects them.

These objectives have something in common with Porter and Teisberg's ideas, as quality is correlated with minimizing the cost of the health outcomes, because the search for an adequate treatment for each pathology contributes to generate good patients' health outcomes; this, combined with efficiency, contributes to improve patient health outcomes per dollar spent. Furthermore, fairness implies giving patients the right treatment at the right time, avoiding waiting lists ordered by time of first diagnostic as it is the usual case in Chile, defining explicit priorities associated with the pathology and aggravating factors; this agrees with their idea of minimizing time for patients and the risk of adverse consequences. They are also related to the Christensen et al. proposal, since, in pursuing quality in the sense just defined, the complexity of the illnesses can be accounted for in finding the right cure. Moreover, the efficiency pushes in the direction of avoiding unnecessary treatments.

The objectives we propose are aligned with a best product positioning Strategy, including operational effectiveness (efficiency) and unique attributes due to quality and fairness.[61]

The Business Model[62] behind such objectives generates value for patients in general by the way of better quality of treatment and, in the case of the Public Sector, fairness that prioritizes patients with a high risk of death, thus generating value for the people and society in terms of increased life expectancy. Value is also generated for customers who pay less for the medical services due to better efficiency that reduces costs and prices.

In what follows, we will consider only our approach, since most of our cases developed follow its ideas; however, when relevant, we will relate our ideas to the other proposals presented earlier. Given this, what are the Capabilities in health institutions needed to make operative the Competitive Strategy and Business Model of such an approach?

Capabilities are provided by the Intelligent Structures and Business Patterns (BPs) that are presented in the next section. Note that, besides proposing good foundations for the design of health services, we provide a mechanism to implement the Capabilities needed to put such principles into practice. This is our differentiation: We not only provide ideas, but also make them operational by means of predesigned structures of processes.

General Architectures for Health Services

Now that we are clear about general health Strategy and Business Model, including Capabilities involved, we provide general architectures for health systems that can serve as a framework of reference for health services design, including the necessary Capabilities within them.

As a part of the framework, Intelligence Structures and BPs are summarized, which were detailed in the previous book mentioned in the Prolog; then we present the general health architectures we propose.

Intelligence Structures and Business Patterns

Intelligence Structures

We now show how Analytics can be incorporated in alternative design structures that offer different complexity levels of techniques used, which can be applied when performing the design levels identified in Chapter 1.

The use of Analytics in our design proposal aims to providing business logic that supports *intelligent* business development and management. In order to formalize the options a service designer has in using Analytics, we propose *Intelligence Structures* that provide several levels with increasing complexity as follows. We start with a basic case, where business processes, which are structured as in the design levels of Chapter 1, have an IT system support providing nonintelligent information that just reports the state of the processes. Then we complement this structure with intelligent support that specifies how such processes, which are in routine execution, can be supported by Analytics and IT. The general structure we propose is summarized in Figure 2.1, where the intelligent support in introduced as a general component that can be implemented with four intelligence levels, summarized in the figure. Such levels are then detailed as four different structures that define how they can be implemented.

Now we give a summary of the structures for the different intelligence levels defined in Figure 2.1; more detail can be found in the previous volume mentioned in the Prolog.

Intelligence Structure I corresponds to the idea of developing and implementing simple business logic that, based on the state of the process,

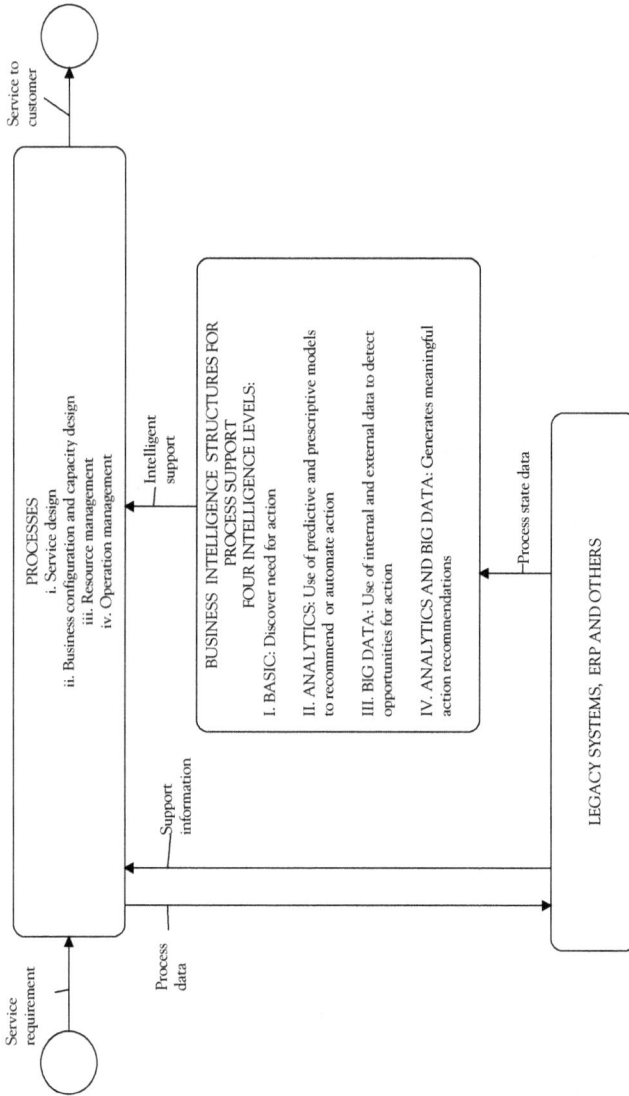

Figure 2.1 General Intelligence Structure

discovers the need for action and, possibly, recommends actions on process execution and management. Logic can be based on several ideas:

- Simple rules based on experience and process metrics, which show that the process is not operating as expected; for example, waiting time before a step of the process that is not according to a service metric in patient treatment in a hospital emergency. There is BPMS software[63] that allows to model and execute this type of processes, using BPMN, including metrics definition and their monitoring.
- Formalization of expert knowledge based on semantic modeling and similar techniques; for example, formalization of medical criteria in an emergency triage to determine illness severity for a patient, which is applied with patient data using a computer program that recommends a priority for him. Similar cases to this are logic for surgical list prioritization and bed management as reported in Barros.[64]
- Use of Balanced Scorecard[65] and similar techniques that specify the expected results of a process, which compared with state data that gives actual results determine which parts of the process are not according to plan.

Intelligence Structure II uses predictive and optimization models allowing to make a well-founded recommendation on how to act on the process, including the possibility of influencing the customer, as presented in Figure 2.1. Barros[66] presents several real cases that also use this structure including cardboard optimal production management, flight demand management in an airline, proactive sales management in an office equipment distributor, chronic disease management in a private clinic, preventive compliance checking of labor law infringements, sawmill optimal production planning, and management of a large workforce in a food distributor; it is also possible to have applications oriented to business developments, such as a real case of use of demand forecasting and simulation models to design an hospital's emergency configuration and capacity.[67] Other well-known cases of this type are Amazon and Walmart on predictive and optimization models use.

Intelligence Structure III builds on Intelligence Structure I by introducing big structured and unstructured data coming from different sources—web, cloud, contact center, sensors, social media, logs, Internet of Things (IoT), and the like—and sophisticated data manipulation and analysis technologies. Examples of such technologies are Hadoop for data storage, advanced multistructure data architecture and in memory databases; high definition models to discover patterns—for example, clicks patterns for customer buying on a commerce site—and find path to purchase, product affinity and shopping cart abandonment; and advanced visualization. Real cases of use of these technologies are a medical supplies company that uses sensors to monitor employees and products movements in a warehouse in order to determine what to do in real time to expedite shipments and make better use of resources; and a Telco that combines web usage with contact center interactions to identify important churn factors, resulting in the identification of hundreds of at-risk churn targets worth millions per year.[68]

Intelligence Structure IV uses Analytics, in advanced versions, over traditional data and big data to generate meaningful actions over the service processes (Levels i to iv), as shown in Figure 2.1. Actions may be generated by advising, recommending, and, in some cases, automating them by means of prescriptive models. Actions may be related to service delivery, service processes management and execution, service capacity adjustments, and new business development, including, for example, creating new Business Models, discovering new services offers, and monetizing data to external companies. The general objective in doing this is to provide business agility at different design levels. The Analytics involved in this include truly intelligent approaches, such as Web Mining, text mining, voice recognition and processing, image recognition, and Machine Learning. These are necessary to make sense of the big data coming from the web, social media, the cloud, mobile devices, IoT, and sensor data a company may collect; for example, the IoT data coming from sensors on trucks to determine their maintenance needs mentioned before. Cases using these ideas are:

- Netflix, which has developed a movie "recommendation engine" based on customer behavior that relies on an algorithm that clusters movies, connects customer movie rankings to the clusters, evaluates ratings online, and considers current use web behavior to ensure a personalized web page for each user; it also has a testing culture for new business developments that uses surveys, website testing, concept development and testing, advertising testing, Data Mining, brand awareness studies, subscriber satisfaction, channel analysis, marketing mix optimization, segmentation research, and marketing material effectiveness. Machine Learning is behind the "recommendation engine" and other analyses.[69]

- Walmart, besides historic use of demand prediction with its own data, has introduced mining of social media data to predict shoppers' purchases and act on that basis to plan logistics, which is also optimized with mathematical models.[70]

- Asthmapolis,[71] an organization that gives services to asthmatic patients in the United States,[72] was motivated by the fact that around 26 million people suffered from asthma in 2003 in this country. The annual cost of treating this condition was estimated at $50 billion for medical expenditure, plus a further $6 billion in additional indirect costs resulting from missed school and days off work. This considerable expense is to some degree due to the patients themselves, who do not follow their treatment procedures properly or are not in regular contact with their health care providers, who then lack feedback on how the treatment is going and under what conditions attacks continue to occur. It has been calculated that if patient treatment could be better monitored, 80 percent of all asthma-related hospitalization could be avoided, and that the mortality rate from asthma could be reduced by 20 percent. The technology that Asthmapolis has developed has several objectives, one of them being to help health care workers to treat their patients more effectively as a result of monitoring their treatment on an ongoing basis and collecting precise data on the environmental conditions under which patients use their inhalers. Aside from enabling patients to manage their own treatment more efficiently, the

Asthmapolis system is also proving very useful for medical staff. It works with a small sensor attached to the patient's inhaler linked to an IoS or Android mobile app and an online platform. Geolocation is integrated into the app, so medical practitioners have access to precise, detailed information on how their patients are using their inhalers. They can also monitor how the treatment is working. Doctors receive this information about their patients on an ongoing basis and can therefore work more closely with them. Moreover, the data collected can indicate those areas where asthma attacks most often occur, thus enabling health practitioners to warn their patients about any danger areas and sending them notifications, suggestions, and advice on the precautions they ought to be taking. Asthmapolis has also entered into a partnership with Qualcomm Life, so that those patients who do not own a smartphone can be alerted by standard phone call, SMS, or e-mail. A pilot study has shown that 60 percent of all patients who embarked on the project were not monitoring their own condition. After three months, 50 percent of these patients were able to track and manage their asthma condition proactively, while 70 percent of all participants in the study stepped up their overall self-monitoring activity.[73]

- A Chilean children's hospital decided to send chronic patients with respiratory problems to their homes to liberate beads. They had a monitoring process designed by the hospital but operated by children relatives, from which need for medical attention was determined. Then we developed a new design based on online monitoring of medical variables—such as temperature, cardiac frequency, and respiratory frequency—and a diagnosis data-based analytical model to determine when the patient is in crisis and needs medical attention. All this is supported by computing and telecommunications technologies that make the process effective. The new process, which will be elaborated in Chapters 3 and 6, is now under implementation at the hospital.

Business Patterns

Now we present the *BPs* that model different structures, using the various Intelligent Structures just presented, from which a business can select to have a first approximation to the Business Design. We give a summary, presenting more details for patterns relevant for health services design. A complete presentation of BPs is given in the previous volume.

For organizations that provide the services we intent to design we propose several BPs abstracted from experience. They show how the components of a service business can be structured in different configurations to generate a desired Capability. The need for such Capability is derived from a Strategy and Business Model and is related to some kind of innovation that an organization wants to perform in its business. Then the BPs will show the new business components that are necessary for particular Capabilities. The more relevant innovations in services relate to the more changing and dynamic demand for services. Moreover, demand, when occurs, is difficult to manage, since there are constraints for its programmed release to "production" that go from cases where demand cannot wait, as in hospital emergencies, to situations where Service Level Agreements (SLAs) must be met. So we need to determine creative ways to tackle such a type of complex demand. As the BPs show, some answers to this challenge are to track and monitor demand using Analytics to predict in advance customers needs; to continuously monitor service processes to know when they are not adequately processing demand and take corrective actions to fix them; and constantly evaluate the services performance to discover opportunities for improved or new services.

The proposed patterns emphasize the introduction of Analytics that will be embedded within the components of the management system, which implies innovation and redesign in the way the business is performed. Such patterns have been developed based on experience and knowledge generated by hundreds of projects; we summarize them here, highlighting the ones we consider have the most potential for innovation in health services.

One such pattern is *Client's Knowledge-Based Selling.* The common aim of the organizations that have motivated this pattern, called Business Pattern 1 (BP1), is to advance to:

- Strategic positioning in the line of giving integral services to clients, as defined by Hax and Wilde and summarized in Chapter 1.
- A Business Model based on providing value to clients by personalized services, in the idea of getting toward lock-in, generating "captive" income, and the advantages of better pricing; for this the key processes are those that implement the Capabilities, which will be discussed later, and the resources are mainly professional people who can develop these Capabilities.

Real cases of use of these ideas are to actively monitor customers to model their behavior and generate customized services; examples of this are the asthma and chronic respiratory patients monitoring in the cases presented for Intelligence Structure IV.

To implement the Strategy and Business Model objectives of this pattern, there is a need to have Capabilities that allow to capture and organize customer data, to process such data with analytical machinery—for example, Data and Web Mining, including analysis of data in social networks, semantic analysis, and the like—and to generate ideas, based on this, for proactive services to clients. A pattern, BP1, for this situation is shown in Figure 2.2, where the key idea is to complement typical components a service has with more advanced and intelligent management elements that define what is required to generate the new Capability. In such a model, a *Value Stream* is a set of interrelated operating activities or processes that go from generating requirements for a client to successfully delivering the service. It has a more restricted scope than the typical Value Chain, defined by Porter and others, and the one we will define later. The *Management System* is a set of interrelated activities, using basic practices, which decides about actions necessary to define and direct the Value Stream to fulfill clients' requirements, including short-term management, such as sales and operations or logistics, in addition to longer-term Strategic Planning, new product development, and other new development Capabilities. Financial, human, and other resources management is not explicitly included. These basic practices are enhanced with new components that have embedded

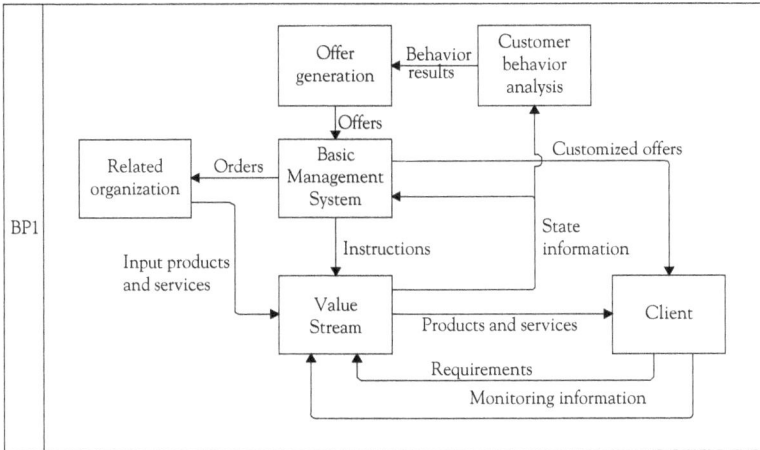

Figure 2.2 Business Pattern 1 (BP1)

Analytics-based models, which allow generating new knowledge about users of the service and actions based on it. For modeling simplification, all the data have been summarized under the label "State information," which includes items such as customers' service history, website navigation logs, and the like. The flows in the model represent the typical relationships among the components; some of them are information flows, such as "Orders" and "Behavior results" and other flows of material things, such as "Input products" and, in some cases, "Products and services."

An implemented case of use of this pattern is the children's hospital that maintains chronic patients with respiratory problems at their homes with a new design based on online monitoring of medical variables and diagnosis data-based analytical models to determine when the patient is in crisis and needs medical attention, presented earlier.

This pattern is an instance of application of the Intelligence Structure II or IV, when big data is present, of the previous section, since it incorporates specific components that allow developing predictive models to provide proactive service to customers. It is oriented to operational design (Level iv).

Following pattern is Business Pattern 3 (BP3): *Internal Learning for Process Improvement.* This pattern is based on the following objectives defined by Strategy and Business Model:

1. The positioning that is selected is best product according to the definition by Hax and Wilde in the variant, also defined by Porter, of operational effectiveness.
2. The value that is to be generated for clients is to provide attributes for the product that are appreciated by them such as low cost, due to better efficiency, quality, on-time delivery, and the like; key processes are related to discovering how to generate more value by operational process redesign and implementing such redesigns; and key resources are again human resources that are able to innovate on processes, including users who have to adapt to new ways of doing things.

The Capability that is needed for such Strategy and Business Model is to be able to systematically analyze the organization processes, in particular, the Value Streams, to detect opportunities for process improvement. This should lead to very effective and efficient processes, which are also convenient for the customer.

The BP3 in Figure 2.3 provides a way to implement such Capability with an emphasis on the use of Analytics to systematically find the origin and possible solutions for process problems using hard data. Real

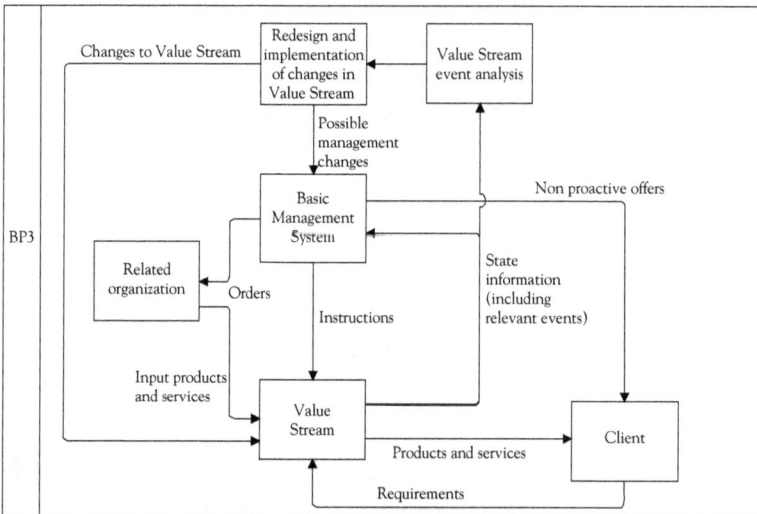

Figure 2.3 Business Pattern 3 (BP3)

cases on which this pattern is based relate to the analysis of events in the workflow of patients in urgency, ambulatory services, and surgical operations in hospitals to discover events that delay or put into risk the treatment of patients to redesign the associated process and eliminate such events.

This pattern covers the possibilities of redesigning the service itself, configuration and capacity, use of resources, and operational processes (Levels i to iv); possible Intelligence Architectures are I, II, and III, with simple rules, predictive and optimization models, and analyses with big data. A case of use of BP3 is the application of DEA, as will be detailed in Chapter 4, to 40 public hospitals, which has shown in practice that measuring efficiency allows to define in a very precise way how hospital services should change to improve their efficiency and assign resources accordingly; we are also currently calculating the efficiency of academic departments at the Medical Faculty of the University of Chile and finding similar opportunities as in the hospital case.

Next pattern is *Optimum Resource Usage*. The common aim of the organizations that have motivated this pattern, called Business Pattern 6 (BP6), is to advance to:

1. Strategic positioning in the line of giving the best product in its version of operational effectiveness.
2. A Business Model based on providing value to clients by means of excellent service at competitive prices, which requires low cost based on good resource use; for this, the key processes are those implemented by the Capabilities that will be discussed later and the resources are mainly professional people who can develop these Capabilities.

Real health cases on which this pattern is based are the following: OR scheduling in a hospital that comply with patients' priorities and optimize resource use and optimal capacity and assignment of OR to specialties to satisfy patients' maximum waiting time. These cases will be presented in Chapters 4 and 6.

This pattern includes Capabilities that allow having the abilities to detect opportunities for better resource usage and the tools to develop models, mathematical or heuristics, to produce optimal use. The pattern, BP6, for this situation in shown in Figure 2.4, where the key idea is to complement typical components that a service has with more advanced and intelligent management elements that define what is required to generate the new Capability.

This pattern aims to redesigning configuration and capacity, use of resources, and operational processes (Levels ii, iii, and iv) using Intelligent Structures II or IV, since predictive models based on internal data or complex analyses of big data and prescriptive mathematical models may be necessary to analyze resources use and design improved processes that optimize their use.

Additional BPs, detailed in previous volume, that cover other design levels and other Intelligence Architectures are:

- Business Pattern 2 (BP2): *Creation of New Streams of Service,* which provides further integration with the customer, in the line of integral services to clients, with new streams of business services that provide innovative added value services to them. Intelligent Structure IV is the one present in this pattern, since powerful Analytics applied on local and external big data are needed to generate new business opportunities; so its aim is business design (Level i).
- Business Pattern 4 (BP4): *Performance Evaluation for Replanning and Process Improvement.* This pattern is centered on the analysis and redesign of the operational processes (Level iv) with simple business logic of the Intelligence Structure I. It is applicable in situations where there is a formal Strategic Planning process that generates formal KPI's or equivalent targets that allow to detect systematic noncompliances and, from there, generate redesign opportunities.
- Business Pattern 5 (BP5): *Product Innovation.* New products or services or both, developed from this pattern, provide high value personalized services, generating a lock-in effect that induces loyalty. This pattern aims to business design (Level i) using Intelligent Structures II, III, or IV, since predictive models or complex analyses on internal data or of big data

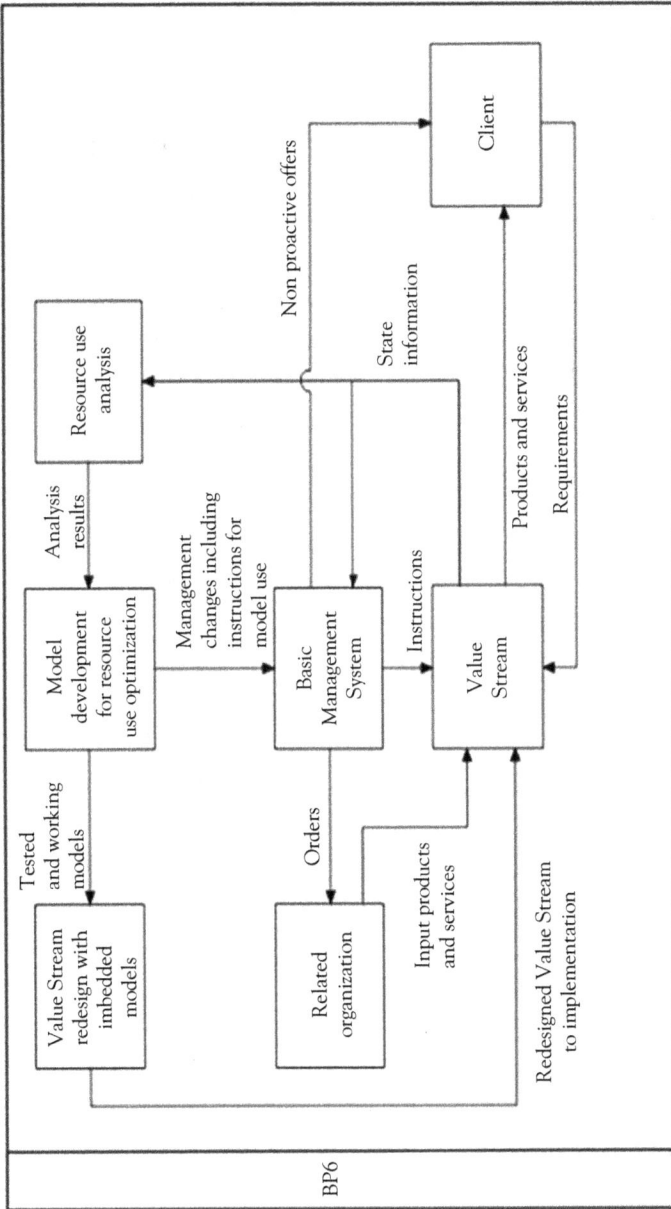

Figure 2.4 Business Pattern 6 (BP6)

may be necessary to identify new service opportunities. A case in which this pattern has been applied is a large private hospital, where the problem solved was to create a Capability, based on this pattern, to manage all investments in assuring the generation, evaluation, planning, and implementation of innovative new health services for their clients. This case was introduced in Chapter 1 and it will be detailed in Chapters 3 and 4.

- Business Pattern 6: *Optimum Resource Usage.* This pattern covers design *levels ii to iv*, by developing predictive and optimization models in the *Intelligence Structure II* style, to assure that the resources needed to provide the capacity necessary to process demand, estimated by forecasting models, is provided at a minimum cost; that resources needed to provide the capacity are deployed dynamically, as needed, at a minimum cost; and that the day-to-day scheduling of demand over the capacity is performed in such a way that demand is satisfied with the best use of resources. Examples were given when presenting Intelligence Structure II.

General Architectures

First general architectures proposed for any business, presented in the previous volume, are summarized.

We propose *Architecture and Business Process Patterns*[74] that can be adapted to any domain in order to model service processes configuration options. So it will be shown that any design based on the BPs can be converted into corresponding processes design by means of an instantiation or specialization of the Architecture and Business Process Patterns that are presented later. All the patterns are based on extensive experience with process design in hundreds of real cases and share the idea that there are four aggregations of processes, called macroprocesses, which exist in any organization; they are:

1. *Macroprocess 1 (Macro1) or Value Chain*: Collection of processes for the production of the services the organization offers to its customers,

which begins with their requirements formulation and ends with the satisfaction of the requests; it includes all the management and operating activities related to marketing, sales, supply, production, and logistics necessary to capture and generate the service. We call this macroprocess *Value Chain*, adopting a definition slightly different from Porter's that includes other processes in it, such as the development of new products and the management of supporting resources, such as personnel and financial;[75] such processes are included as part of other macroprocesses in this proposal. *Value Streams* are contained within Macro1 (Value Chain) and there may be several of them, explained using cases in the following chapters.

2. *Macroprocess 2 (Macro2) or New Capabilities Development*: Collection of processes for the development of new Capabilities that the organization requires to be competitive, such as new products and services, including new Business Models; necessary infrastructure to produce and operate those products, including IT infrastructure; and new business processes to assure operational effectiveness and value creation for customers, establishing, as a consequence, IT-based systems.

3. *Macroprocess 3 (Macro3) or Business Planning*: It contains the collection of processes that are necessary to define the direction of the organization, in the form of strategies, materialized in plans, programs, and budgets with well-defined objectives.

4. *Macroprocess 4 (Macro4) or Support Resource Management*: Collection of support processes that manage the resources necessary for proper operation of the other macroprocesses. Four versions of these processes can be defined *a priori*: financial resources, human resources, infrastructure, and materials.

These process aggregations are called macroprocesses because they contain many related processes, subprocesses, and activities that are necessary to produce key services, for internal organizational use or external clients, such as those offered to customers, strategic plans, and new facilities.

The four macroprocess patterns just presented can be combined into different structures depending on the type of businesses. We call these structures Process Architecture Patterns, modeled in BPMN as explained in the previous volume. The most basic pattern is shown in Figure 2.5 where only one instance of each macroprocess is included and therefore there is only one Value Chain; also the relationships with clients, suppliers, and other entities are not shown in detail. In real complex cases, there may be several Value Chains, each of these containing several Value Streams, integration of processes with clients, suppliers, and business partners and other relationships.

All the architecture patterns we define are based on the general structure in Figure 2.5, which shows the interaction of the different macroprocesses with markets, customers, and suppliers by means of information flows and the internal flows, such as "Plans" generated by Macro3 that direct the behavior of the other macroprocesses; "Needs" that request "Resources" to Macro4; flow of "Resources" and feedback flows of "Ideas and Results" to monitor processes and initiate new plans in Macro3 and change in Capabilities in Macro2.

Since our patterns model business practice, they must represent different business structures. Here we define structure types based on the classification developed at MIT,[76] which was reviewed in the previous volume. This classification defines the following business structures: Diversification, Unification, Coordination, and Replication.

Then we consider the following architecture types:

1. Businesses with just one Value Chain of the Macro1 type.
2. Businesses with several Value Chains, each of which operates independently (Diversification of MIT's classification).
3. Businesses that have several Value Chains, each of which operates independently but may share some supporting central services, such as business planning (Macro3), product design (Macro2) and financial, IT, and human resources services (Macro4); they may also use instances of centrally defined processes in their operations (Coordination and Replication of MIT's classification).
4. Businesses that have several Value Chains, which share some of their internal processes—which are common services such as logistics, IT, and supply, some of which may be outsourced—and supporting central services (Unification of MIT's classification).

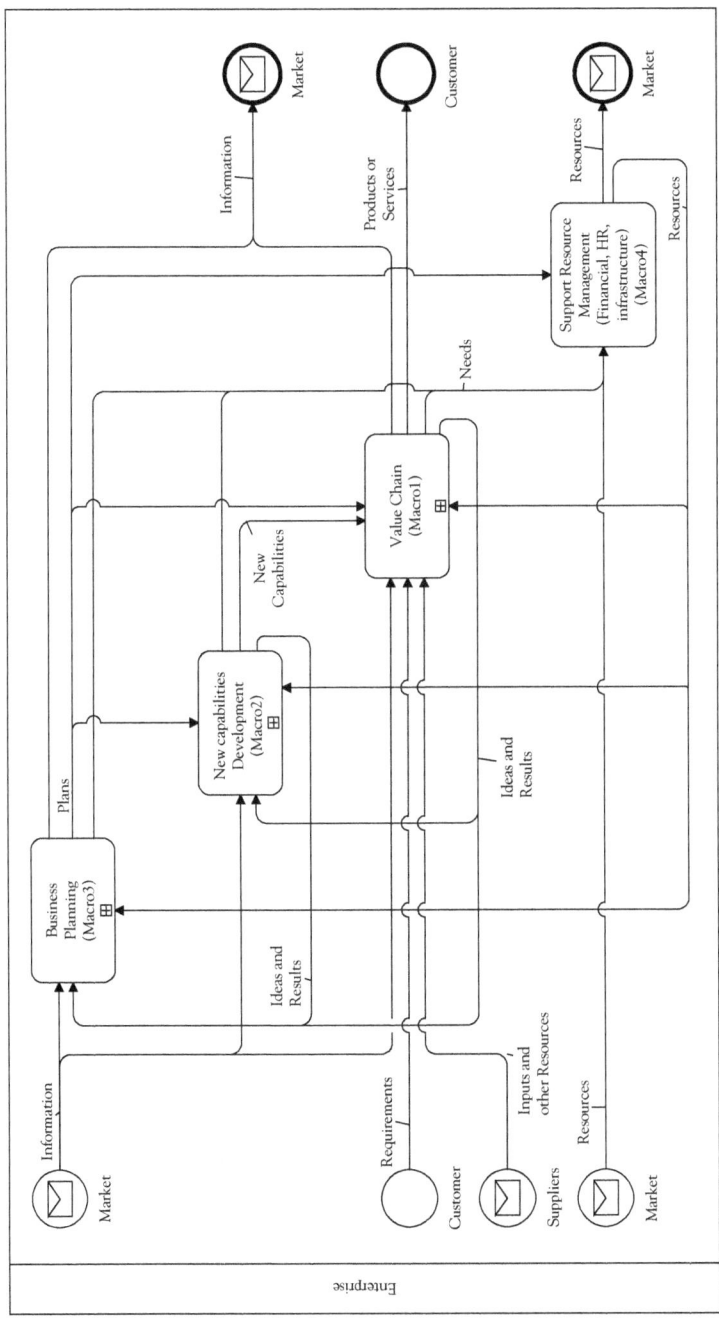

Figure 2.5 Macroprocesses Architecture Pattern

The Process Architecture Patterns types can be modeled in similar way to Figure 2.5, which we do not show here. We will only present the pattern more relevant to health institutions, which is the one in Figure 2.6. The basic idea of this pattern is to factor out the different Value Chains (i), which generate the services organization offers, several Internal Services (j) that may be centralized because of economies of scale or scope, transaction costs, agency advantages, and other economic reasons.[77] For example, laboratories, ORs, beads, cleaning, and IT support in hospitals. We notice that some of the shared services can be outsourced to suppliers. Later, in Chapters 3 to 6, the application of this architecture to several cases will be presented.

The Process Architecture Patterns proposed are Enterprise Architectures with emphasis on the dimension of processes; but other architecture dimensions, such as organizational structure, which were outlined in Chapter 1, are present in the proposed structures. The dimension of IT architecture is more hidden, but, for example, shared services imply a centralized structure of systems, data, and infrastructure to support the shared services. It implies that the process structure dimension, corresponding to an explicit business design, determines the other dimensions of organization and IT structure, as modeled in Figure 1.1.

Hospital Architecture

We propose a general process architecture for hospitals based on the Shared Services Architecture Pattern presented earlier. Shared services are part of hospital practices, as all the existing Value Chains that provide different services for patients—emergency, ambulatory services, and hospitalization—use several internal common services, such as laboratory services, ORs for surgeries, food services, and cleaning services. Therefore, our architecture pattern applies directly to this domain. Specialization of such a pattern to hospitals then results in the architecture of Figure 2.7.[78] This architecture has been fully validated by the management of several representative public hospitals and also by the staff of one of the largest private hospitals in Chile. In such an architecture, the Capabilities associated with "Product innovation" are taken care by the macroprocess

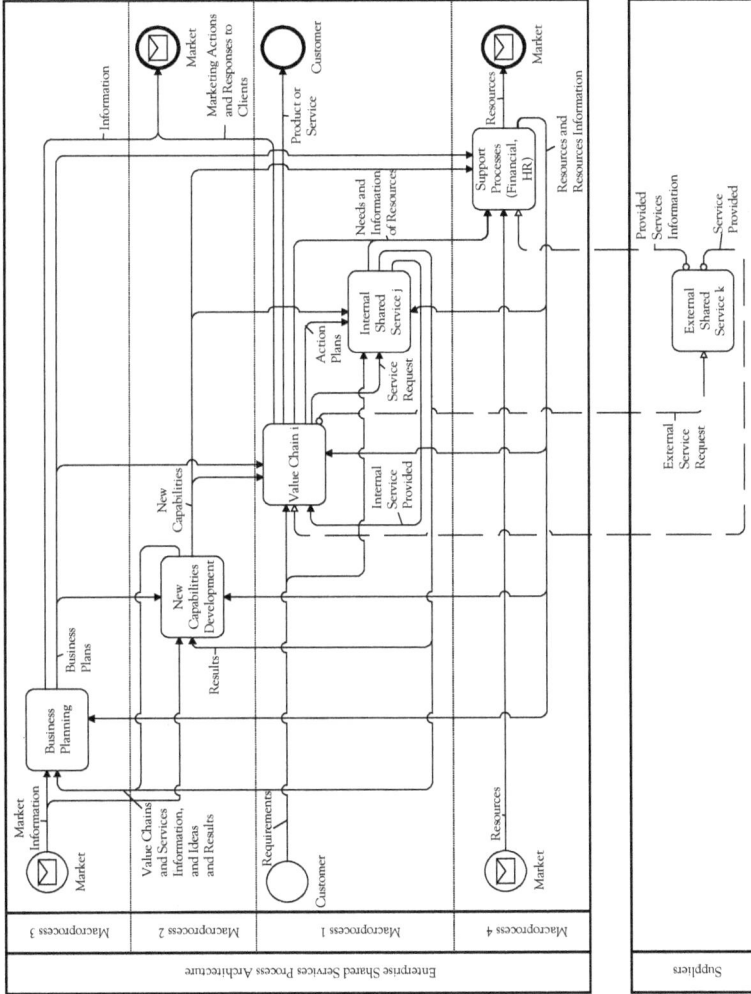

Figure 2.6 Shared Services Process Architecture Pattern

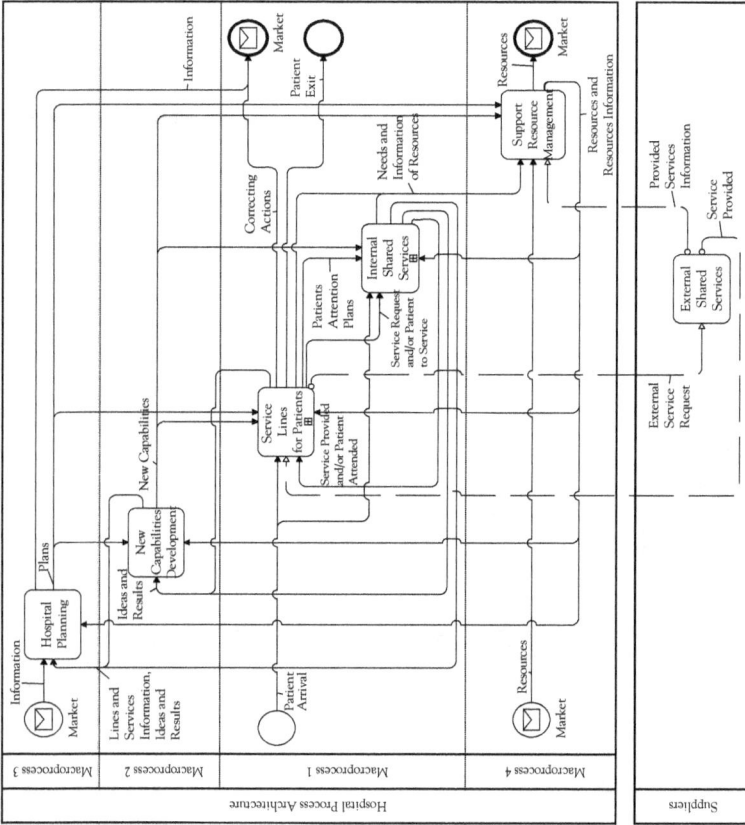

Figure 2.7 Process Architecture Pattern for Hospitals

"New Capabilities Development," where processes are designed and projects are implemented that assure constant innovation that takes care of the variables of quality and fairness by, as shown in Figure 2.7, monitoring the Value Chains in "Services Lines for Patients," by means of "Ideas and Results," and redesigning them as needed to improve such variables. Moreover, the variable efficiency is present since, when redesigning, Value Chains and "Internal Shared Services" will be designed to make best possible use of resources, using Analytics as exemplified in the Intelligence Structures of previous section. In designing the macroprocess "New Capabilities Development" that provide innovation of a health service, the pattern for Macro2 defined earlier provides the guidelines on how it should be structured, as described in the first case of the following chapter.

The macroprocess "Hospital Planning" in Figure 2.7 also contributes to the improvement of the variables selected by providing "Plans," which are, first, guidelines on which lines of innovation are more pressing or profitable, possibly in a social sense, and second, feedback on proposals that "New Capabilities Development," "Services Lines for Patients," and "Internal Shared Services" submit to be considered in the plans. In the first case in the next chapter, interaction among the three macroprocesses of pattern in Figure 2.7 is clearly shown following the guidelines just presented. In the second case in the next chapter, the role of "Hospital Planning" is much more important; since it is a public case where the key decision is on how to assign resources to Chilean hospitals, part of the public health system. This assignment is for innovating in selected hospitals on the variables of quality, efficiency, and fairness in a coordinated way, concentrating on those hospitals with the best possibilities of social value return.

Further details of the architecture will be exemplified by decomposing "Services Lines for Patients" and "Internal Shared Services" in Figures 2.8 to 2.11. When performing such decompositions, the general process pattern developed for Macro1 is used, as detailed in previous volume. For example, processes such as "Demand Analysis and Management," "State Updating Service," "Demand Forecasting and Characterization," "Define Correcting Actions," "Demand Analysis," and "Operating Room Scheduling" are instances or specializations, in our terminology, of generic processes

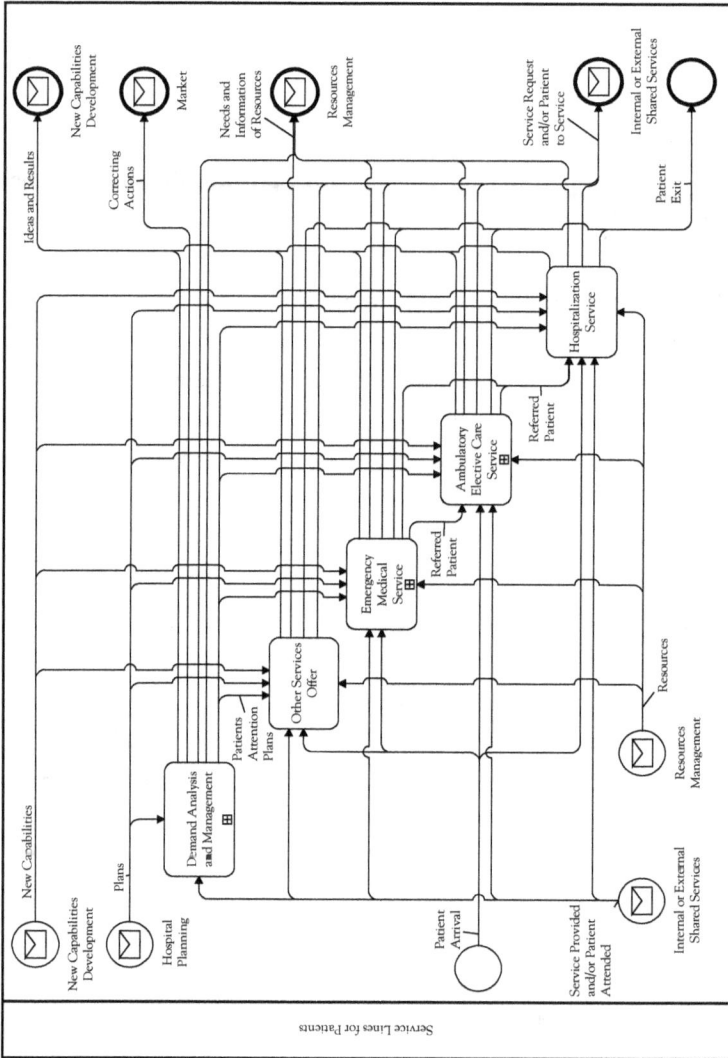

Figure 2.8 Detail of "Services Lines for Patients"

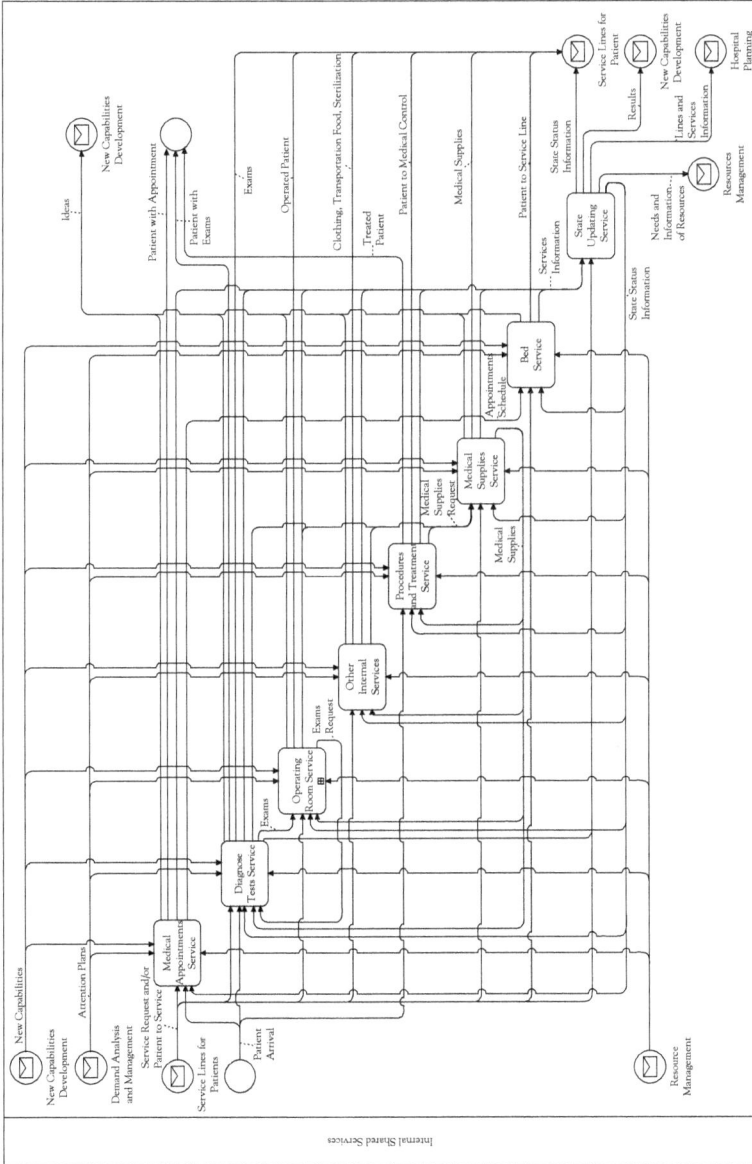

Figure 2.9 Detail of "Internal Shared Services"

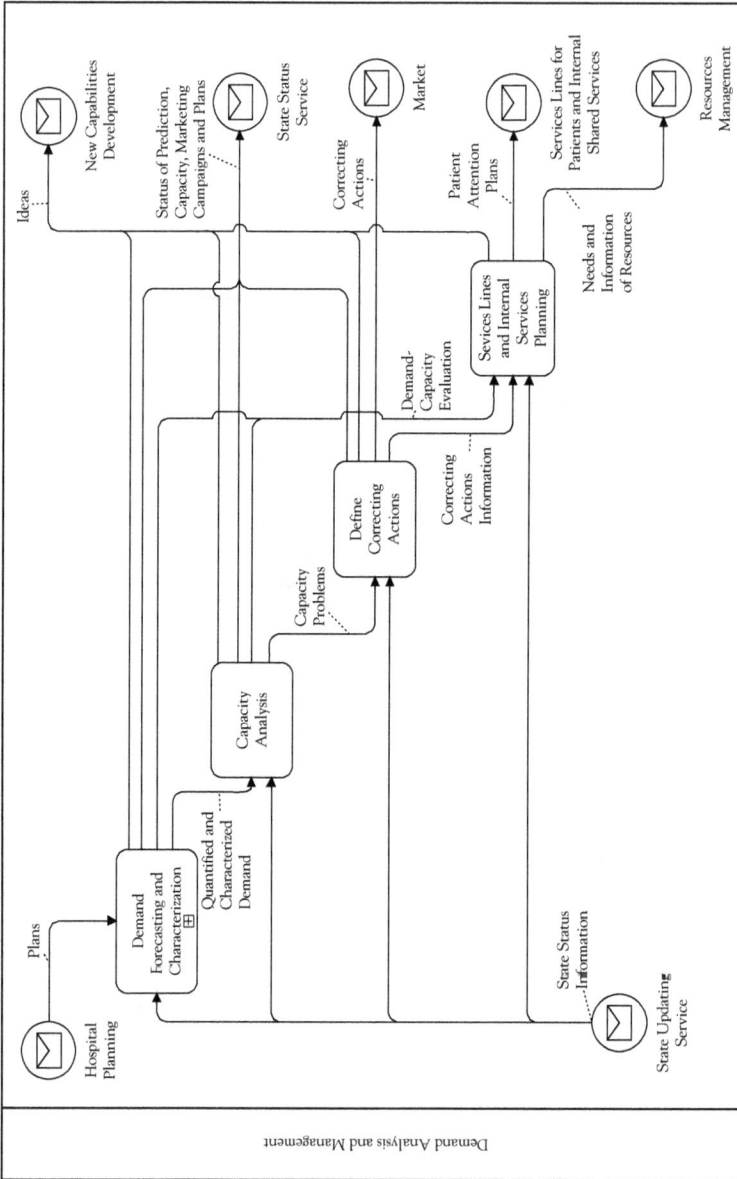

Figure 2.10 Detail of "Demand Analysis and Management"

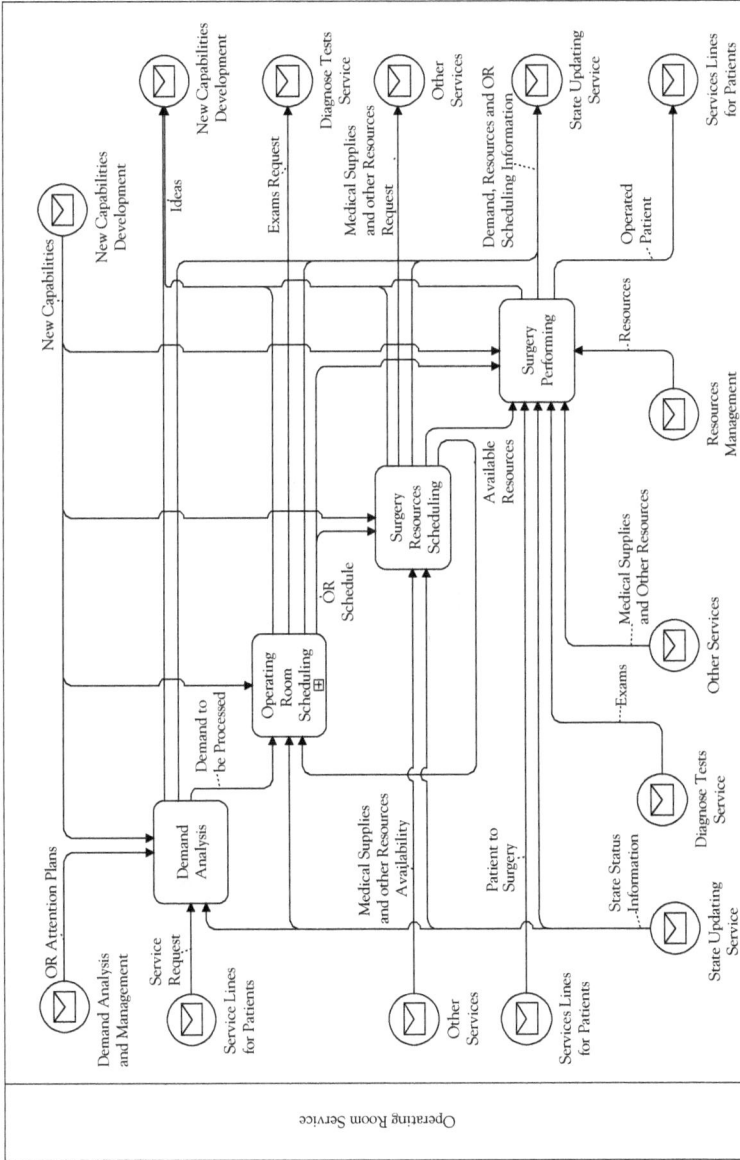

Figure 2.11 Detail of "Operating Room Service"

or subprocesses defined in Macro1; also many of the flows in these decompositions are specializations of general flows defined in the pattern.

Figure 2.8 presents the decomposition of "Services Lines for Patients." There are three main service lines at the hospitals we have studied, to which patients may access directly or by being referred from another service line. These lines are:

1. Emergency Medical Service: Attends nonelective patients, for example, those who require urgent medical attention and, as a consequence, cannot be programmed with anticipation. Each patient who arrives to this service line is categorized according to the severity of its illness, in such a way that more urgent patients are attended to with priority. Here the patient may also be referred to any of the other service lines in case the patient needs to be hospitalized or requires specialized medical attention.

2. Ambulatory Elective Care Service: Attends elective patients, for example, those patients whose medical attention can be programmed in advance. In this line, a medical consultation is made and some procedures are performed.

3. Hospitalization Service: Attends elective and nonelective patients who must be hospitalized, either to prepare to or recover from a surgery or a procedure.

In addition to the aforementioned service lines, other complementary services might be offered to single patients or groups; for example, health insurance plans for specific patient's classes or certain company employees. This process takes place in the "Other Services Offer" line, where such services are typically found in the private health system.

The process "Demand Analysis and Management" is defined as a shared process for all service lines in such a way that it captures the behavior of their demand, allowing to plan their resources in a coordinated way to attend to such a demand.

Figure 2.9 shows the decomposition of "Internal Shared Services." These services are shared by all the service lines mentioned earlier and they constitute a fundamental part of the activities they perform; such services are the following:

1. Medical Appointments Service: Assigns to patients a medical appointment for any kind of elective medical attention: diagnosis, exams, procedures, and so forth. The patient may request the appointment directly to the service or through the service lines.

2. Diagnose Tests Service: Performs all necessary tests to diagnose the patient. For example, blood tests, X-rays, lab analysis, among others.

3. Operating Room Service: Receives and prioritizes the waiting list for surgery, schedules the ORs, and performs the programmed surgeries.

4. Other Internal Services: Contains other services shared by the services lines for patients, such as blood bank, internal and external transportation of patients, food and cleaning service, sterilization, and so forth.

5. Procedures and Treatments Service: Provides procedures and treatments to patients who do not require a doctor. For example, wound-healing treatment, physical therapy, and vaccination.

6. Medical Supplies Service: Provides the medical supplies requested from the service lines and internal shared services.

7. Bed Management Service: Provides and manages different bed types for the service lines and internal shared services. Its principal goal is to locate each patient on the right bed at the right time, according to the complexity of the patients' pathology and its expected evolution.

8. State Updating Service: Updates and provides the state of every process of the hospital, which makes it a shared information service.

"Demand Analysis and Management," of Figure 2.8, is the process defined to forecast the demand for hospital services and manage such demand and the hospital capacity to ensure that an adequate balance is reached. The basic idea is to proactively create the conditions for all the relevant demand to be processed with a required quality of service (variable quality) and that large current lists of patients waiting for services are eliminated (variable fairness). Our experience so far is that a better distribution of the existing resources should increase customers' satisfaction, without additional investments in capacity (variable efficiency), which has been proved true in the cases we present in the following sections. The details of this process, shown in Figure 2.10, are as follows:

1. Demand Forecast and Analysis: This process uses a forecast and analytical model that allows the hospital to anticipate the behavior of the demand through its periodical execution and the analysis of its results.

2. Capacity Analysis: Evaluates if the capacity of the hospital will be adequate to attend to the demand forecasted in the previous process, depending on the resources required for each category of patients. If lack or excess of capacity is concluded, then actions are taken in order to increase capacity or decrease the expected demand.

3. Define Correcting Actions: Defines the correcting actions to decrease the demand for services or adjust capacity. For example, to inform nonelective patients with certain pathologies that they can be attended to in other health services.

4. Services Lines and Internal Services Planning: Analyzes the impact that previous correcting actions will have on the forecasted demand, in order to design plans that improve the quality of service for the new demand expected.

"Operating Room Service" is the process that prioritizes and schedules the incoming demand for surgical interventions in such a way that maximum waiting times, defined by medical experts, are met and the use of resources associated with the facilities is optimized. The detailed process of the same is shown in Figure 2.11 and its subprocesses are as follows:

1. Demand Analysis: In this process, medical orders for surgery are added to the waiting list and then prioritized, according to the medical criteria previously formalized as business logic, which is directly related to the variable fairness presented earlier. Subsequently, a waiting list analysis determines if the resources will suffice to attend such demand on time or if additional resources are required to achieve this objective.

2. Operating Room Scheduling: Generates the OR schedule using the waiting list prioritized in the previous process. Although the scheduling maximizes the use of facilities, attending to the variable

efficiency, it also includes good medical practices to decide the order and time of surgical interventions, which relates to quality.

3. Resources Scheduling: Schedules the resources that are necessary to perform the surgical interventions schedule, optimizing their use, which leads to efficiency.

4. Surgery Performing: Executes every surgery scheduled, which includes the preparation of the patient, the surgical procedure, and recovery. After surgery is performed, the procedure protocol information is registered and the patient is removed from the waiting list.

The Process Architecture Pattern that has been presented is only a partial selection of the complete model and emphasizes the processes and subprocesses that are used in the cases to be presented in the next chapters. The complete architecture includes the details of all the components in the general architecture of Figure 2.7.[79]

Health Network Architectures

Hospitals in public health services are part of a complex network, which include a central management, usually a high government office, subnetworks geographically defined that have a decentralized management and primary services that refer patients to hospitals; these primary services may belong to the subnetworks or be decentralized and locally managed, for example, by counties. We have had some experience in trying to apply our proposal to the design of Chilean Health Network, which has allowed us to define the Network Architecture we present as follows.

The architecture we propose is based on a general architecture pattern for multilevel structures that appear in complex organizations, such as holdings, businesses with several product or service lines and government services, which, besides health, include justice, education, and various others. The general architecture is included in the previous volume where an application to public health system planning was also presented. Here we present the application of the general architecture to model the problem of subnetwork management. We use as reference the case of the Chile's Public Health System and, in particular, the operational management of a geographical defined subnetwork, which is a grouping of hospitals and primary health services, operating units, that are located in a given region and, in the case of a big city, covers sectors of the same. The key structure design decision in this case is the degree of management decentralization, since there are two hierarchical levels, overall health system and subnetwork management, above the operating units that provide the health services. In principle the management of the system is decentralized, since most of the hospitals are defined as self-managed units and primary health services are run by counties. But there are still many coordination issues that need to be centralized, such as referrals among units within a subnetwork and among subnetworks; management of waiting lists; and share of scarce resources such as beds. We will not go into these coordination issues but focalize on how to make possible that the units' performance is maximized. This analysis of management centralization of complex systems has recently been studied under the flexibility and complexity theory mentioned before. Health structure is layered, which tends to be centralized, so the question is how to decentralize but maintaining flexibility, which is the advantage of layering, and also align results with the interests of the health authorities.

The current solution to this decentralization issue in Chile is "management by commitments," where health system central management negotiates with network and units' management production targets and associated operating budget; then a unit commits a given production in accordance with the budget. This practice has two problems: there is no way to calculate the right performance, with optimum use of resources, and no well-founded method to determine the correct budget. We have proposed a structural solution to this problem based on hospitals' efficiency measurement by means of DEA and budget assignment based on this, which is detailed in other publication[80] and will be presented as a case in the next chapter. Here we consider the situation of subnetwork central management, where the short-term operations management is analyzed. One design consideration is to provide means to assure that "commitments" negotiated with health system management are met. Such design is shown in Figure 2.12.

The management by commitments is simple and follows the idea of Intelligent Structure I, which is to monitor results, compare with goals and determine actions to correct deviations. It is shown in Figure 2.12 by

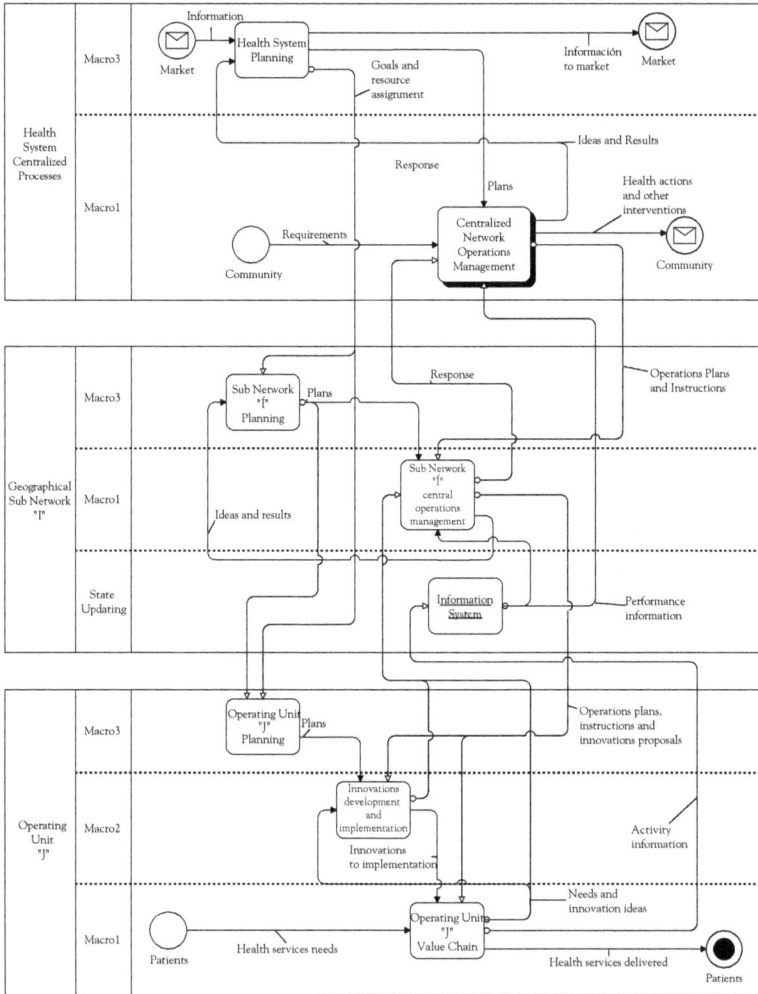

Figure 2.12 Network Operations Management Architecture

several flows among levels that inform commitments, report results, and provide instructions to correct deviations from plan. More interesting is the possibility that subnetwork management learns from results and discovers opportunities of changes in the operating units by using best practices that increase quality of service or improve use of resources or both. The flows related to this idea are "Activity information" from "Operating unit j Value Chain" to "Information System" and then from there the flow "Performance information" to "Sub Network i central operations management," where the data is analyzed and operations improvements determined, which are then proposed as "Operations plans, instructions, and innovation proposals" to "Innovation development and implementation" (Macro2) of the operating unit. We worked on this idea with one subnetwork in Chile and found many opportunities for improvement, which will detailed in a case in the next chapter.

Design Levels for Health Services

We defined a hierarchy of design levels in Chapter 1; here we complement such definition, including the role of Analytics in each level. The use of Analytics in our design proposal relates to providing business logic that supports *intelligent* business decision making and operations and also business development using well-founded designs; we define this concept as truly BI, as opposed to simpler methods based only information displays of the dashboard type. The central idea is that, in executing services delivery and related processes, business logic is necessary to formalize certain routines that use models to assure that certain objectives are attained. Models can be predictive, such as Data Mining to investigate customers' behavior or sales forecasting models, or prescriptive to advise or automate decisions, such as optimal assignment of resources by means of mathematical optimizations models. Also service development, improving current services and designing new ones, is possible by the right use of Analytics. There are several levels of complexity at which Analytics can be applied, from very simple rules to complex optimization models, with only internal or big data. We have formalized such levels in what we call Intelligence Structures, which were summarized in this chapter. In the cases we present in Chapters 4 to 6, the use of Analytics in all these versions will be illustrated.

The design levels and the role of Analytics in each of them are as follows:

i. *Service Business Design* that delivers the structure of components of the service–production, management, supporting, and others–and their relationships, together with the interaction with the environment that generates a business Capability, which provides value to customers according to Strategy and Business Model. It represents *what the business does* and does not yet map to organizational units, area, or product. For example, the case of the private hospital we have presented shows that the Business Model of leading on medical treatments and technology requires new Capabilities in the form of new activities that discover and manage innovations of this type. Analytics may have an important role at this level when there are customer data, both internal and external big data, which can be used to develop new services. This requires the ability to formally perform what we have called "design of the service itself" and its production, which is similar to the product and production engineering that traditional manufacturing does with well-known practices. The difference here is that services in general and health in particular do not have well-defined processes to do this and service design is the result of experience and tradition. This has the added complexity that health services are always changing because of scientific and technological advances and that, in many cases, health services cannot be designed in advance in terms of the specific treatment a patient will need and this has to be determined for its particular needs. So the challenge is to have a process that continuously generates health services that provide innovation and the possibility of dynamic adaptation to the particular patients' needs. This idea is present in the private hospital case of Chapter 3.

ii. *Business service configuration and capacity design,* which includes, when necessary, the detail *design of the service and its production process*, as will be exemplified with cases in the following chapters; it also covers the identification of the management processes that should be present to assure that the service is provided in an effective and efficient way; and also the determination of what capacity each process should provide in order to be able to attend the demand according to desired SLAs. This level is based on a Process Architecture design. This design has two versions: the first is when there is a one-time redesign of the service and, due to the dynamics of the market, it is not expected to change in the short time. The other case is when, due to demand behavior changes or possible frequent innovations in service technology, it is necessary to continuously redesign the service and its production and management processes; this means that another level of processes is required, designed to produce service designs (design for producing designs recursively), which provides a *continuous Capability* for doing this, generating innovations *required to keep the service competitive*. Analytics is relevant to discover new service opportunities with internal and big data analysis, for example to model behavior of chronic patients to support preventive treatments as a new service and to model demand and determine optimal service capacity.

iii. *Resource management process design;* that is people, equipment and supplies that are necessary *to provide the capacity established in (ii)*. For example, in hospitals, number of doctors of different specialties that will work in each shift. This requires well-designed processes that, based on Analytics, forecast demand, plans and assigns resources in such a way that capacity is dynamically provided at the minimum cost. Such processes are executed regularly with a frequency that depends on the dynamics of the demand. The use of Analytics is relevant here to optimize capacity available.

iv. *Operating management processes design*, such as processes, are necessary for the day-to-day scheduling of the demand over the resources in order to provide the required level of service and optimize their use. For example, in public hospitals there are usually waiting lists of surgery patients that should be scheduled in ORs in such a way that priorities associated to the severity of the patients illnesses is met and use of facilities is maximized. The use of Analytics is relevant here to optimize resource use.

This can be interpreted *as a hierarchical top down approach*, where business service components are progressively designed in increasing levels of detail, always starting with previously defined components and processes. In an ideal world, this assures a systemic, consistent, and efficient *global health service design*. However it is not necessary to do it all at once; the advantage of a top-down approach is that, once upper levels of design are performed, detail design may proceed with selected components of global design, as it will be shown in the examples to be presented in next chapters.

Alternatively one may take any lower level of design, ii to iv, without having a global business-service design, as defined earlier, and proceed with a design at such level, accepting what will not be designed as given and determined by previous decisions on how they are structured and performed. We will call this a *local design* case. This situation arises when priority, timing, resources, and other restrictions do not make viable a more systemic approach. The design proposed for these levels is applicable independently of no having made the design of the previous levels.

We will present cases of both of the previous approaches in the following chapters.

It is important to notice that design levels i and ii may be executed just one time to generate a new business design, configuration, and capacity, which will get implemented, possibly, with new resource management and operating processes that execute the new business-service design. On the other hand, levels i and ii can generate new processes designs that are routinely updated when the dynamics of the business require continuous innovation, as exemplified in some cases before and that will be present in more cases in what follows.

Design Methodology

Based on the ideas in previous section our proposal for service design is as follows.

At the outset we assume that the business under design is looking for innovations in their services to make it more competitive, which may imply going from increasing its productivity to changing in a fundamental way the offer and value to clients or to provide entirely new services. To accomplish this we define the following steps, not necessarily sequentially implemented:

1. Start with an innovative Strategy and Business Model.
2. Derive the need for new Capabilities to implement the Business Model; this implies defining new practices over existing activities or new activities that are created for this purpose. For example, new BI practices to develop customers' predictive models to be able to make service offers adapted to their needs.

3. The business is designed to include such Capabilities using BPs, presented in this chapter; the design defines how the new Capabilities are inserted into the current business structure or form a new structure. This may require the redefinition of the service itself; for example, the case of a financial information processing organization that has one Value Stream executing a traditional model of mechanical credit card transaction processing for banks with low added value, which has decided to implement another Value Stream that makes proactive offers related to credit cards to banks' customers, based on BI predictive models developed with the transaction data, generating a high value for them; this case was presented in detail in the previous volume. This step covers a *Level i* design, as defined in previous section, and generates a first approximation to Business Design using a BP.

4. Process Architecture designs are generated, including configuration and capacity of its components; they should be aligned with the preceding, possibly including additional detail design of the service as well as its production processes, as will be exemplified in next chapters. For example, hospitals emergency services may have different configurations in terms of its processes: among others use of a Triage (patient classification), a fast track line and several different lines of service; once components are determined, enough capacity has to be provided in order to have a desired patient average waiting time. This step covers a *Level ii* design, as defined in previous section.

5. Detail design that makes operational the architecture of previous step is performed, including processes that manage the resources required to provide the service efficiently and with adequate quality. Also the operations management processes are designed. It covers *Levels iii* and *iv* designs.

These ideas are summarized in the conceptual model of Figure 2.13.

Figure 2.13 shows the components of the structures and patterns, defined in previous section, that support each of the steps of the methodology. In the cases we will present in the following chapters, we will show how they are applied in producing a design. In their application we will use the logic and set of rules that follows.

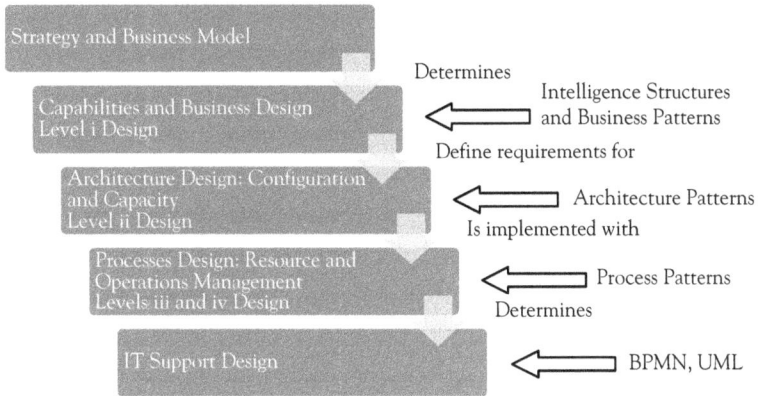

Figure 2.13 Service Design Methodology

First we consider how to determine the Capabilities and the BP that are required according to Strategy and Business Model. For the Capabilities we only provide a guide, considering certain typical situations that illustrate the line of reasoning that should be applied. Most frequent cases of Strategy we have found consider the positioning of best product, with variants of operational effectiveness and differentiation, and integral solutions to clients with variants of redefining clients' relationship and integration with clients,[81] as outlined in Chapter 1 and detailed in previous book.

With the positioning of operational effectiveness, the emphasis is on price competition with services that are usually a commodity; so the value provided to customers is mainly low price, with quality according to market standards. Then the main Capability the business needs has to do with being able to lower costs as much as possible, without compromising quality. For this there are two approaches: (a) to redesign the production of the service, using a Level ii design, or (b) to concentrate on optimizing the use of resources, using Levels iii or iv designs. In terms of intelligence needed, Option (a) needs Analytics as proposed in Intelligence Structure II, in previous section, which allow optimizing configuration and capacity of production of the service. For Option (b) relevant Analytics are the ones of Intelligence Structure I, to identify and correct situations of waste of resources and eliminate them, or Intelligence Structure II to optimize the use of resources. So if we select the positioning of operational effectiveness we end up with clear options of the design level in which to concentrate and the Intelligence Structure that should be used.

For differentiation positioning, the Business Model should be to offer, ideally, a service that is unique and provides more value to clients than any alternative. For this the necessary Capability is being able to continuously improve the service, adding features that increase value, for which a Level ii design is required to redesign the service itself and its production process, as defined in previous section; however, complementary, design Levels iii and iv are necessary to put into practice the service design. As to intelligence needed, Analytics as proposed in Intelligence Structures II or IV, as defined in previous section, are needed that allow to determine customer service's evaluation and preferences and to optimize the configuration and capacity of the production of the service; what structure is more relevant will depend on the importance of big data to study customer behavior.

For integral solutions to clients in the variant of redefining clients' relationship, the key is to know the client in order to offer customized services to people or other businesses. Then the necessary Capability is being able to process information available for clients and discover behaviors that suggest services he will appreciate. A Level ii design is required if it is necessary the redesign of the service itself and its production process, as suggested by customer's behavior. Then in order that a new service design is well managed, Levels iii and iv designs are necessary to put into practice the required processes. However there may be cases in which only Level iv is required, since there are situations in which, without a complete redesign on the service, we can introduce Analytics into current marketing and sales processes to offer the same service, but personalized; for example, the product suggestions that Amazon does. Intelligence needed, as it is clear from previous analysis, is Intelligence Structure II or IV, depending on the relevance of big data to develop customer's behavior models.

For integral solutions to clients in the variant of integration with clients, the aim is to be part of the client's Value Chain, performing services that provide high added value to the served business. Clearly we are in the case of a B2B situation; then the necessary Capability is to be able to process information available for clients and discover situations that suggest services he will appreciate. A Level i design is required in cases in which the service needs a new business line, and a Level ii to design the service itself and its production process according to customers' needs; however, complementary, design Levels iii and iv are necessary to put into practice the product design. Analytics needed are the ones included in Intelligence Structures II or IV, depending on the relevance of big data to develop customer's behavior models.

In all the Strategy and Business Models variations analyzed earlier we conclude, from the Capabilities needed in each case, which are the levels of design that should be performed and the Intelligence Structure that applies in order to comply with a required positioning and value to be generated for customers.

Now we show how to determine the BP that applies to define a first approximation to Business Design. For this we start with the design level and Intelligent Structure that apply to the business situation under analysis, determined as just explained. For each combination of design level and Intelligent Structure, the possible BPs that apply were discussed when the BPs were presented; thus, for example, BP1, Clients' Knowledge-Based Selling, applies for Level iv design and Intelligent Structure II or IV, and BP3, Internal Learning for Process Improvement, applies to all design levels and Intelligence Architectures I, II, and IV.

Next the relationship between Business Design, materialized in an instantiated in a BP, and process architecture is examined. The selected BP is implemented through processes, for which the following rules apply:

1. BP "Client's Knowledge-Based Selling" (BP1) implies a redesign of Macro1, as will be shown in the case of the in-home patient monitoring to detect treatment needs by means of predictive models in next chapter; so the Process Architecture is just Macro1. This applies only when there is not a need for structural changes of the Value Chain, which is so in cases where the Analytics can be readily inserted in its current processes, and also clients' predictive models are stable and do not need continuous review.

2. All the other BPs require that the design includes the ability to continuously reconsider, through several means, the situation and performance of the Value Streams and, based on this, propose changes

to such streams or new ones. Hence, a structure that generates new designs for the streams is required. This implies that Macro2, "New Capabilities Development," must be a part of the Process Architecture, together with the Value Streams of Macro1, which are to be continuously changed. This can be relaxed when any of the following conditions apply:

a. Structural change is made just one time, since there is not a need for reconsideration.

b. Stable environmental conditions make unnecessary continuous change.

c. Improvements can be part of Macro1 or Macro4.

3. In architectures derived by Rules (1) and (2), Macro3, "Business Planning," may appear when changes to Macro1 should be aligned with Strategic Planning; this is particularly required in the BP "Performance Evaluation for Replanning and Process Improvement" (BP4). Also BP "Product Innovation" (BP5) usually requires an architecture with Macro3, since this type of innovation should be aligned with or approved by the strategic level.

4. In all the aforementioned architectures, Macro4, "Support Resource Management," may appear in the architecture depending on the need to assure that a certain resource is available to supply the other macros in the architecture; a particular case in which Macro4 may be the main macroprocess is when, under the BP "Optimum Resource Usage" (BP6), a particular Value Stream of Macro4—for example, human resource provision, financial management, or equipment maintenance—is the one under design.

Cases that illustrate the use of all these rules will be presented in the following chapters.

CHAPTER 3

Health Service Business Design

Real cases of health services Business Design, based on the foundations presented in the previous chapter are the subject of this section. They illustrate how, having a clear Strategy and Business Model, a Business Pattern that provides a first approximation to a Business Design model can be selected and specialized to make positioning and value to clients operational, following the methodology of Chapter 2.

Service Innovation in a Private Hospital

First, we present the case of a private hospital, one of the largest in Chile and considered among the best in Latin America, summarized in Chapter 1, which has defined the following Strategy and Business Model:[1]

1. This hospital wants to be distinguished as the one that provides the best treatments with the best required technology; so they are clearly in the line on best product positioning with an emphasis on differentiation based on continuous innovation on the services they provide.
2. The value they aspire to offer is to assure patients the right treatment that minimizes health risks for them at a competitive price.

Then the Capabilities this hospital needs are (a) the possibility to evaluate the performance of the several Value Streams that provide services to patients, (b) to identify opportunities for improvement of the medical procedures and introduction of new technology—for example, a new imaging equipment or a robot to perform surgeries—that make a difference for the patient, (c) to be able to formalize all these opportunities as formal investment project and rigorously evaluate them to determine the ones to execute subject to budget limitations, and (d) design, plan, and execute the selected projects that create or modify the corresponding streams, which implement the new ideas. Of the variables defined in the section "Competitive Strategy and Business Model for Health Care Services" of Chapter 2, we concentrate on quality, with the possibility of also introducing the ideas of Porter and Teisberg, and Christensen et al. to gain competitive advantages. This can be done by identifying niches such as chronic diseases—for example, diabetes and hypertension—where models for predicting patient risks are possible to develop for generating preventive actions that increase the value defined by Porter and Teisberg, and generate simpler, lower-cost treatments for less complex diseases as proposed by Christensen et al.; for example, treating patients at their home, as it will be exemplified for a public hospital case in this chapter. In improving quality, as just outlined, also efficiency is to be dealt with to assure costs that make competitive pricing possible. In doing all this the opportunity exists to use formal Analytics to forecast needs, evaluate investment projects and plan them; then the Intelligence Structure II applies. Notice that some of the innovations imply change in the medical practices, which means we are redesigning the service itself and its production processes. All this clearly points to Business Pattern 5 (BP5), "Product innovation," presented in Chapter 2.

The situation in the hospital before the reported design was that ideas and projects were informally defined and presented in an annual budgetary procedure to the Board, which decided on which projects to execute without any formal evaluation.

The specialized BP5, shown in Figure 3.1, defines a first Business Design, establishing requirements for new business components as follows:

1. "Service performance and use analysis" implies the need of learning how to evaluate services based on observation and analysis of the use and performance characteristics of the current services, which can be supported by Analytics on well-structured data.
2. "Design of improved or new service" requires to set processes that take results from (1) and discover opportunities for service innovation, which can go from improving medical practices that are not

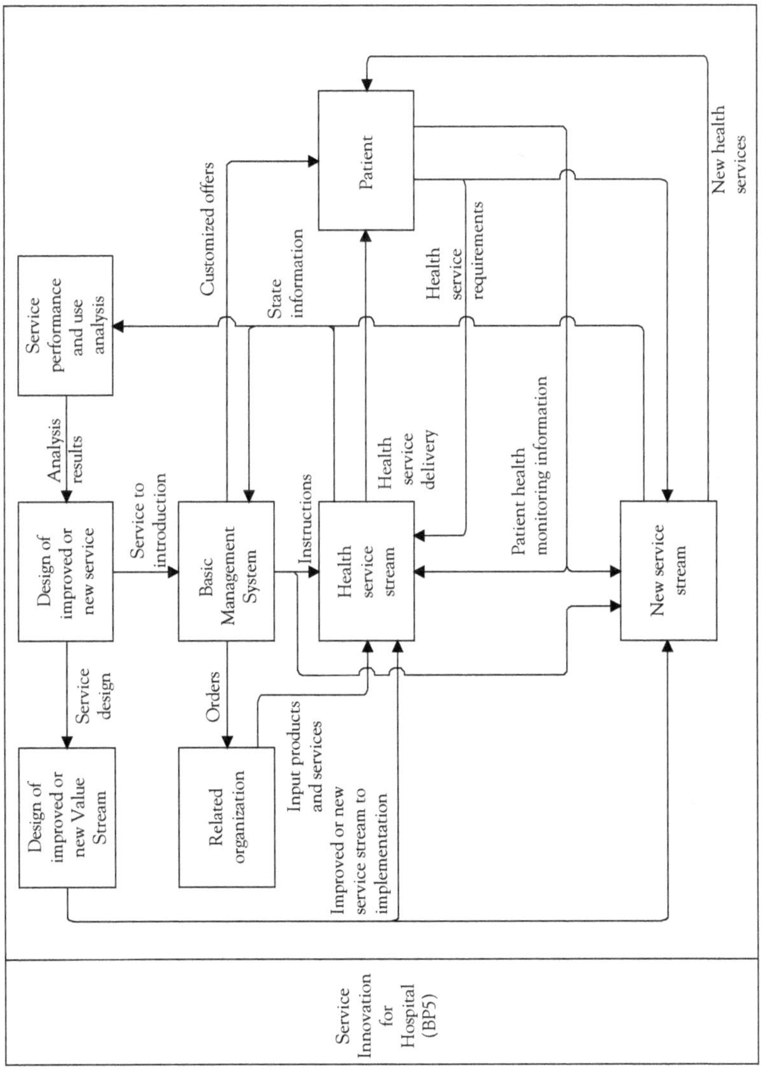

Figure 3.1 Business Design for the private hospital case

producing good results or introducing new practices, due to medical or technological advances, to completely new treatments for old or new pathologies, which may generate new Value Streams. This requires the ability to formally perform what we have called "design of the service itself," which is similar to the product engineering that traditional manufacturing does with well-known practices. The difference here is that services in general and health in particular do not have well-defined processes to do this and service design in the result of experience and tradition. This has the added complexity that health services are always changing because of scientific and technological advances and that, in many cases, health services cannot be designed in advance in terms of the set of specific treatments a patient will need and this has to be determined for the particular situation. So the challenge is to have a process that continuously generates health services that provide innovation and the possibility of dynamic adaptation to the particular patients' needs.

3. "Design of improved of new Value Stream" is the design of the service production and it is similar to the production process in manufacturing, but with the complications we identified in (2), in that the service needs adaptation in its production for each patient; this requires well-defined processes that include the design of the detail flow of the service, from the arrival of the patient to conclusion of its treatment, and all the management of the operations of the service, including demand management, scheduling of patients, resource assignment, and flow monitoring.

The design that allows making the previous operational requirements will be detailed in the next chapter by defining an architecture and configuration that makes its implementation possible.

Resource Assignment in the Public Sector

Next, we focus on public health Business Design, where an overall analysis for the public health system in Chile is performed and a design developed to promote a coordinated solution for innovation resource assignment.

This case illustrates a situation of a complex multilevel architecture, mentioned before.

Public hospitals have to usually cope with more demand than their capacity allows, generating waiting lists of patients who cannot be attended immediately; hence they need to optimize the use of such capacity and must have means to manage priorities, which means efficiency and fairness. In doing this, one of the best possibilities of improvement is to modify the logic behind the decision on the resources hospitals receive. The idea is assigning resources in a way that promotes efficiency and, at the same time, improves quality.

The state of the health system in Chile in connection with resource allocation oriented to improve efficiency and fairness of the hospital services is as follows:

For the improvement of the efficiency, the current method of resource assignment to hospitals is primarily historical and includes important distortions related to demand. It is based on the idea of "management by commitments," which are basically goals measured in quantity of medical interventions of different types that the hospital promises to execute to receive a certain amount of resources in any given year. This method fails on several accounts: (a) failure to set goals that consider the true capacity of the hospitals, (b) within a given type of medical interventions the easier cases are selected to formally meet the goals, (c) there is no measure of quality of the intervention, and (d) no incentive to do more than the goal; in fact, there is a disincentive, since more production than the goal means a higher goal for the following year. Obviously, there is no guarantee that a hospital operates at the "right" efficiency level, according to the resources they have. Furthermore, the objectives of fairness and quality are negatively affected because of selection of patients with no priority, but less difficult to treat.

For the improvement of fairness, the processes and practices that currently govern the management of waiting lists should be reformulated; it is necessary to change from attention according to order of arrival to one that ensures the timely delivery of the service, considering formal and objective medical criteria. It is also important to discourage the selection of cost-effective hospital treatments, which implies selection of patients that are easier to treat, by transferring the complex cases to other higher-level hospitals; this increases the count to the goals explained earlier with lower costs, but increases the costs of transportation of patients in complex conditions, owing to nonpayment of the hospital transferring the patients.

We now analyze how hospitals should be managed as a system, particularly in the assignment of resources, to avoid the situations reviewed earlier.

From a strategic point of view, they should follow the positioning of best product and operational effectiveness, as defined by Porter and complemented by Hax and Wilde. This Strategy requires evaluating services provided and improving them to provide better quality as well as use the resources in the best possible way to provide such services at the lowest possible cost (efficiency). As for the Business Model, they should provide value to patients (customers) by executing medical services and management processes in such a way as to guaranty the treatments that patients need with the required quality and at the right time (quality and fairness). Here the ideas of Porter and Teisberg[2] and Christensen et al.[3] can be considered to provide the right value and adapt practices to disease complexity.

Thus, the Capabilities that hospitals need, according to the preceding Strategy and Business Model, are to be able to measure current efficiency and quality levels to assign resource in such a way that there is an incentive for the hospitals to improve. This means using Analytics of the Data Envelopment Analysis (DEA) type, summarized in Chapter 2, to rigorously measure efficiency and determine what improvements are necessary to increase it. So Intelligence Structure II is needed. This combined with the level i of design we are performing, means that the Business Pattern 3 (BP3), "Internal Learning for Process Improvements" applies. BP3 provides the Capabilities to improve efficiency of health services that produce better quality and fairness to patients. It is also correlated with the proposals by Porter and Teisberg and Christensen et al., since the Capability to innovate on health services provided by this pattern is at the heart of changing medical and management practices that contribute to minimize the cost of the health outcomes and adapting them according to the level of complexity. A specialization of BP3 to this case is shown in Figure 3.2.

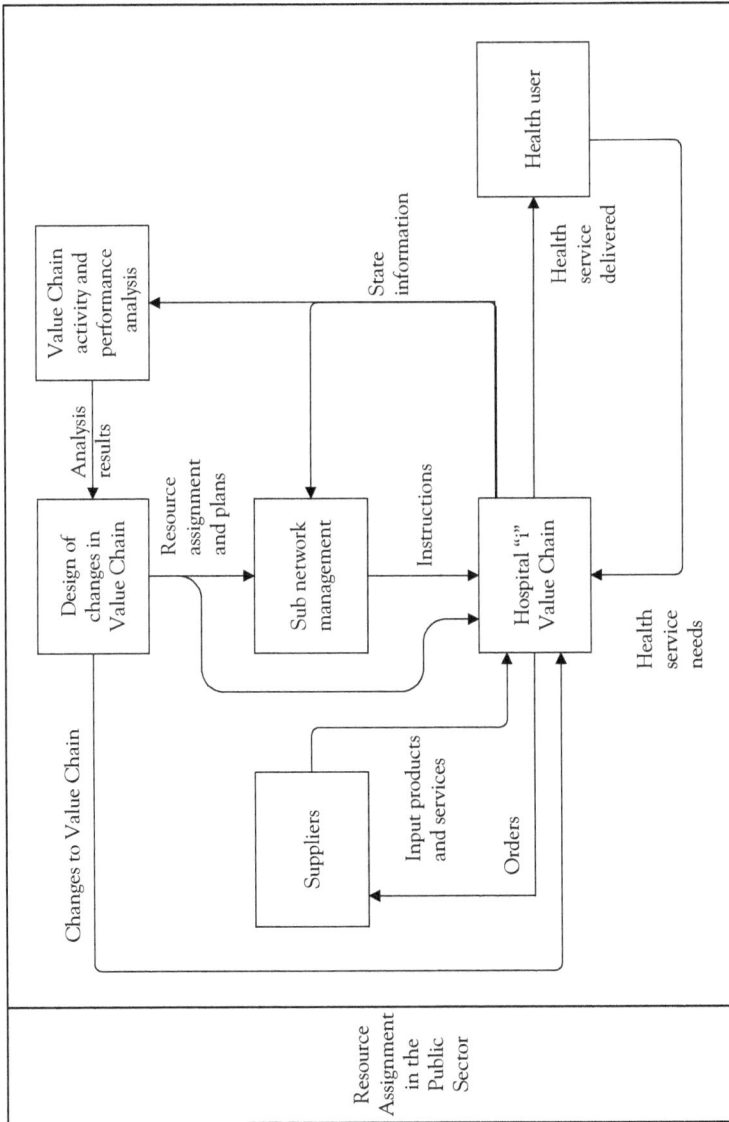

Figure 3.2 Specialized BP3 for health system resource assignment

The model in Figure 3.2 defines the new components the health system needs to continuously innovate by assigning resources where the best possibilities are of increasing efficiency, with adequate consideration of quality. Requirements are:

1. "Value Chain activity and performance analysis" implies the need of learning how to measure health services efficiency based on observation of the performance of the current services, which can be supported by Analytics on well-structured data.

2. "Design of changes in Value Chain" requires to set processes that take results from (1) and discover opportunities for service innovation, which are oriented by the results, since adequate Analytics should indicate which variables explain current efficiency and which changes on them would increase it; for example, patient scheduling practices and resource management that assure its good use. This requires the ability to formally perform what we have called "design of the service itself." This is particularly difficult in health services that do not have well-defined processes to do this and service design is the result of experience and tradition. This has the added complexity that health services cannot be designed in advance in terms of the set of specific treatments a patient will need and this has to be determined for its particular situation. So the challenge is to have a process that continuously generates health services that provide innovation and the possibility of dynamic adaptation to particular patients' needs. This must be complemented with the design of the service flow and its management to assure that health care is efficiently delivered and with proper effectiveness.

This design centralizes resource assignment and project definition on the idea of agency theory that this is the only way to assure that principal's interests are taken care of; also there are economies of scale in defining improvements on the Value Chains of several hospitals by sharing their experiences, formally considered in the comparative efficiency measurements that DEA performs as will be illustrated in Chapter 4. But improvement projects' execution is decentralized also following agency theory[4] in that opportunity costs are reduced, since agents have better knowledge of implementation details. Another theory that supports the decentralization approach is complexity in layered systems, which argues that for such systems, in particular health, there are advantages in such a solution.[5]

Design in a Public Health Network

As presented in Chapter 2, we consider the case of the Public Chile Health Network and, in particular, the operational management of a geographically defined subnetwork, which is a grouping of hospitals and primary health services that are located in a given region and, in the case of a big city, covers sectors of the same. The key design decision in this case is the degree of management decentralization, since there are three hierarchical levels: overall health system and subnetwork management, and the operating units—primary health and hospitals—that provide the health services. In principle the management of the system is decentralized, since most of the hospitals are defined as self-managed units and primary health services are run by counties. But there are still many coordination issues that need to be centralized, such as referrals among units within a subnetwork and among subnetworks; management of waiting lists; and share of scarce resources such as beds. We will not go into these coordination issues but center on how to make possible that the units' performance is maximized. The current solution to accomplish this objective is "management by commitments," where health system central management negotiates with a sub-network and its component units production targets and an associated operating budget; hence a unit commits a given production in accordance with the budget. This practice has two problems: there is no way to calculate the right performance, with optimum use of resources, and no well-founded method to determine the correct budget. We have proposed a structural solution to this problem based on hospitals' efficiency measurement by means of DEA and budget assignment based on this, which was presented in the previous case and will be detailed in Chapter 4. Here we consider the situation of subnetwork central management, where the short-term operations management is analyzed. The problem is then to design a business structure, assigning roles to the different management levels, such that the idea of decentralization is maintained, but that, as agency theory studies, the principal's interests expressed by means of commitments are met by the operating units; we also consider a decentralization approach, since as mentioned in previous case, complexity in layered systems supports this idea. Then we focus on what should be the role of sub-network management and, in particular, its responsibility in operations management.

First we define the strategic positioning, which is best product with emphasis on efficiency as discussed in the previous case. As to Business Model, the idea is to provide value to users by executing medical services and management processes in such a way as to guaranty the treatments that patients need with the required quality and at the right time (quality and fairness). Then the Capabilities needed are to be able to generate good information on the performance of the hospitals' Value Chains; process such information with the proper Analytics, determining opportunities for efficiency improvements; and design improvements in Value Chains according to such opportunities.

Previous analysis implies that the Intelligence Structure II is the one applicable in this case and this, as a consequence, determines that the Business Pattern that should be used is "Internal Learning for Process Improvements," BP3. This pattern is thus specialized to this case, resulting in the design in Figure 3.3. This design implies requirements as follows:

1. "Value Chain activity and performance analysis" implies the need of learning how to measure health services and be able to generate good information on the performance of the hospitals' Value Chains, such as commitments satisfaction, resources available and degree of use, waiting lists, complaints, and the like, which can be supported by Analytics on well-structured data.

2. "Design of improvements in Value Chain" requires to set processes that take results from (1) and discover opportunities for service improvements, which are oriented by the results, since adequate Analytics should indicate which parts of the Value Chains need better practices to assure good resource use or provide better service; for example, best practices for demand prediction and capacity planning, using simulation, for surgeries to reduce excessive waiting lists; analyses of users' formal complaints to identify opportunities

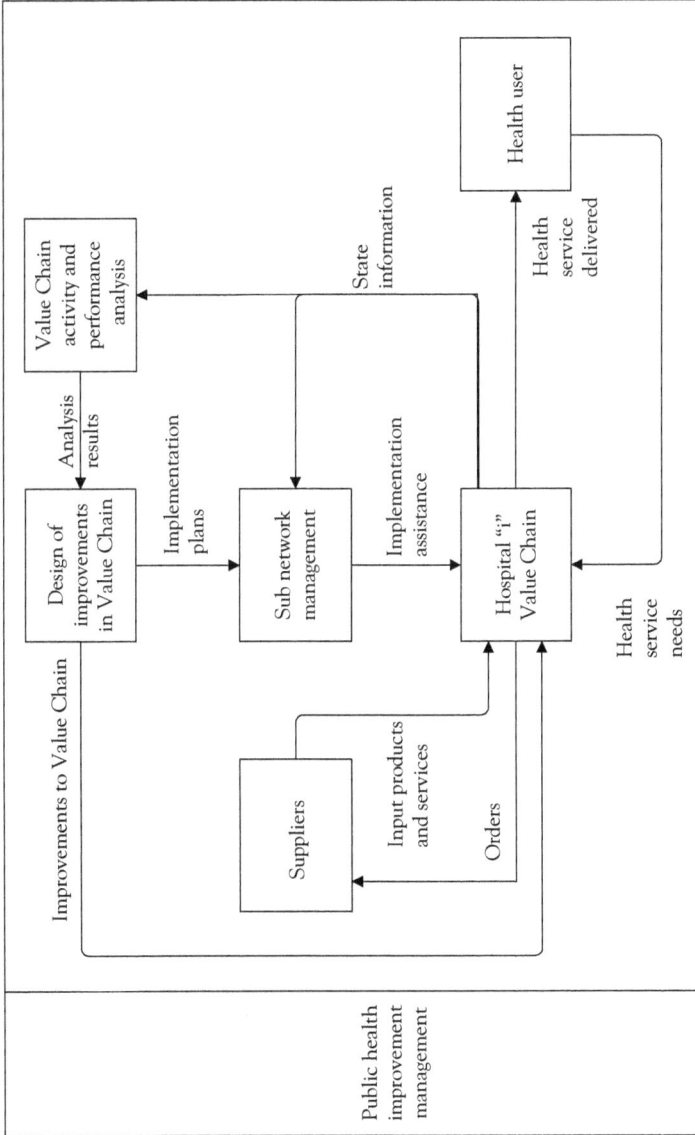

Figure 3.3 Business Design for subnetwork improvement management

for process improvements leading to eliminate such complains; and human-resource planning for emergency services according to forecasted demand to improve service. So the challenge is to have a process that continuously generates process improvements on the hospitals' Value Chains that provide innovation and the possibility of dynamic adaptation to the particular patients' needs. Also there is the need to create processes that implement the changes in such chains.

We worked on this design with one subnetwork in Chile and found many opportunities for improvement that were discovered, designed, and implemented by the subnetwork management, in collaboration with the hospitals. We found that this is the right place to do this since analyses can be made with data from several hospitals, comparing situations and developing solutions that can be used in several of them; practices that have worked well in one hospital can be disseminated to others; and hospitals do not have the resources to rigorously do this innovation by design. This is also supported by the agency and complexity theory in layered systems analysis in the same way as in the previous case. So the architecture design shown in Figure 2.12 of Chapter 2 is justified as well by the analysis we have just performed.

Design of Emergency Service

This case corresponds to the emergency service of a University hospital. It was motivated by a serious quality of service problem, whose worst effect was service denial to patients because of extreme congestion, including closing the doors of emergency facilities. The positioning strategy must then be best product with emphasis on quality differentiation or improvement, but efficiency should also be considered due to the high costs and large deficit the hospital has. So the Business Model should be to generate value for patients with on-time services, according to the severity of their condition, without loss of quality in the health service itself, and making a good use of resources.

The Capabilities this hospital needs, for the aforementioned purposes, are to be able to predict emergency demand; transform this demand on requirements of different resources, such as nurses, doctors, boxes, beds, and others; and continuously adapt resource capacity to provide a response time to patients according to their needs. So Intelligence Structure II is the relevant to model demand and assign resources optimally; hence the Business Pattern that applies is BP3, "Internal Learning for Process Improvements." This pattern is thus specialized to this case, resulting in the design in Figure 3.4. This design implies requirements as follows:

1. "Emergency Value Stream activity analysis" implies the need of learning how to predict emergency services demand and be able to generate good information, which can be supported by Analytics on well-structured activity history; also resource use should be analyzed to determine how to convert demand on resource requirements; and information on delays processed to determine where in the Value Stream are the most acute problems.

2. "Design of improvements in Value Stream" requires to set processes that take results from (1) and design service improvements, which are oriented by the results, since adequate Analytics should indicate which parts of the Value Stream need better practices to assure good resource use or provide better service; for example, emergency extreme congestion prediction to prevent closing; best practices for capacity planning based on demand models, using simulation, to reduce excessive waiting time; and continuous monitoring of service flow to detects congestion problems in advance to improve service and also detect unnecessary delays, for example, on medical exams, to speed up patients and make a better use of facilities. So the challenge is to have a process that generates improvements on the hospitals' emergency Value Stream. Also there is the need of to create processes that implement the changes in such chain.

Work was successfully done by implementing innovation processes that redesigned the Value Stream and continuously monitors online its performance to discover problems that need to be dealt with, producing immediate improvements in service, including avoiding closing.

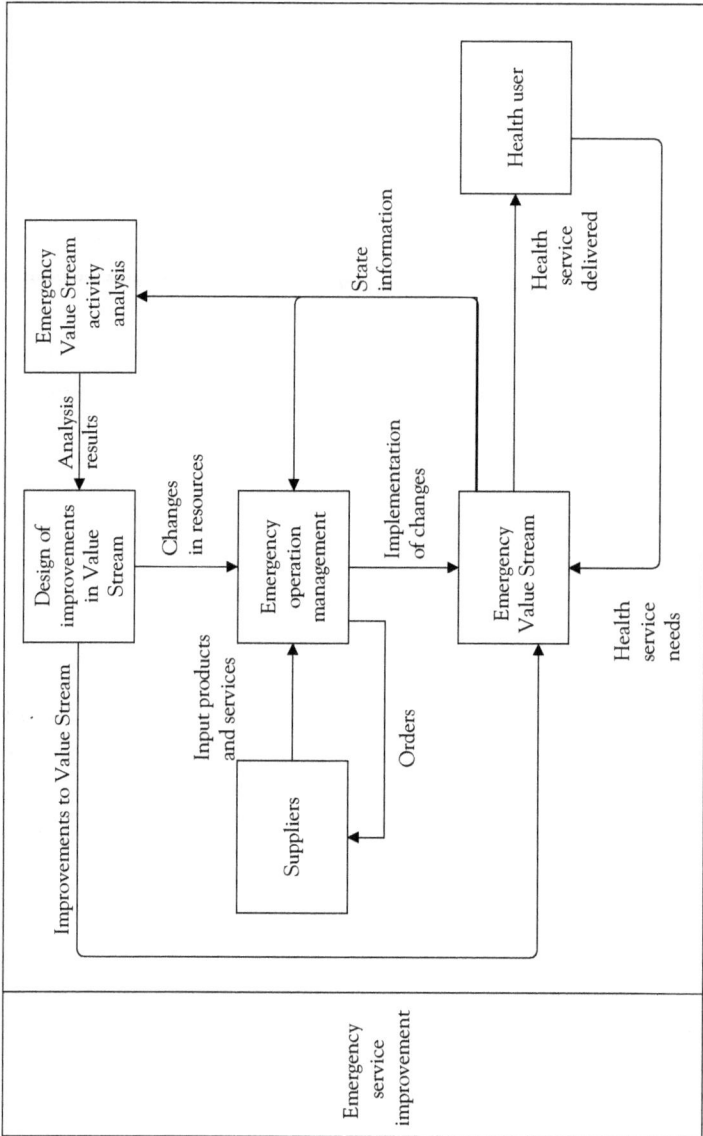

Figure 3.4 Business Design for emergency service improvement

Design of Services for Patients at Home in a Public Children Hospital

Now we present the case of a children's hospital which has chronic patients with respiratory problems that need permanent monitoring, spending most of their time at the hospital using beads, which is a very scarce resource. So the challenge was to perform a Business Design that provides a solution for keeping the children at their homes with the proper attention that assures their well-being. So this hospital wanted to evolve to personalized added valued services according to the following Strategy and Business Model.

The Strategy is to deliver integral services for children at home and use the hospital only for emergencies. The Business Model is to provide value through new services that allow to diagnosis the children at home and then provide adequate care that can be given there; also to detect crisis that require treatment by hospital professionals; all this to be executed by a new service line under design. This means that hospital has to generate the following Capabilities:

1. Be able to structure a solution to collect patient data at his or her home and discover, by means of Analytics, predictive models for children that alert the hospital of health problems.
2. From behavior results, go on to determine the right actions when crisis are forecasted and carry on with such actions.
3. Finally, create and maintain the necessary Value Stream to put into practice the attention at home, which today does not exist.

To provide these Capabilities the Intelligent Structure IV is needed, since not only the normal patient data is relevant, but continuous data coming from instruments at the patients' home, in the idea of Internet of Things (IoT), are needed, which is big data. By combining the design level i, the Intelligent Structure IV, and the emphasis of this case in a new business line that necessarily will need a new Value Stream, the right Business Pattern is BP2, "Creation of new streams of service"; hence, this pattern can be specialized to this case as shown in Figure 3.5.

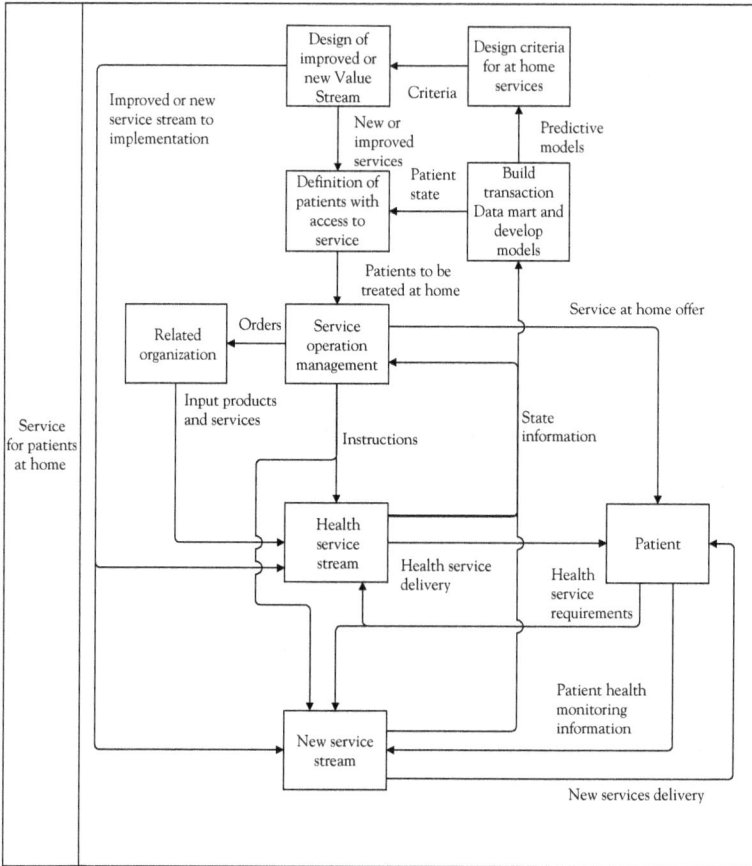

Figure 3.5 Service design for patients attended at home

The specialized BP2 requires the following components to be designed in detail:

1. "Build transaction Data mart and develop models," which determine the variables to be monitored, transfer it to a Data mart to build predictive models for patients' crisis, and make data available for model operation.
2. "Design criteria for at home services" uses predictive models to define criteria for advising medical professionals on actions to be taken, who decide on and execute such actions.
3. "Design of improved or new Value Stream" including design and development of new evaluation processes, software support, human

resources provision, and other resources needed—to put into practice the attention at home, which today do not exist.

4. "Definition of patients with access to service," which determines the chronic patients in the hospital that are subjects for service at home.

These processes were developed including online monitoring of medical variables—such as temperature, cardiac frequency, and respiratory frequency—and a diagnosis data-based analytical model to determine when a patient is in crisis and needs medical attention. More detail for this case will be given in Chapter 6.

Design of Medical School Service Improvement

From a strategic point of view, this medical school should follow the positioning of best product and operational effectiveness, as defined by Porter and complemented by Hax and Wilde. This Strategy requires evaluating services offered and improving them to provide better quality as well as use of the resources in the best possible way, generating such services at the lowest possible cost (efficiency); this is particularly relevant for this school due to the large operational deficit it carries. As for the Business Model, they should provide value to students by providing a state of the art curriculum that gives them the right preparation for successful career; to society, medical research that advances the medical standards of the country and gives the proper foundation for teaching; and to client population the best services through an associated clinical hospital.

Thus, the Capabilities the school needs, according to the aforementioned Strategy and Business Model, are to be able to measure current efficiency and quality levels of its about 50 departments to determine which ones are not providing good academic services or do not properly use resources, or both, to take corrective actions. This means using Analytics of the DEA type to rigorously measure efficiency and quality and to determine what improvements are necessary to increase them. So Intelligence Structure II is needed.

This, combined with the level i of design we are performing, means that the BP3, "Internal Learning for Process Improvements," applies, which provides the Capabilities to improve efficiency and quality of academic services. Then it can be specialized to this case as shown in Figure 3.6.

The model in Figure 3.6 defines the new components the medical school needs to continuously innovate where the best possibilities are of increasing efficiency, with adequate consideration of quality. Requirements are:

1. "School Value Streams efficiency analysis" implies the need of learning how to measure the efficiency and quality of the academic services that are provided through various Value Streams—medical undergraduate and graduate formation, research, and extension—based on observation of the performance of the current services, which can be supported by Analytics on well-structured data.

2. "Design of improvements in Value Chain" requires to set processes that take results from (1) and discover opportunities for service innovation, which are oriented by the results, since adequate Analytics should indicate which variables explain current efficiency and quality and which changes on them would increase it; for example, increase the faculty academic qualifications or provide better research support.

The processes necessary to satisfy the previous requirement have been designed and successfully tested in practice, showing that DEA models correctly measure efficiency and gives hard support for taking specific actions to improve departments' performance; they are currently under implementation at the medical school.

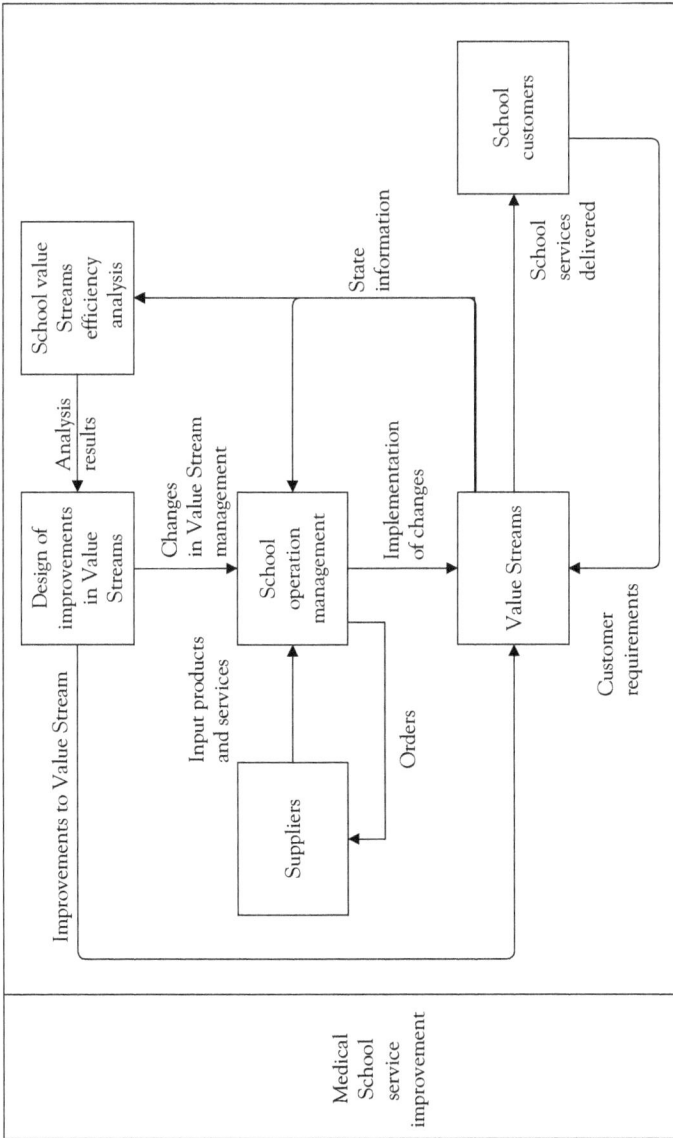

Figure 3.6 Specialized BP3 for medical school service improvement

CHAPTER 4

Health Services Configuration and Capacity Design

This chapter presents cases in which the Business Design of the previous chapter is converted into a process architecture that makes it operational, performing what we defined as a Level ii design in Chapter 2. Also a case which does not have a previous Business Design is presented, illustrating what we defined as a local case.

Service Innovation in a Private Hospital

Taking as a starting point the Business Design of the previous chapter in Figure 3.1 and the requirements derived from it, a process architecture is designed. Mapping the Business Pattern (BP) in Figure 3.1 to the processes needed is straightforward, by rules given in section "Design Methodology" of Chapter 2. They are clearly included in the general macroprocesses defined in Figure 2.7: "New Capabilities Development" (Macro2) and "Hospital Planning" (Macro3) interacting with Macro1 to collect performance and use data and change hospital services as designed. Here the idea implies recursively generating a Capability that is able to generate new Capabilities when it is routinely executed. The mapping is done by specializing these macros to this case, resulting in Figure 4.1, where the two macroprocesses, "Strategic Planning" and "New Capabilities Development," to be designed are included. A detailed design was performed, including a formal strategic planning procedure that provides guidelines for the generation of innovation project proposals that results in the flow "Investment budget, Objectives, and metrics" and "Accepted projects." In addition "New Capabilities Development" was created, which, based

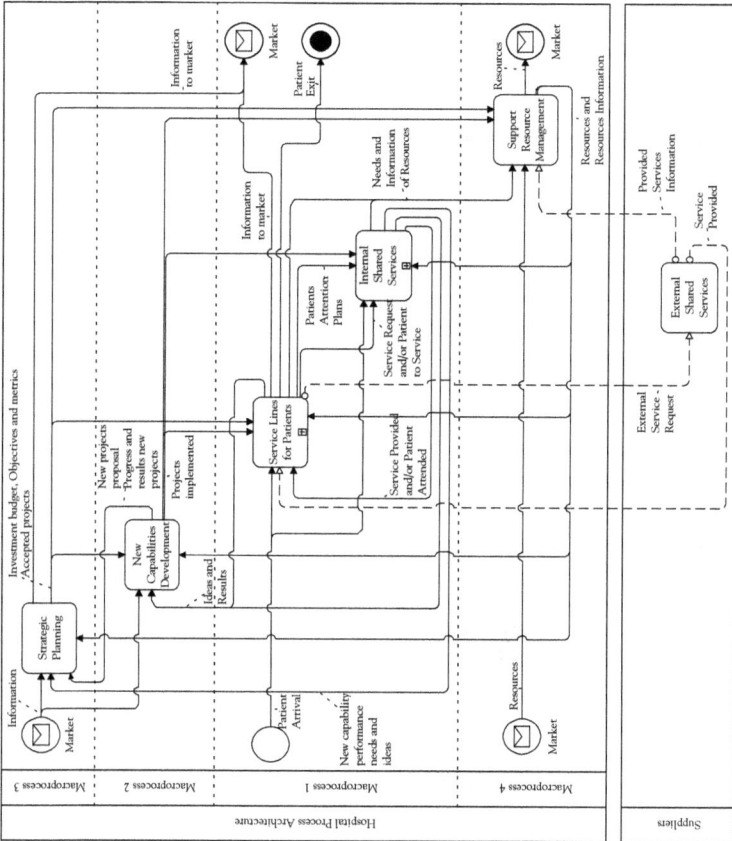

Figure 4.1 Architecture design for the private hospital case

on aforementioned guidelines, produces the "Projects implemented" and interacts with "Strategic Planning" by means of the flow "New projects proposal" and "Progress and results new projects." Both of these macroprocesses interact with the other processes in the architecture through "New Capability performance" and "Needs and ideas." What we have then is a sequence, which is implicit in Figure 4.1, because it is a nonsynchronous representation, where first "Strategic Planning" will issue guidelines; based on this and "Ideas and results" arising from other processes, "New Capabilities Development" generates new projects ideas that will be submitted back to "Strategic Planning," which will then define the projects to be implemented. Later, projects will be designed and constructed by "New Capabilities Development" and implemented on the other processes. Finally, during all the preceding sequences and after the project is implemented, a monitoring of the progress and result of such projects will be performed. This sequence is formalized and made explicit in the more detailed levels of design presented next.

To illustrate the following level of design, we use "New Capabilities Development" for which a general pattern for a macroprocess of this type is used.[1] Such pattern is instantiated for this case, resulting in Figure 4.2, where the first process is "Generation of new projects proposals" that, based on guidelines arising from "Strategic Planning," does a formal definition and evaluation of projects, interacting with the "Other macroprocesses" and acquiring market information; this interaction means an active participation of the Heads of the medical and other services operating units in generating new project ideas. Now this hospital has a strategic alliance with the medical school of a private university for training their medical school students; then such school may participate in the generation of medical innovations that can be considered in the project generation. The first result of its effort is "New Capabilities ideas" to be considered by "Strategic Planning," where the projects to be implemented are decided. For such projects, the process "Manage design and construction of new capability" is executed, which generates "Design and construction plans" to be executed by "Design and construction of new Capability." The business logic to be executed by these two processes is essentially good project management practices as proposed by the Project Management Body of Knowledge (PMBOK).[2] All these processes have feedback flows that allow

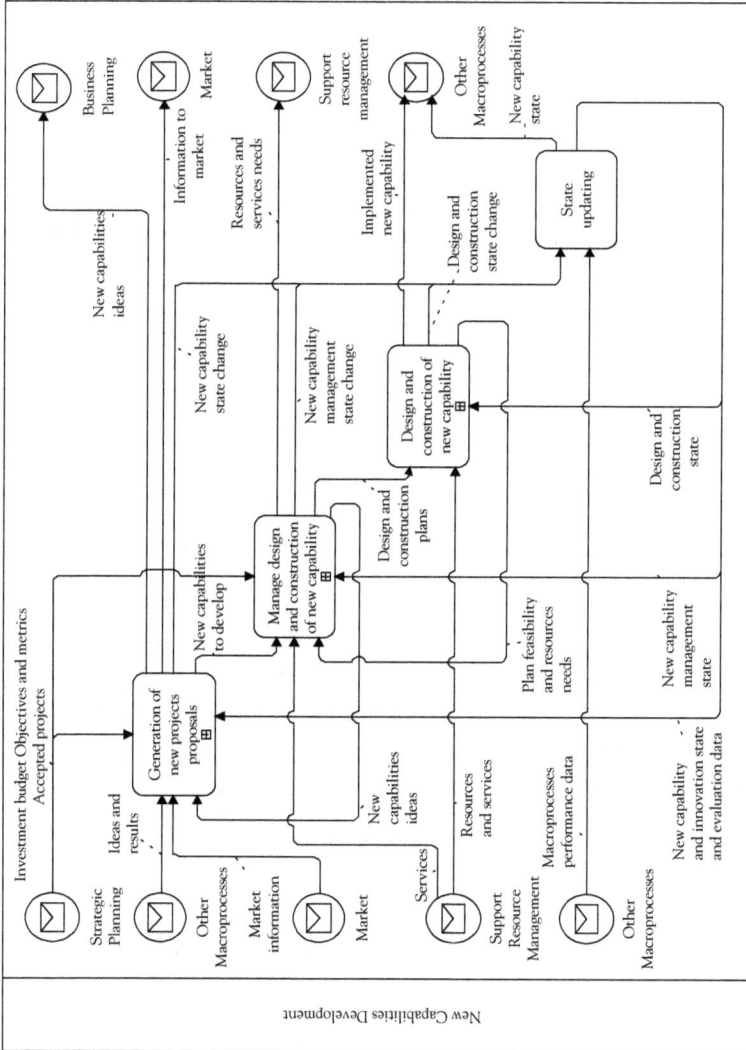

Figure 4.2 "New Capabilities Development" design for the private hospital case

monitoring and correcting actions, such as "Plan feasibility and resources needs." To provide the adequate system support there is the process "State updating," where all the information about projects in their various states, plans, and resources are maintained up to date.

"Design and construction of new capabilites"in Figure 4.2 is where the detail design of the service itself and its production is performed as defined in Chapter 2 in "Design Levels for Health Services."

There are several levels of design details, as will be exemplified in later cases, which define the operation of the processes and the business logic that is executed, but are not included for this case.

The project reported earlier was developed during approximately 18 months, where formal processes of planning and management of strategic projects were designed and implemented, which did not exist before this effort, with a custom-made information system support. Moreover, a formal effort was implemented that took care of the factors of change management within the organization. Such effort made a difference in this case, since it is difficult to change management practices in a radical way in a medical environment, where doctors emphasize mainly their discipline. In making the innovations feasible, the support from the Board of Directors and the active participation of the medical unit heads were the key factors. As a result of this design, the visibility of plans and projects' execution was considerably increased; also the communication between the Directors and the section heads improved. Finally, the results motivated the creation of a Project Management Office that supervises and leads the innovation initiatives. It is convenient to emphasize the enormous cultural change that this project produced in the executives of the organization, including its board and all the medical unit heads, which had to change their practices of planning and management of projects in a fundamental way, a great merit in a medical atmosphere, where they tend to subvalue the improvement in the management practices.

This case proves again that a profound and good Business Design involves integrated and systemic changes in the structure of the organization, the process architecture, and IT support; that is, true Enterprise Architecture.

Innovation Resource Assignment in the Public Sector

Based on the BP presented for this case in the previous chapter we propose an architecture based on the general health multilevel architecture of Figure 2.12, which should exist at the top of the public health system to guide its development with an emphasis on resource assignment for innovation projects on existent hospitals. Hence, we overlook features such as ordinary annual budgeting, investment in new facilities, health campaigns, and many other activities that are necessary in a centralized country health management, which are summarized in the "Other processes" component of the architecture. We also do not consider the level of subnetwork in Figure 2.12, which are groups of hospitals managed by a centralized authority, since they do not play a significant role on resource assignment.

Our selection of innovation resource assignment is based on the execution of many projects with hospitals, where the implementation of well-selected projects, which change in a radical way the medical and management practices of services in hospitals, has generated significant social value.[3] Thus, our key idea is to generalize and extend our experience to the public hospitals system.

In the architecture in Figure 4.3, which is an instantiation of the general pattern in Figure 2.12, the main idea is that, besides "Regular planning and budgeting" oriented to continuing operation, Macro3 of the central level includes a new process of "Innovation planning and budgeting." Such process executes a logic, which will be explained later, to determine the innovation projects that are to be executed in selected hospitals in trying to maximize the value associated with the objectives stated earlier. This innovation relates to new Capabilities to be developed for hospitals in a similar way to the previous case of the private hospital; the difference in this case is that we are dealing with all the hospitals in the Chilean health system in a centralized planning approach for this type of innovation. Then the projects are defined in detail by "Innovation projects organization and monitoring," which determines the budget and the possible external services suppliers that can execute them. Next, the projects are communicated, by means of the flow "Project definition and budget" to the selected hospitals, determined as explained in the

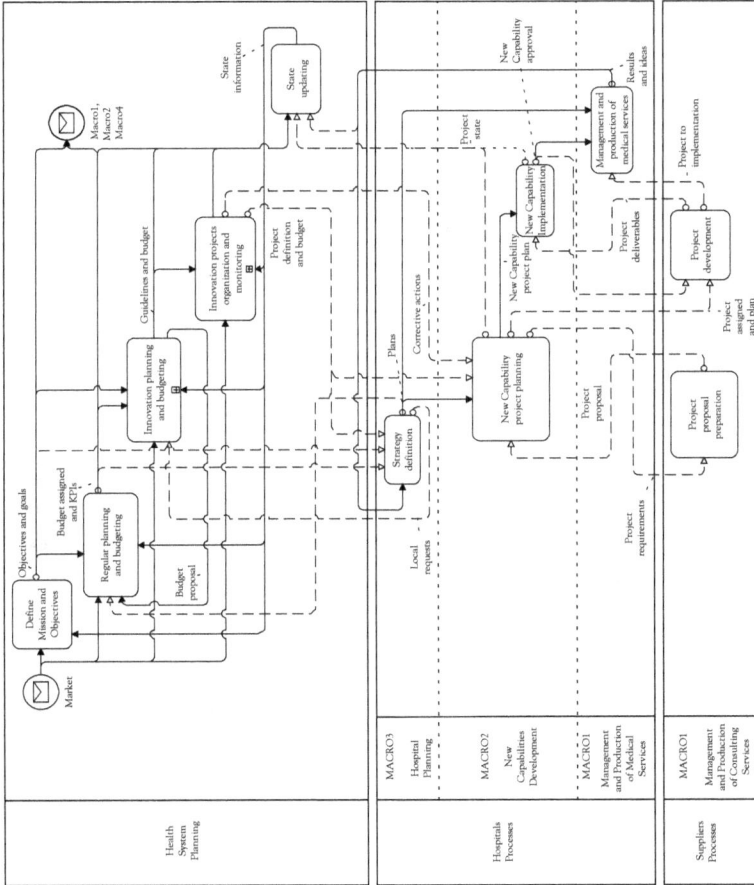

Figure 4.3 Design for resource assignment in the Public Sector

following, to be defined in detail by them with the collaboration of the "Suppliers Processes," which are academic or consulting services specialized in the types of projects to be defined. The idea behind this proposal is that hospitals do not have health innovation and project management specialists, so the projects should be executed by means of externalized services, as it has been the case in many historical projects dealing with IT support or process design. In implementing this approach, hospitals need, as shown in Figure 4.3, three new processes: (a) "Strategy definition" that, besides doing the current budgetary planning, which includes resources and other medical factors, will perform the overall planning to execute the projects assigned to the hospital, (b) "New Capability project planning" that requests proposals for executing projects from external suppliers, evaluates them, and decides which consulting group will actually develop the project; and (c) "New Capability Implementation" that will coordinate with suppliers and the people from "Management and production of health services," who will execute the new Capability, and put the project into practice. Similar examples of such Capabilities will be presented when the logic that defines which new Capabilities are to be implemented is specified. Besides, the processes just explained for "Health System Planning" in Figure 4.3, the design includes "Define Mission and Objectives" that provides a frame of reference for the rest of the processes and "State updating" that carries out its usual task of keeping up to date and reporting the status of the all the processes in the design; in particular, the situation and results of each innovation project.

Notice that this architecture is centralized on decision of funds assignments to innovations projects that maximize efficiency improvements on hospitals and its justified by agency theory that says that principal (government) interests are better taken care of with this option.[4] But execution of projects is decentralized, since the same theory says that this is better because operators (agents) know more about these implementations issues and if principal tries to manage them he would incur in severe opportunity costs due to lack of information.

The key business logic that makes possible the implementation of the aforementioned architecture is the one that, in "Innovation planning and budgeting," measures efficiency of the hospitals and determines which projects to develop in the less efficient ones to make them improve. Such logic was developed by measuring the efficiency, based on the Data Envelopment Analysis (DEA) analysis, for 40 hospitals and it is detailed as follows.

As stated in Chapter 2, we pursue three objectives: quality, efficiency, and fairness in designing health services. This is a multicriteria problem for which it is impossible to find a solution that optimizes all the objectives simultaneously; thus, a possibility is to prioritize the optimization of an objective and then take into consideration the others. Hence, the logic proposed for the design of new Capabilities for innovation projects generation, in "Innovation planning and budgeting" of Figure 4.3, is founded on the idea that it is possible to measure and compare the efficiency of the hospitals by using the economic theory of efficiency frontier as presented by Farrell,[5] which takes into account such variable. Subsequently, based on efficiency comparisons, take into consideration the fairness and quality variables as we explain later. Next, we briefly summarize the economic theory used for the efficiency measurement and comparison.[6]

According to economic theory, a unit is efficient when it is able to produce, relatively to comparable group, a greater amount of product for given resources, or to use a smaller amount of resources for a given production. One formal approach to measure efficiency is the one of Farrell, which is based on the empirical results of the units and not on the possible ideal or optimal results. For this reason, the levels of efficiency of the units are defined in relative terms, given the information available. Thus, the most efficient units are those that define the productive frontier. According to Farrell, three types of efficiency can be distinguished: technical, allocative, and scale. The technical efficiency is obtained when a unit obtains the maximum results with its resources. The allocative efficiency is obtained when a unit uses its resources in the optimal proportions and maximizes results. Finally, the scale efficiency occurs when both types of efficiency are obtained.

In 1978, Charnes et al.[7] generalized the proposal of Farrell with a mathematical nonparametric model, called DEA. This model constructs the technical efficiency frontier on the basis of the provided data (inputs and outputs) that can be of constant returns to scale (CRS) and variables (VRS), which is an extension of Banker, Charnes, and Cooper.[8] In calculating the technical efficiency frontier, inputs can be minimized or outputs can be maximized. The first calculation looks for the breach between the evaluated unit with respect to the amount of resources established by the efficient frontier, given a production level and the second looks for the optimal production amount, given the level of resources.

Some advantages that distinguish DEA from other methodologies of efficiency calculation, like the Stochastic Production Frontier,[9] are: (a) it does not assume a form of the production function on the basis of the resources, (b) it is possible to use different measurement units for the inputs and outputs amounts and multiple inputs, and (c) outputs can be integrated.[10] The limitations are that the DEA is very sensible to the sample; it does not allow identifying the theoretical maximum efficiency, interprets any deviation from the frontier as inefficiency, and it is complex to perform sensitivity analyses.[11]

A graphical interpretation of an efficiency frontier, in the simple case of just one input and output, is shown in Figure 4.4, where the curve that envelopes the pairs of inputs and outputs that define the data points is the frontier. Data points on the frontier are efficient and those under the frontier are inefficient.

The efficiency frontier can be calculated by solving the following optimization problem:

$$\text{Max}_{u,v} \; h_k = \frac{\sum_{r=1}^{s} u_{rk} y_{rk}}{\sum_{i=1}^{m} v_{ik} x_{ik}}$$

subject to:

$$0 \le \sum_{i=1}^{m} v_{ik} x_{ij} - \sum_{r=1}^{s} u_{rk} y_{rj}; \; j = 1, \, \ldots, \, n, \; k = 1, \, \ldots, \, n, \; u_r, v_i \ge 0$$

Where there are n decision units that generate similar products and the evaluated unit is the kth; each unit consumes diverse amounts of m

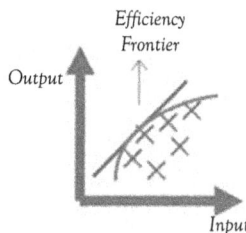

Figure 4.4 Input, output, and the efficiency frontier

different resources to produce s different products; x_{ij} is the amount of the resource i that uses the jth unit; y_{ij} is the amount of product r of the jth unit; and v_i and u_r are the weights associated with resource i and product r, respectively.

The model evaluates the n units, one at a time, and, in each iteration, it looks for the set of weights that maximizes the efficiency level for each evaluated unit k. Such levels are in fact the values of efficiency for each unit. According to Dyson et al.,[12] the flexibility in the election of the weights is a weakness and simultaneously the strength of this approach. It is a weakness because the model can arbitrarily consider that a unit is not related to the value of some resource or product, allowing it to appear as efficient, which is possible to correct. It also shows strength, since if a unit, in spite of getting the most favorable weights, turns out to be inefficient and implies a breach between that unit and the more efficient ones. Thus, DEA can be used in those cases where the different resources and products from the units are valued accurately and also when there is a high degree of uncertainty or disagreement on the values of some resources or products.

The DEA methodology has been extensively used internationally to compare the efficiency of hospitals; thus Hollingsworth[13] makes a revision of 317 international studies where 75 percent of them use DEA to measure efficiency in health units.

The AP model, named after Andersen and Petersen proposal, is an extension to the original formulation of DEA[14] because it allows discriminating in a more effective way the possible errors of the data.[15] In this model, when the evaluated unit is the same as the compared unit, the weights may take values greater than one, which are then known as super-efficiency levels. The AP model is criticized because the units that emphasize a single resource and a product in the results, also known as "mavericks," tend to obtain higher efficiency values, as found by O'Neill and Dexter.[16] Thus, O'Neill and Dexter proposed an indicator of robustness based on an adaptation to the model AP,[17] which indicates if the hospital is a maverick.

To apply the DEA model, appropriate software to manage the data and solve the optimization problem is necessary. Of the many alternatives available, General Algebraic Modeling System (GAMS)[18] was used, because it is easy to use and more convenient than other programs.

In applying the DEA analysis to Chilean hospitals, it is necessary to measure their output. For this, and in order to standardize the production of multiple different outputs, a weighted measure has been proposed, which is called *Diagnosis-Related Group* (DRG). In the literature, the use of DRG as an adjustment of hospital's production is common,[19] since it has been empirically observed that the relative weights of the DRG are correlated with the real cost of a hospital.[20] The creators of this methodology at the University of Yale were Fetter and Thompson.[21] They managed to generate 465 DRG using the historical data of patients by classifying them into groups with similar patterns in the use of resources and with clinical coherence.[22] The groupings were obtained based on the time of hospitalization of the patients and validating those groups by means of their cost. Also, to generate these groups, they produced an indicator that identifies the Potential relative consumption of the resources for a DRG, which is estimated with the expected cost of the DRG based on the average cost of the hospitalized patients.[23] Currently, Chilean hospitals use an international version of the DRG developed by the 3M Company, called International Refined DRG (IR-DRG), that defines 1,077 different types from groups of related diagnoses differentiated by severity levels, discounting the cases with ambulatory medical services.[24] The DRGs are being used in the great majority of the hospitals of high complexity.

Now, given that we have the basis to measure hospital production or output using DRG, we define the data to apply the DEA analysis. The variables used to make the DEA analysis of Chilean hospitals is summarized in the Table 4.1 and in Table 4.2, where the descriptive statistics of such variables are given.

Then using the data just presented, the obtained efficiencies, calculated with the DEA method, are shown in Table 4.3 and Figure 4.5.

With these results we now come to the key question: Which variables explain such results and what actions can be taken over such variables to increase efficiency? At the same time quality and fairness issues too are to be considered. In answering the preceding question, 240 variables associated with the hospitals that may affect efficiency were considered; for example:

1. Social-delinquency vulnerability index of the population attended by the hospital, which may decrease efficiency because the health of the population is poor.

Table 4.1 Variables definition for the DEA model

Variable	Definition
DMUs or decision units	Self-managed hospitals with sufficient data during the period October, 2011 to September, 2012. Altogether, 40 hospitals.
Input	• Number of doctors who discharge hospitalized patients from the hospital. • Number of registered beds.
Output	Amount of discharged patients adjusted by clinical complexity (DRG), differentiated by: • Simple interventions (DRG weight less than 1). • Medium complexity interventions. • Complex interventions (DRG weight greater than 4).
Type of orientation	Orientation to the input, because the hospitals accept demand for health services, which is an exogenous variable; however, the resources are handled by the hospital.
Type of returns	CRS, since, *a priori*, the level where the (des) economies of scale happen is not known, but explanatory variables related to the size of the hospital are considered.

Table 4.2 Variables' statistics

	Inputs		Outputs DRG weighted discharges		
	Doctors	Beds	Simple	Medium Complexity	Complex
Minimum	65	130	1,388	1,362	5
Maximum	566	870	20,118	14,018	4,742
Average	198	384	8,014	4,848	1,535
Standard deviation	107.49	183.32	3,806.83	3,103.49	1,213.55

Table 4.3 Efficiency results with constant returns to scale

	Efficiency (CRS) calculated with DEA model (CCR[25])	Efficiency (CRS) calculated with AP model
Minimum	0,634	0,661
Maximum	1	1,511
Average	0,8212	0,913
Standard Deviation	0,1092	0,191
Hospitals in and over the efficiency frontier	6	7

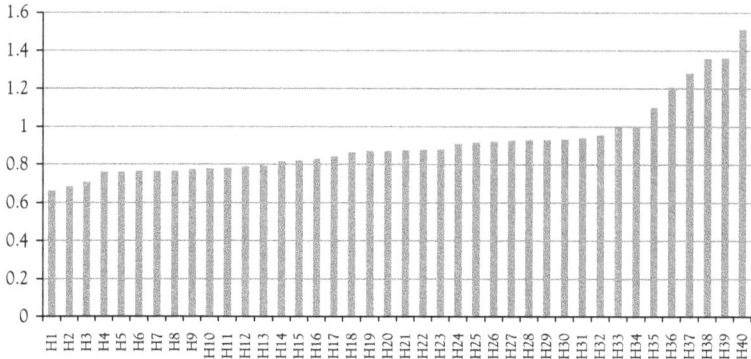

Figure 4.5 Efficiency results with AP model for hospitals

2. Percent of child births, because it is a complex medical procedure that may also affect efficiency.

3. Patients without social security—also an adverse factor to efficiency.

4. Percent of programmed patients, which means that medical procedures are planned in advance, as opposed to urgency patients, which favor efficiency.

5. Children hospital.

6. Patients coming from emergency services.

Further, by using a statistical procedure proposed by O'Neill and Dexter,[26] which detects outliers, correlated, and nonsignificant variables, 13 variables were determined as good candidates to explain efficiency and hence possible to be manipulated, if possible, to increase efficiency in a hospital. These variables are shown in Table 4.4.

In selecting hospitals where manipulation of variables in Table 4.4 may provide better results, we come back to the comparative hospital efficiencies to prioritize them for intervention. A simple rule used for intervention is by selecting the hospitals that have an efficiency of less than 0.80, which means that one-third, or 13, of the hospital are prioritized for improvement as shown in Figure 4.5.

To further refine the selection of variables to be considered for intervention, the opinion of health experts was requested, who selected six variables they thought that hospitals could possibly manage to improve efficiency. Then each of these variables was analyzed for its impact on

Table 4.4 *Main explicative variables*

No	Name	Category	Correlation	p-value for significance
1	Social-delinquency vulnerability index	Social factors	−0.40	0.012
2	Percent of programmed patients	Patient management	0.44	0.005
3	Patients coming from a lower level in health network	Network integration	0.35	0.026
4	Meeting payment deadlines with suppliers	Supply and financial management	0.40	0.013
5	Patients coming from an emergency service	Demand behavior	−0.39	0.012
6	Hospital with breast surgery	Hospital structure	−0.36	0.021
7	Hospital with maxilla-facial surgery	Hospital structure	−0.40	0.011
8	Hospital with neurosurgery	Hospital structure	−0.45	0.003
9	Percent of adult patients	Demand behavior	−0.38	0.016
10	Percent of child births	Complex variable	−0.47	0.002
11	Date hospital started with self-management	Complex variable	−0.49	0.002
12	Children hospital	Demand characteristics	0.38	0.015
13	Rotation index	Complex variable	0.34	0.033

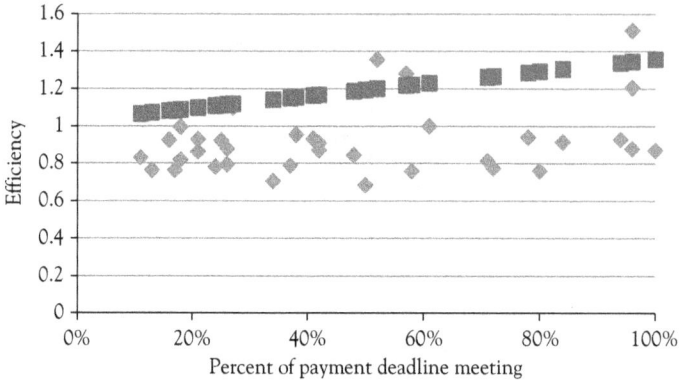

Figure 4.6 Relationship between efficiency and the variable "Meeting payment deadlines with suppliers"

efficiency. For example, in Figure 4.6, the impact on efficiency of the variable "Meeting payment deadlines with suppliers" is shown, where the rhombuses are the values of efficiency for each hospital and the squares are the tendency line of the efficient hospitals; this line represents the value the less efficient hospitals could achieve if properly managed. By constructing the same curves for the six selected variables, it was concluded that only five have possibilities to improve the hospitals efficiency. With this analysis, a Potential for efficiency improvement for each variable and hospital can be calculated with the following expression:

$$\text{Potential}_{ij} = (e'_{ij} - e_i)\frac{(1 - e_i)}{\sum_j (e'_{ij} - e_i)}$$

Where j is the index of the Potential variable, e_i is the efficiency of the ith hospital, and e'_{ij} is the value of the efficiency of the tendency line of the hospitals in the efficiency frontier, which the ith hospital could achieve.

The calculation of the Potential for each of the 13 prioritized hospitals for each variable allows constructing Figure 4.7, where it is apparent how by making effective the Potentials for each hospital, its efficiency can be improved from its current value to close to one.

Finally, by selecting the variables with greater improvement impact, projects can be defined to make effective the Potential and improve

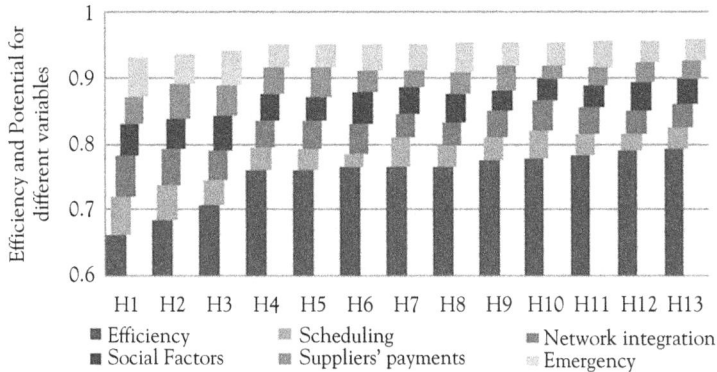

Figure 4.7 Efficiency and Potential for each variable and hospital

efficiency, the outcome of which is expected. For example, the variable Programming or "Percent of programmed patients" has a relatively large Potential for low productive hospitals, which implies that if processes incentivizing programming are introduced, efficiency will improve. If, at the same time, formal programming methods are introduced, which these hospitals do not have, the efficiency improvement can be reinforced. We have performed many projects related to programming in several hospitals, some of which will be reported in the next chapters, where we have introduced processes to characterize demand, prioritize, and program it on hospital facilities: ambulatory services, urgency, beads, and operating rooms. In all cases, the result has been a large improvement in use of facilities, thus increasing the efficiency. But, at the same time, better service has been provided by defining explicit medical-based priorities for patient treatment, assuring attention at the right time and reducing waiting times. Therefore, quality and fairness can be improved in parallel with efficiency, as they usually go hand in hand.

A more systematic procedure to define projects is to select variables that experts evaluate as more feasible to manipulate to generate increased efficiency. A preliminary list of such variables, discussed with some health authorities and derived from the data in Figure 4.7, is shown in Table 4.5.

Typical projects consistent with the list in Table 4.5 and which have increased efficiency in specific cases are:

Table 4.5 Candidate variables for project definition

No	Categorization	Projects
1	Social factors	- Patient education
2	Patient management	- Train support personnel to schedule patients with medical criteria - Ambulatory patient programming - Bed management
3	Health network integration	- Preventive examinations and treatments - Interconsults and contra reference management - Waiting list management

1. Ambulatory patients' prioritization managed on a first-come-first-served basis. A case in this same chapter shows this is inefficient and unfair. As a result, there is a huge Potential for efficiency improvement by applying these ideas in hospitals that are low as shown in Figure 4.7.

2. Predictive models for chronic patients to detect critical situations in advance, avoiding crisis and expensive treatments. This has a lot of Potential because chronic diabetes and hypertension patients constitute a significant part of the hospitals' costs. Besides, this idea was tested for diabetes in a private hospital and proved feasible, as will be shown in Chapter 6. Currently, this idea is being implemented in a children's hospital for patients with respiratory problems that can be treated at home, as presented in Chapter 3 and will be detailed in Chapter 6, for which predictive models are being developed that, based on line monitoring, will give suggestions to doctors when there is any risk for such patients. The goal is to encourage home treatment for chronic diseases to improve fairness and efficiency.

3. Bed management at the level of the health system, monitoring availability, and assigning patients centrally to the right hospital that has the possibility of attention. This has been used for several years and produced good results.

4. Operating room management, including patients' prioritization, operation scheduling, and intervention monitoring. We have performed projects of this type in several hospitals that show benefits; we will present a case proving this in Chapter 6.

The approach proposed in this section has as an important by-product the possibility of learning from hospitals that are more effective and efficient, those at the efficiency frontier, and share medical and management solutions that have proved successful for them. This can generate a virtuous circle due to the centralized assignment of innovations resources oriented to improve efficiency, taking into account quality of service, which will move lower-performing hospital to the efficiency frontier. This will generate a powerful learning process that will improve the transference of proven methods to other hospitals in future innovation resource assignments.

Operating Room Capacity and Assignment

We present what we defined as a local case, in "Design Levels for Health Services," where there is not a Business Design and Configuration Design, since current situation is taken as given. However, the Strategy and Business Model are still relevant to guide the definition of the appropriate capacity and its assignment. Then, the positioning in this case should be best product with an emphasis on operational efficiency, since operating rooms are a very scarce resource, and value to be provided to users is on-time delivery of the surgery, according to maximum waiting time (MWT) associated to the patient illness. The main Capability necessary to accomplish these objectives is being able to design an operating room capacity according to demand, so as to assure meeting of MWT, assigning and using it in the best possible way. So an Intelligent Structure II is needed to provide the required Analytics and the relevant BP is BP6, "Optimun Resource Usage." This BP maps directly into Macro1 specialized for hospitals as shown in Figure 2.9, where the "Operating Room Service" is defined in the context of hospital's operation, and its detail design given in Figure 2.11. In this case we concentrate on "Demand Analysis," which forecast demand for surgery and determines the necessary resources to be able to process such a demand according to the aforementioned objectives, the design of which is given in Figure 4.8. We will design the details of this process to be executed periodically in time to determine adjustments to capacity and its assignment, according to the dynamics of the demand.

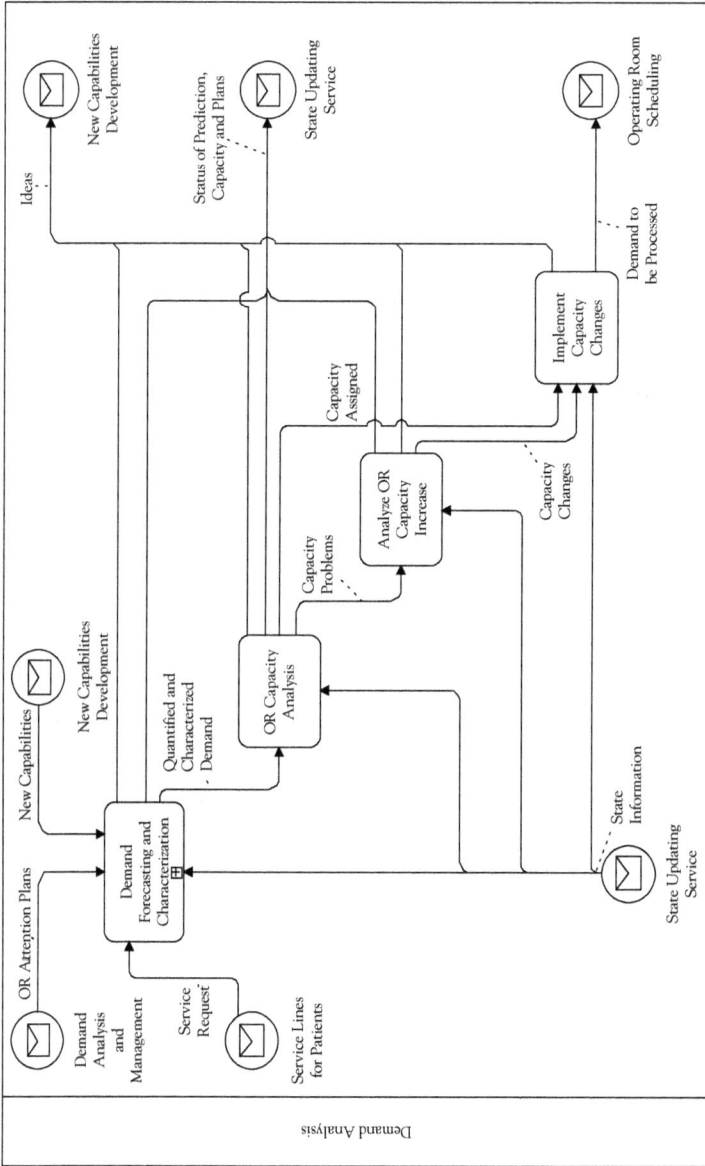

Figure 4.8 Design for "Demand Analysis"

"Demand Forecasting and Characterization" in Figure 4.8 is the sub-process that provides a forecast that allows the hospital to allocate OR resources in "OR Capacity Analysis." In particular, it is determined if current capacity of the hospital is enough to meet the demand or if it is necessary to change it. If more capacity is needed, the possibility of doing so should be studied in the subprocess "Analyze OR capacity increase." Finally, changes and assignments are implemented in "Implement Capacity Changes." What we need then is a business logic to perform such subprocesses, which is defined as follows.

There are two ways to perform the assignment of operating rooms to specialties that use them: block assignment, in which fix duration of time on given days are schedules for each specialty, and case scheduling where individual surgical operations are assigned independently. In both cases all capacity would be used up, because there are waiting lists due to lack of enough capacity.

Currently, in the hospital under study, capacity is assigned as shown in Table 4.6, where the different specialties that require OR service are: General Surgery (GS), Urology (Uro), Trauma, Traumatology Cord (TC), and Plastic Surgery (PC).[27]

This is a typical static block assignment and there is no formal method or criteria to justify it in this hospital, having only a historical justification. So, in particular, there is no way to prove that this assignment contributes to fairness, which is one of the relevant objectives in this case. Therefore, considering the high number of people on the waiting lists for the different specialties, no assurance exists that patients are being operated according to the required MWTs determined by their pathology.

Therefore, what is proposed for this case is a design of OR capacity and its assignment in such a way that patients are operated meeting a required MWT and that different specialties have the same possibilities to operate their patients according to their demands (fairness); also capacity should be used in an efficient way, which relates to one of the other objectives we defined at the beginning of this section.

The process "Demand Forecasting and Characterization" is designed in detail, including the business logic that will be executed, where the services demanded by patients are determined and described according to

Table 4.6 Current OR capacity assignment

	Monday morning	Monday afternoon	Tuesday morning	Tuesday afternoon	Wednesday morning	Wednesday afternoon	Thursday morning	Thursday afternoon	Friday morning
OR 1	GS	Uro	Uro		Uro		Uro		Uro
OR 2	GS	GS	GS	GS	GS	GS	GS	GS	GS
OR 3	Trauma	Trauma	TC	TC	Trauma		Trauma		Trauma
OR 4	PC		PC		PC	PC	PC		PC
OR 5	Trauma		Trauma						

various attributes, such as of MWT category. This subprocess is modeled with BPMN in Figure 4.9.

In Figure 4.9, historical data is first prepared, where only the useful information to generate forecasts is considered, leaving aside attributes such as name, ID, or the patient's address. Then the model to be used is selected from a set of alternatives previously developed and its parameters are set to run it and generate a forecast. Finally, the forecast is approved and sent to "OR Capacity Analysis." The data and models that are used are presented later. Once the prediction and characterization of demand is obtained, the subprocess shown in Figure 4.10 is performed. First the forecast is requested; then the allocation of a percentage of surgical time for each OR is assigned to each specialty to meet the objectives set by the hospital, which is determined through an Integer Linear Programming (ILP) model, which will be explained later. The assignment can be run again with different information and model parameters if the result is not satisfactory in terms of meeting hospital performance objectives. If it is satisfactory, the next question is whether more capacity is needed to reduce the overall excessive waiting time for patients. In the case in which more capacity is necessary, the subprocess "Analyze OR capacity increase" is executed according to the design shown in Figure 4.11. In this subprocess, the main activity is the use of the same ILP model of "OR Capacity Analysis" within a simulation that evaluates possible increases in capacity in "Run model to evaluate Scenario." Such Scenario defines which forecast will be used, parameters of the ILP model and other parameters, as detailed next.

Next, the details of Analytics that are used in the subprocesses are presented. As in all the cases we have included in this book, this a key component of the design, assuring that the objectives of the process, in this case, fairness for patients and efficiency in the use of resources, are accomplished.

For "Execute Demand Forecast and Characterization Models," part of the subprocess of Figure 4.9, regression, moving averages, Neural Networks, and Support Vector Regression[28] are considered. Given the objectives of the case and also considering the information available, its quality, and finally the volume of demand for the various specialties, the forecast is done on a monthly basis. Historical information regarding

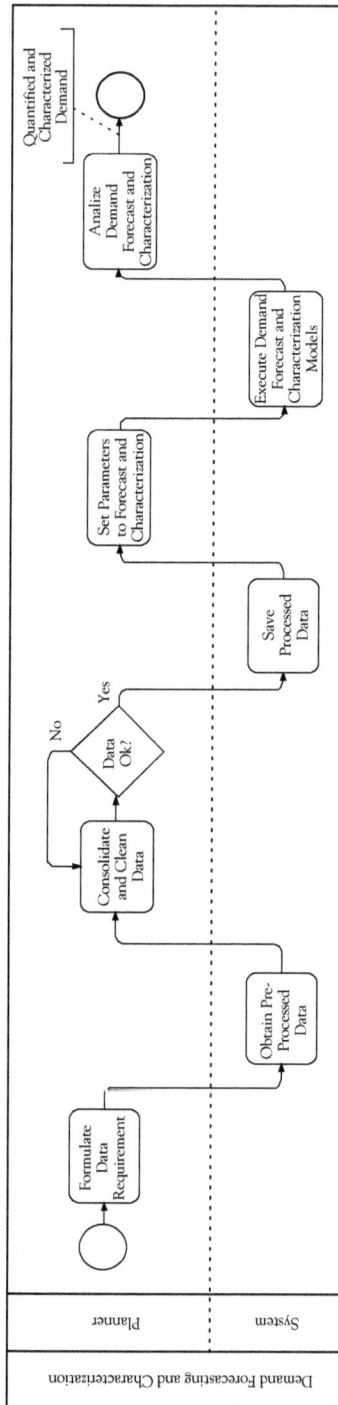

Figure 4.9 Design of "Demand Forecasting and Characterization"

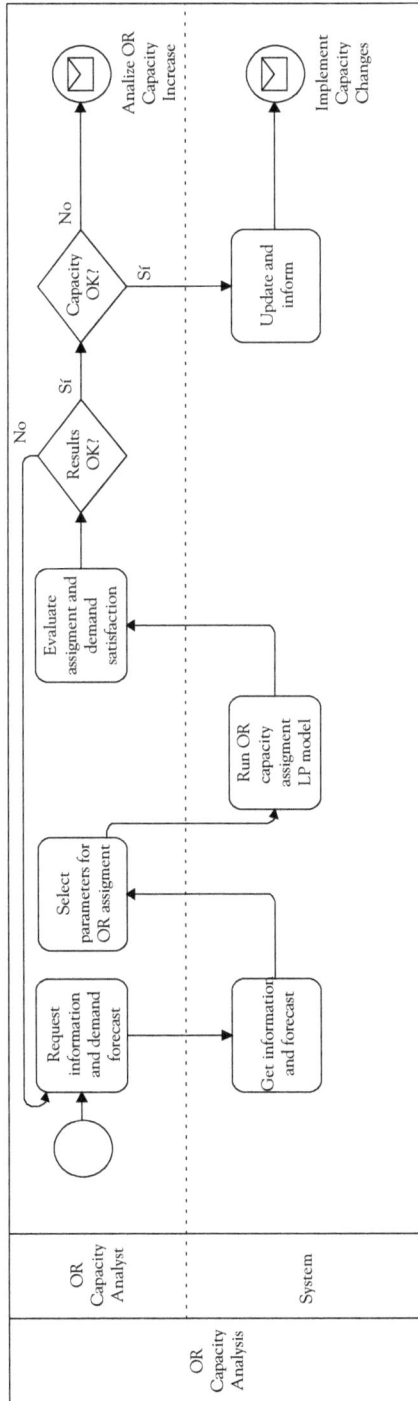

Figure 4.10 Design of "OR Capacity Analysis"

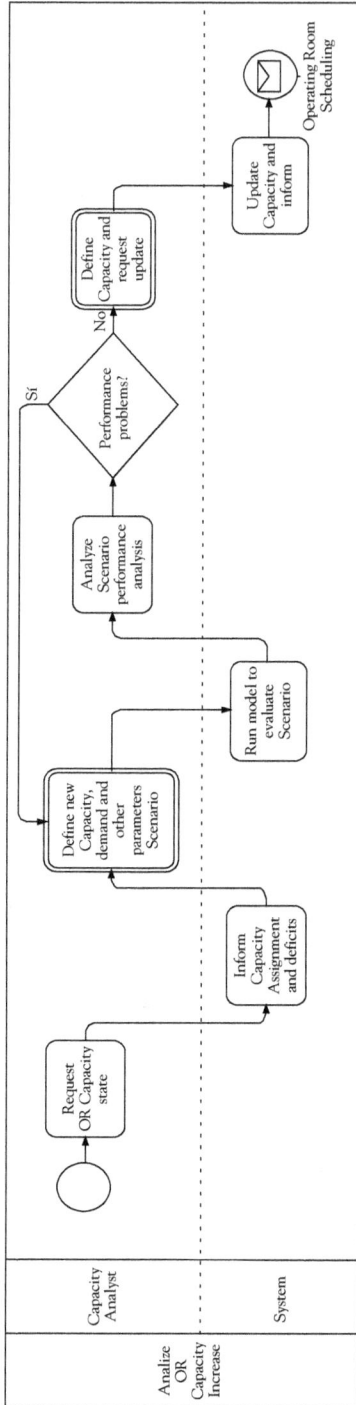

Figure 4.11 Design of "Analyze OR capacity increase"

the number of patients admitted to waiting lists is available for the different specialties: Plastic Surgery, General Surgery, Traumatology, and Urology.

Analysis of the information provided by the hospital is presented. This is done through the study of the waiting lists, categorizing each diagnosis presented by the patient according to the four different specialties mentioned earlier. The information is recorded every day, so it is aggregated on a monthly basis and presented graphically, as shown in Figures 4.12 and 4.13 for General Surgery and Urology. Characteristic behavior patterns can be appreciated on a monthly basis as the graphs of 2004 to 2010 show:

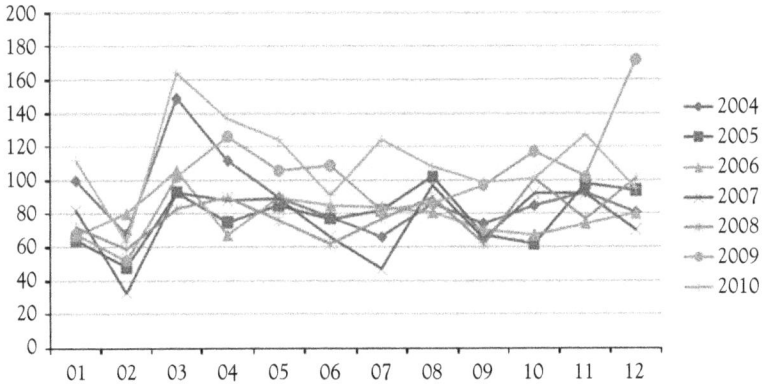

Figure 4.12 Admission to General Surgery waiting list

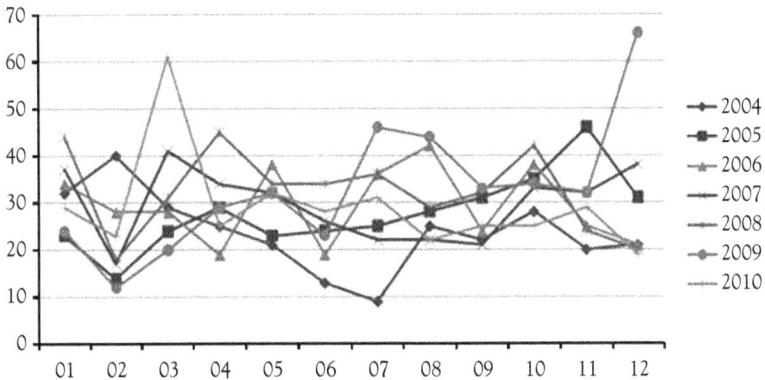

Figure 4.13 Admission to Urology waiting list

1. In all specialties, a decrease in patients admitted to waiting list for the summer months of December to February is observed, showing a considerable drop in the month of February (vacation month in Chile).
2. An increase is observed in all the specialties to waiting lists for the month of March.
3. In general, good quality of data is available without a large amount of outliers, which are eliminated manually to avoid errors in the forecast.
4. Specialties, such as Urology, Traumatology, and General Surgery, are much more stable in contrast to Plastic Surgery, which has more variation.

Forecasting models are developed separately for each specialty, since they independently manage their waiting lists and each of them has characteristic behavior patterns. To develop such models, and based on previous experience with forecasting, several variables are considered as possible determinants of future demand behavior, such as the demand of the previous month or two previous months to the one to be forecasted; the value of the demand for the same month last year or two or three years ago; and the difference between the current and the previous month in the year prior to the month to be forecasted.

Then the different models are estimated with the data, leaving a set of data unused in order to test for models errors. The results for each model in terms of forecasting quality measured by forecasting error mean absolute percentage error (MAPE) of the forecast, as shown in Table 4.7.

Table 4.7 MAPE for the different forecasting models

	Neural Network (percent)	Linear Regression (percent)	Support Vector Regression (percent)	Moving Averages (percent)
General Surgery	38	18	28	23
Plastic Surgery	71	58	46	92
Traumatology	20	11	12	71
Urology	12	22	14	50

The models finally chosen correspond to those having lower MAPE. The high value of this error in Plastic Surgery is explained by the number of patients who enter the waiting list, which is very low; so a little difference in these forecasts can have a big effect on the error.

Given a forecast, we present the business logic (based on Analytics) that allows assigning a percentage of surgical time to each specialty, as required in the subprocess of Figure 4.10, in order to comply with the already stated objectives of the hospital. To perform such assignment, a multicriteria ILP model is used.

First, a set of criteria is defined to assign the OR capacity. They are based on the objectives described at the beginning of this section: fairness in relation to the patient and efficiency in the use of resources for the hospital and, hence, for the public health services. This is detailed in the criteria explained later.

The first criterion relates to the characteristics of the patient, that is, the complexity of the pathology involved, the category of MWT for the surgery that determines the opportunity, and finally the total surgical time. The determination of complexity is done by the DRG—explained in the case "Innovation Resource Assignment in the Public Sector" in this chapter—of the surgical intervention. The opportunity is defined in terms of the characterization of each specialty based on the MWTs for surgery defined for Categories A, B, C, D, and E. These categories are defined in terms of the risk the patient has if he is not operated: A is maximum risk and E is minimum. Of course, MWT allowed before surgery should be low for A and high for E. This time is determined based on medical factors by doctors and also depends on aggravating factors such as age and general health of a patient. The application of this idea in current practice is shown in Figure 4.14, where real waiting times for categories are presented, which show that the idea is present but not fully applied. This work creates conditions for the MWTs of the different categories to be duly followed.

As for the total surgical time for specialty for the patients, statistical analysis shows a great variability, so they must be described by probability distributions. For example, Urology has the surgical time distribution as shown in Figure 4.15. Now what is needed is the distribution for each

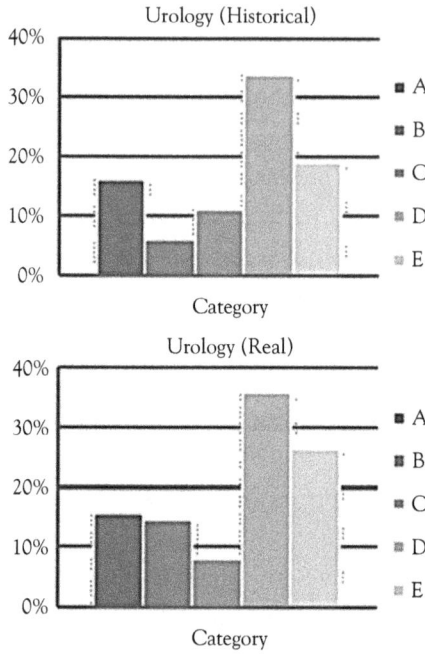

Figure 4.14 Categorization of patients on waiting list Historical and current in Urology

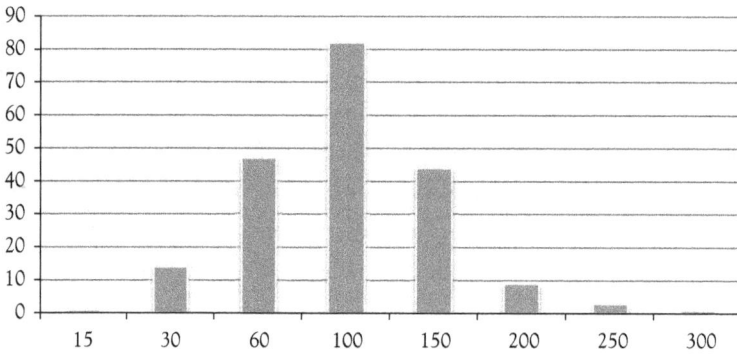

Figure 4.15 Distribution of surgical time in Urology

category: A, B, C, D, and E. On the basis of historical data, such distributions were normal with different parameters for each category.

Now the different categories have the distributions as shown in Figures 4.16 and 4.17 for Urology. These are approximated to normal with parameters given in Table 4.8.

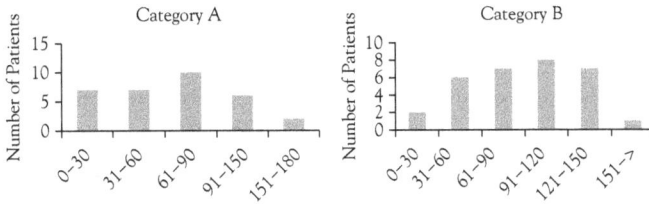

Figure 4.16 Distribution of surgical time Categories A and B

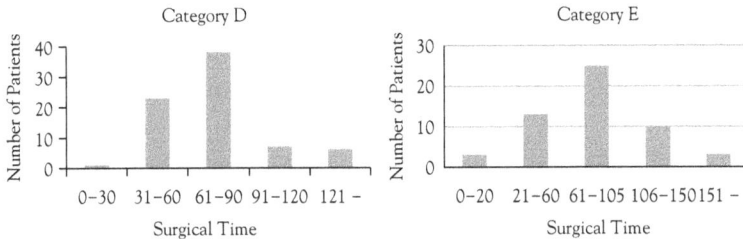

Figure 4.17 Distribution of surgical time Categories D and E

Table 4.8 Distribution of surgical times by category

Category	Distribution
A	Normal(80.4;46.6)
B	Normal(102.2;39.8)
D	Normal(89;42.8)
E	Normal(91.5;42.5)

The second type of criteria considered is the interests of the hospital and of the health system. On the one hand, the hospital has economic interests because it has a variable income, besides the regular budget, paid by health authorities for specific surgical interventions, including a tariff and a target number, which correspond to central health policies explained in the case "Resource Assignment in the Public Sector" in this chapter. Also the hospital may have some target for the reduction of its surgical waiting lists and the government may also require the reduction or elimination of waiting lists for certain pathologies defined as a priority to treat in the health system.

All the factors in the previous criteria should be considered in the assignment of OR capacity to specialties. This is done by the ILP model with the following variables, parameters, objective function, and constraints.

The model, which is based on Zhang et al.[29] aims to ensure the service for patients in the waiting lists, either through compliance with the MWT for the category of his pathology or, if not possible, minimizing the tardiness in operating the patient after MWT has expired. Hence, the first term of the objective function to be minimized models the cost of not satisfying MWT demand as:

$$\sum_{m \in M} \left(\sum_{j \in J} \theta_{Vjm} \left(\sum_{k \in D} u_{jkm} \right) \right)$$

where

u_{jkm}: unfulfilled demand for patients from specialty j, category m that have their MWT expired the day k

θ_{Vjm}: economic cost of not satisfying the demand of patients having its MWT expired in specialty j and category m

The second term of the objective function that model the cost of not satisfying demand for patients who have not yet got to MWT has a similar form:

$$\sum_{m \in M} \left(\sum_{j \in J} \theta_{NVjm} \left(\sum_{k \in D} v_{jkm} \right) \right)$$

where:

v_{jkm}: unfulfilled demand for patients from specialty j, category m who do not have their MWT expired at day k

θ_{NVjm}: economic cost of not meeting the demand of patients of specialty j, category m who do not have their MWT expired

The three other terms of the objective function include the cost associated with the postponement of a surgical intervention of patients with MWT expired and not expired and a cost associated with not meeting a desired level of capacity assignment to a given specialty. The cost parameters of this objective function depends on fairness and the economics interests of the hospital, since the costs considered may have a component associated with the patients' well-being and another with the economic losses a hospital incurs because of the postponement of certain surgical interventions, that is, the ones to which government has given priority.

Besides the variables and parameters in the objective function, other parameters include: number of OR of a given type, number and amount of available OR hours per day per type, demand of patients who have their MWT expired for specialty j, category m in day k measured in hours of OR and demand of patients who do not have their MWT expired for specialty j category m in day k, measured in hours of OR. The main variable is

x_{ijk}: number of OR of type i assigned to specialty j on day k

where x_{ijk} must be a nonnegative integer.

Then the constraints model relationships such as:

1. An OR can be assigned to just one specialty on any given day;
2. Relationship among OR assignment, postponed demand for patients with overdue MWT, and for patients not overdue and OR time available per day for each specialty and day; this constraint defines the values of u_{jkm} and v_{jkm}, among other variables;
3. Maximum time over MWT that a surgery can have; and
4. A specialty should not be assigned to more than a given number of ORs on a given day.

To have a benchmark to compare the ILP, Table 4.9 shows both the assignment and the average occupancy of the OR. From this, it can be concluded that the final percentages of assignment and use for each specialty are practically the same; this implies that the hospital follows the criteria of maintaining such percentages, since they are considered to be at an adequate level.

Now, the ILP assignment model is applied to the same conditions for which results in Table 4.9 have been obtained for different number of days. The resulting assignment is shown in Figure 4.18.

The figure indicates that the assignment of the model is not too different from what there is today. Therefore, the most important question is the one posed in the activity "Run model to evaluate Scenario" in the subprocess of Figure 4.11, that is, how the behavior of waiting time for patients is affected by an optimal assignment and how more capacity

Table 4.9 Average assignment and occupation of OR

	Average percentage of OR assignment (percent)	Average percentage of OR occupation (percent)
General Surgery	31	29
Plastic Surgery	30	30
Urology	19	20
Traumatology	19	20

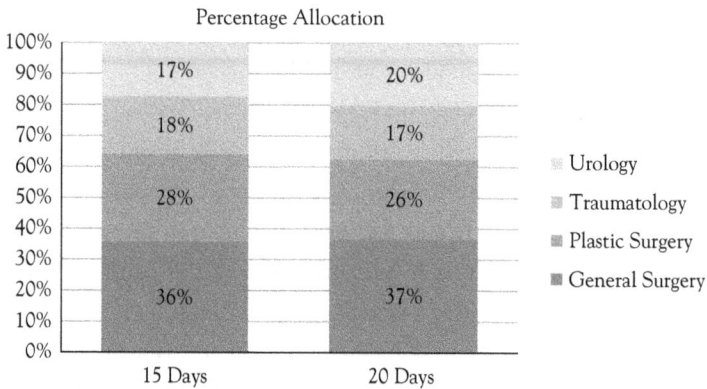

Figure 4.18 Percentage capacity assignment to each specialty

should be assigned to best improve the meeting of MWT and the reduction of waiting time in general? The logic behind the answer to such
question is a simulation model, which has as a component the optimal
assignment model just presented.

In the simulation model, which is presented in Figure 4.19, the following modules are considered:

1. Admission of patients to the waiting list; in this case, it is necessary
   to consider two factors: patients who are currently on waiting lists,
   which are assigned to each specialty, category, and surgical time; and
   a forecasting of patients who will enter waiting lists, which will be
   determined with the forecasting models described at the beginning
   of this case, also assigning to them a specialty, category, and surgical
   time.

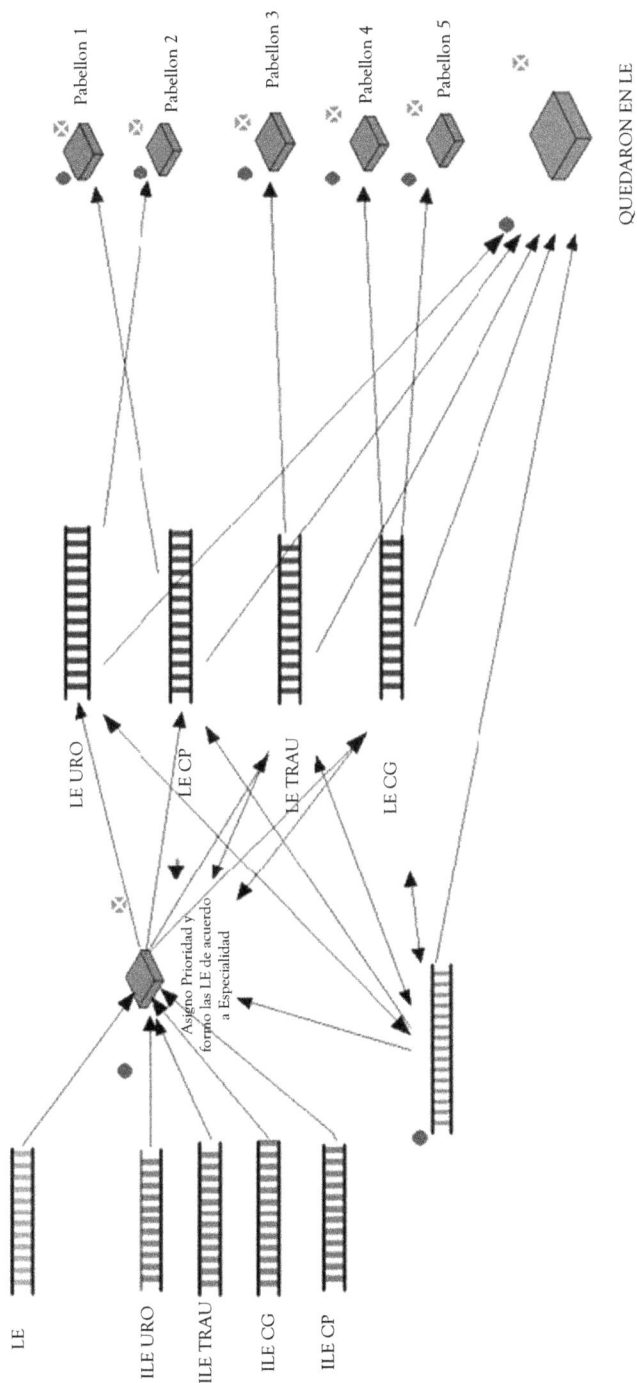

Pabellon 1

Pabellon 2

Pabellon 3

Pabellon 4

Pabellon 5

QUEDARON EN LE

LE URO

LE CP

LE TRAU

LE CG

Asigno Prioridad y
formo las LE de acuerdo
a Especialidad

LE

ILE URO

ILE TRAU

ILE CG

ILE CP

Figure 4.19 Simulation model for OR capacity evaluation

2. Assignment of priority; in this step, each patient is assigned a priority according to the following factors: category (MWT), MWT expired, and MWT not expired.

3. Assignment of patients to OR; here the patients in the prioritized waiting list for each specialty are assigned to an OR according to the ILP presented earlier.

4. Surgical intervention in the OR; this is characterized by a time that follows a probability distribution, statistically determined for each surgical step.

In the simulation model, ILE TRAU - CP - CG - URO simulates the admission of patients to the waiting list. It uses the forecasting model by specialty and is carried out on a monthly basis; LE represents the current waiting list that the hospital keeps; in the priority assignment and formation of waiting lists, the logic of prioritization of patients according to their category and time on waiting list is used, which is done weekly; LE URO - CP - CG - TRAU represents the weekly ranked waiting list, which means that patients are selected to be treated surgically on OR according to such lists; for comparison, statistics of patients remaining in waiting lists are collected, including those who were not present during the simulation.

The simulation model was built using ProModel[30] and several runs of such a model allowed evaluating various scenarios. The main variable manipulated in the model was OR capacity. For example, in Figure 4.20, the average opportunity for patient care is represented according to the current assignment of OR in the hospital. This opportunity is defined as the average percentage of the MWT a patient waits before surgery. The x-axis of the figure shows the capacity represented by the number of OR morning and afternoon shifts the hospital will have during a week. This capacity goes from 6 shifts (according to the minimum allocation of pavilions that can be performed) and a maximum of 50, limited by the number of ORs the hospital has. The ordinate axis shows the average opportunity of attention in percentage as compared to MWT for a category; for example, it can be observed that for a capacity of 18 OR shifts, there is an average opportunity of 250 percent approximately; this implies that the hospital takes 2.5 times more than the maximum time allowed

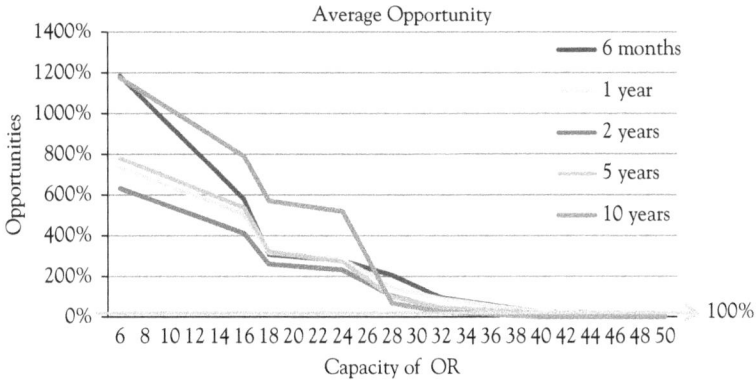

Figure 4.20 *Average patient care opportunity*

according to the category of prioritization, that is, for a patient of Category A, who has a MWT of 15 days, the hospital takes on average 52 days in taking care of him. Finally, different simulation horizons ranging from 6 months to 10 years are shown.

Next a validation of the simulation of the current situation of the hospital is presented. Currently, the hospital has an OR capacity of 16 to 19 shifts, which implies, according to the simulation model, an average opportunity of patients between 400 and 250 percent approximately. These values are in agreement with the average delay beyond MWT patients have today. While it is observed that from a number of shifts equal to 32, the hospital would be meeting the attention opportunity defined according to the category of prioritization for each patient based on his diagnosis and aggravating factors.

However, the concept of average opportunity attention has the problems of considering on an equal footing the different categories of MWTs; this is not right, since it has been determined that it is more damaging that seriously ill patients requiring immediate attention are served late than those who are not so ill. Therefore, a new indicator that considers the opportunity of caring for patients in a weighted manner, giving more weight to the more risky categories from A to E, is built. Considering this, it can be seen in Figure 4.21 the weighted opportunity as a function of OR capacity. This chart presents the effect that produces the weighting of categories of MWTs. Thus, for a smaller quantity of

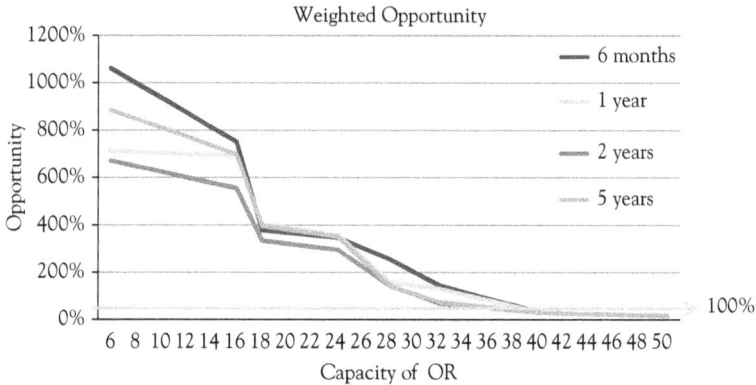

Figure 4.21 Weighted patient care opportunity

OR the weighted opportunity is higher than the average opportunity in Figure 4.20; for a greater capacity, the weighted opportunity decreases. The weighted opportunity in this sense is a better indicator, since lower capacity accounts for the fact that only patients of more risky categories (e.g., A and B) are attended to, who have lower MWTs and hence have a higher probability of being overdue. The figure confirms that for more than 32 shifts the opportunity of attention is close to the MWT, and this is the recommended capacity.

Another analysis that can be carried out is to see how it changes the weighted opportunity for patients' attention, given a fixed capacity of OR, for different time periods of evaluation horizons. This situation is shown in Figure 4.22.

Figure 4.22 presents the weighted chance to care for patients for a capacity of between 16 and 28 of OR shifts. Here it can be seen how, for the two-year simulation horizon, the opportunity for each defined capacity is lower than for other evaluation horizons. This behavior will be named as the "Prioritization effect" and represents how, in this evaluation horizon, patients are attended in an orderly manner according to the waiting list prioritization. Then, when the point is reached where all these patients who initially were on waiting list (where the opportunity is minimum) are attended to and, given that the capacity offered is less than the demand even during the period when the patients were still being updated in the waiting list, it can be seen that they begin to accumulate and therefore the weighted opportunity increases.

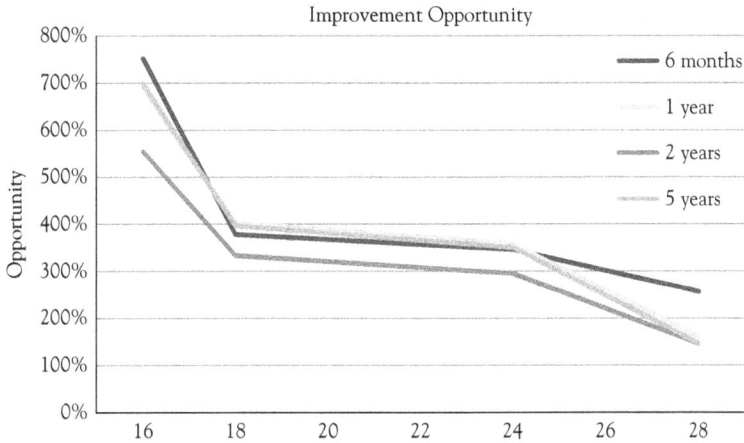

Figure 4.22 Weighted opportunity of attention for capacity of 16 to 28 OR shifts

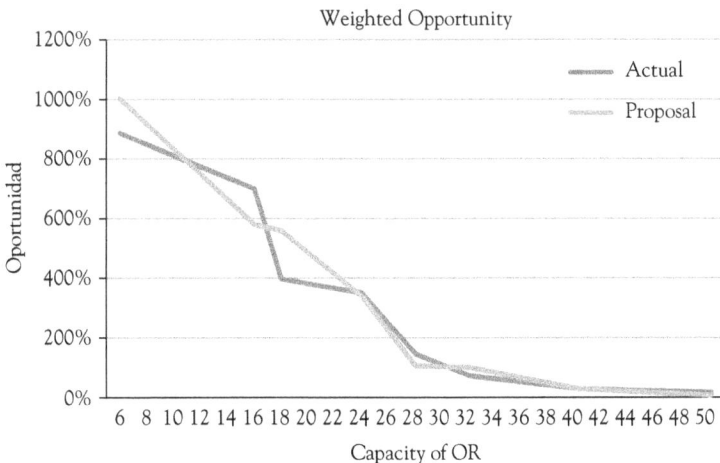

Figure 4.23 Weighted opportunity for current allocation compared with proposed allocation

Finally, the difference between the current assignment and assignment proposed by the model is evaluated. This analysis has been made considering a simulation period of five years, because, as shown earlier, a two-year period is necessary for the waiting list to be ordered according to priorities. The behavior of the weighted opportunity for the current and proposed assignments is presented in Figure 4.23.

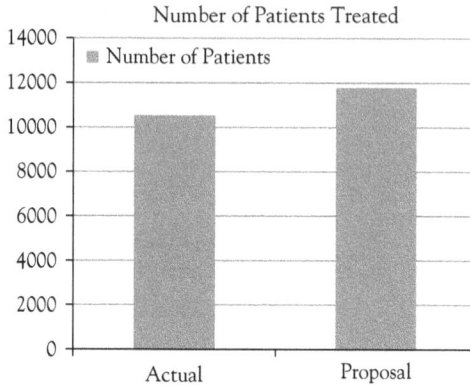

Figure 4.24 Number of patients operated for a capacity of 23 days of ORs

Since assignments are very similar, it is expected that the opportunity of a patient is maintained in the same value. This can be checked visually by looking at the graph and observing an average improvement of about 2 percent in weighted opportunity patient care. While this value is small, the proposed assignment has not only managed to reduce the average opportunity to care for patients, but also allowed to increase the number of operated patients by 10 percent, which mainly belong to the D and E prioritization categories, as it can be seen in Figure 4.24 for the case in which the OR capacity is 23 shifts.

As already commented in previous cases, this type of design clearly includes organizational design, since by periodically executing the processes presented, with the analytical support, the structure of the OR service, including the determination of the human resources needed, can be dynamically adapted to new conditions, assuring defined levels of service and good use of resources. Moreover, in executing the processes, the roles in the lanes of the BPMN diagrams have been assigned specific tasks in the execution of the process, which also defines organization. Furthermore, IT support is also specified precisely for data processing and, more importantly, as a container for embedded logic that allows optimizing resource assignment, which defines integration with current systems and analytical tools for forecasting and simulation.

CHAPTER 5

Health Service Resource Management Process Design

This chapter presents a case that performs a Level iii design and does not have a previous Business Design, illustrating what we defined as local case, when design levels were presented in Chapter 2.

Here the strategic issue is to generate the best possible service by having the right capacity and determination of resources accordingly to assure a service time; the value that can be generated for patients is to improve the service in terms of waiting time and providing the right service. For this Intelligent Structure II is required, since we need predictive and resource optimization models to provide a required level of service at a minimum cost. Hence, BP6, "Optimum Resource Usage," is applicable. Therefore from this we design a new process configuration for the service that reduces waiting time and improve service, besides evaluating them for a forecasted demand. Such design is based on representing the design problem by means of a process architecture. To do this the Shared Services Architecture Pattern, adapted to hospitals as in Figure 2.7, is used. To exemplify this design of configuration and capacity, we concentrate on the "Services Lines for Patients" in the figure, detailed in Figure 5.1, selecting the "Demand Analysis and Management" process in relation to the "Emergency Medical Service." This process needs the subprocess of "Demand Forecasting and Characterization," including business logic, which will be detailed in what follows.

To be able to forecast effectively, one of the key factors is the quality of historical data. In addition, the hospital operating conditions and environment should remain relatively stable for the data to be representative. This work focuses on two public pediatric hospitals: from now on referred to as HLCM and HEGC, and a general purpose hospital, HSBA. On arrival at the emergency facilities each patient is registered, including

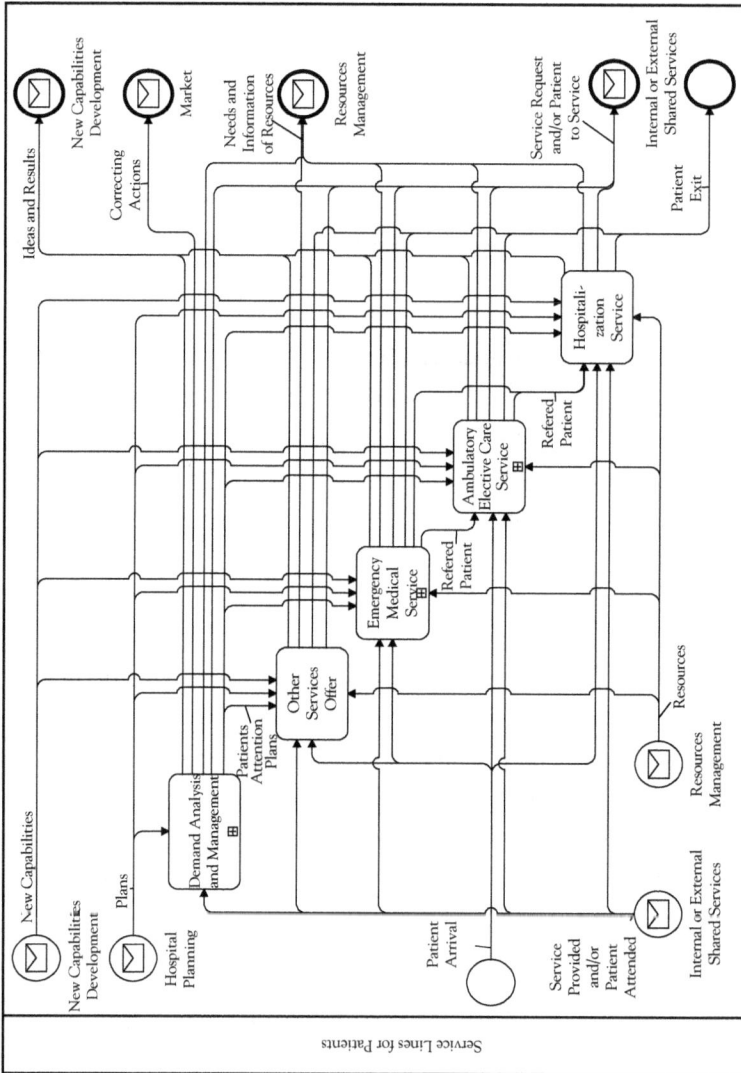

Figure 5.1 Detail of "Services Lines for Patients"

personal data, time of arrival, diagnosis, and classification according to severity of illness. All the historical data for the three hospitals was obtained for the purposes of this work and are as follows:

- HLCM: from January 2001 to December 2009
- HEGC: from January 2001 to July 2009
- HSBA: from January 2000 to December 2009

Since these hospitals could provide high-quality data regarding their emergency operation, we could infer historical demand with forecasting Analytics, reviewed in Chapter 2. We used monthly aggregated demand as a basis to construct predictive models.

However, to convert historical data into useful input information for the forecasting models, further analyses and a series of transformations were necessary. By analyzing the demand that arrives at the emergency department outliers were detected as shown in Figure 5.2. Visual inspection of aggregated demand as shown in such figure for one of the hospitals reveals a strong seasonal pattern. We observed a low demand during the summer months (December, January, and February in the Southern Hemisphere) and a high influx of patients during the winter season (May, June, and July). In general, a downward trend can be observed over the years.

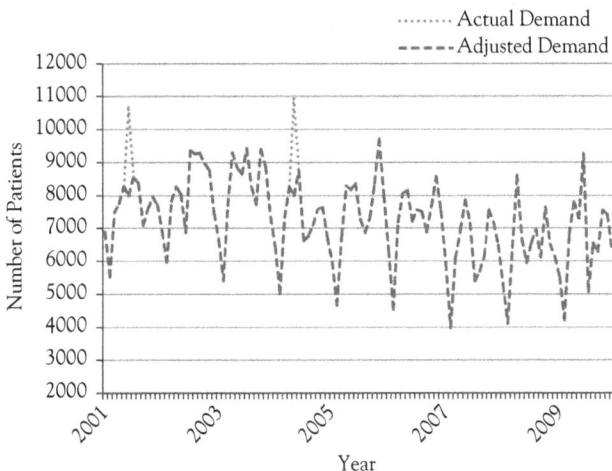

Figure 5.2 Actual versus adjusted demand per month in HLCM

When data is disaggregated by pathology type we notice huge differences, as shown for medical and surgical demand in Figures 5.3 and 5.4. The first is much more volatile over the years since it depends on factors such as temperature and flu-like illness rate, while the second is more stable over the years. We also conclude that medical demand comprises 70 percent of the emergency cases and surgical demand corresponds to 30 percent of the cases.

Demand at HEGC and HSBA shows behaviors that are very similar to the demand at HLCM. Four forecasting methods are applied: Linear Regression, Weighted Moving Averages, Neural Networks, and Support Vector Regression (SVR). The first two are well-known techniques used for forecasting and described in the literature.[1] Neural Networks and

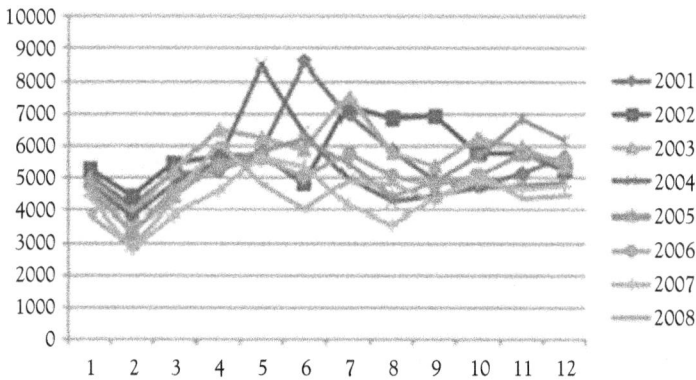

Figure 5.3 Medical demand for HLCM

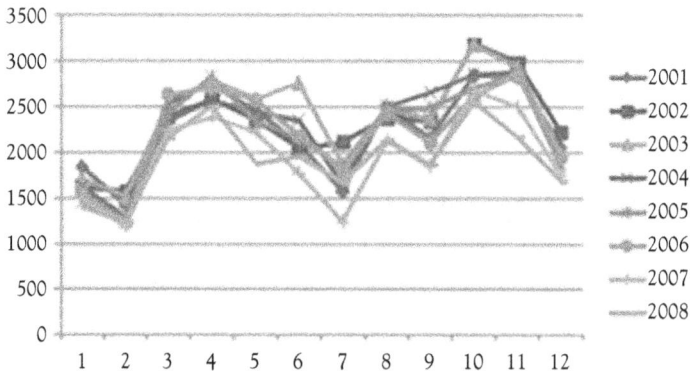

Figure 5.4 Surgical demand for HLCM

SVR are techniques that are increasingly used for forecasting.[2] We used Mean Absolute Percentage Error (MAPE) and Mean Square Error (MSE) as performance measures to determine model accuracy. For the Linear Regression, Weighted Moving Average, and SVR, the same inputs as the ones described for the Neural Network are used. Results obtained using these four methods for the validation sets of all hospitals are shown in Table 5.1. As observed in this, in five out of seven cases, best results are obtained with SVR, when using MSE as criterion to compare the different models' performance. When using MAPE as criterion for comparison, SVR appears as the best option for demand forecasting in all cases.

Given the results described earlier and based on the fact that SVR is built on a solid theoretical foundation, we conclude that it is the most appropriate method for predicting demand in emergency rooms. For practical use, we recommend to additionally consider using simpler methods, which produce results that can be acceptable under certain conditions.

Just having a forecast for the number of patients arriving at emergency rooms is not sufficient for capacity management; also needed are the different kinds of resources necessary to attend the patients. Following the health care conventions used in Chilean hospitals, patients are classified into four categories according to the severity of their illness, as shown in Table 5.2. Each category is associated with different uses of the medical resources, as explained in the following.

As shown in Figure 5.5, the illness severity distribution varies over the different months of a year. Nevertheless, the severity distribution per month remains relatively stable over the years. Therefore, in the following calculations, each month will be considered to have a deterministic distribution of patients for each category.

Given the emergency patients forecast and the illness severity distribution, the expected number of patients per category can be calculated. To determine the number of doctors required to attend such demand, the next step is to characterize the behavior of the attention time for each category. For this purpose, a representative sample of C1, C2, C3, and C4 individuals was used.

Each C1 patient is referred to the reanimation room for resuscitation, upon the patient's arrival to the emergency service. When this occurs, and depending on the complexity of the surgery or diagnosis, between

Table 5.1 Forecast errors on validation sets (best results in bold)

	Linear Regression		Weighted Moving Average		Neural Network		SVR	
	MAPE (percent)	MSE	MAPE (percent)	MSE	MAPE (percent)	MSE	MAPE (percent)	MSE
HLCM Medical Demand	12.67	150,686	7.53	144,729	7.45	161,689	5.61	154,86
HLCM Surgery Demand	6.54	27,097	7.36	20,137	8.99	22,947	5,09	25,199
HEGC Medical Demand	15.91	3,114.37	16.5	1,978.33	7.7	1,043.75	6,86	606,32
HEGC Surgery Demand	8.55	14,302	8.96	11,730	8.3	12,155	5.88	8,120
HEGC Orthopedic Surgery Demand	8.41	35,940	8.60	28,247	5.12	29,851	4.44	25,460
HSBA Medical Demand	8.27	3,125.07	11.83	850,342	7.9	1,226.16	6.97	643,98
HSBA Maternity Demand	10.54	23,738	6.98	12,408	10.6	38,629	3,24	7,867

Table 5.2 Category types and description

Category	Description
C1	Extreme-Risk Patient
C2	High-Risk Patient
C3	Low-Risk Patient
C4	No Risk Patient

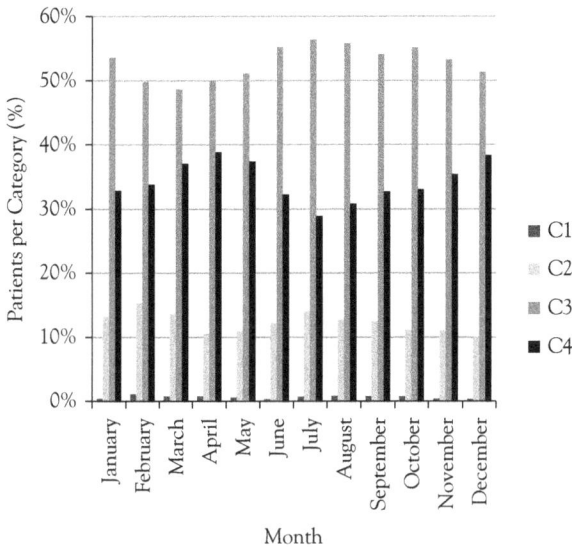

Figure 5.5 Monthly categorization distribution

one and three of the doctors currently working in the attention cubicles immediately set aside their activities to focus on the extreme risk patient. After the medical attention, the time required to stabilize and treat the C1 patient is registered in a logbook, along with the names of the doctors who performed the medical procedure.

Using this information, we run a K-S test to determine the distribution of the C1 patients' attention time. We concluded that it has a log normal distribution with a mean of 108 minutes and a standard deviation of 121 minutes. We also noticed that the number of doctors required to attend these patients had a highly concentrated distribution in two doctors; therefore, this value was used for the following calculations.

When trying to characterize the consultation of C2 patients, the data used did not provide enough information to determine a distribution of the attention time. However, in a discussion with the doctors, a consensus was reached where the average time to attend C2 patients is 60 minutes, with a standard deviation of 20 minutes. A normal distribution was chosen to represent the behavior of this attention time.

Finally, and with a high level of confidence, we determined the distribution of the attention time for C3 and C4 patients as log normal with means of 10 and 7 minutes, and standard deviations of 7 and 3 minutes, respectively. All non-C1 patients are attended by only one doctor.

The time distributions presented earlier provide a basis to estimate the time that doctors will spend to attend the patients from each category, expected to arrive to the emergency room. A summary of the attention time distributions found for the different severity categories and the number of medical doctors required to attend each patient per category is presented in Table 5.3.

An analysis of patient arrivals at different times of the day was performed, as shown in Figure 5.6. This study concluded that 59 percent of the patients arrived at the emergency service between 12:00 and 20:00 hours. Using a representative sample we found that this distribution does not vary significantly among different days of the week or among the same days of different weeks. Therefore, this distribution is considered as fixed for every day of the year.

Now, given a forecast, the subprocess "Capacity Analysis" for the configuration design within the "Demand Analysis and Management" process in relation to the "Emergency Medical Service" in Figure 5.1 is needed, as explained next.

In the literature, several proposals for the configuration of emergency services are defined[3] of which we selected the Option b in Figure 5.7, which considers a Triage, for patient pre-evaluation, and a fast-track line for patients that according to evaluation are more critical; this was complemented with parallel medical facilities for less urgent patients. For such a configuration we developed a simulation model, shown in Figure 5.8, which evaluates waiting time for a given demand. The simulation model incorporates the stochastic behavior of the demand. Since the waiting time and length of lines have shown to be significantly higher for medical

Table 5.3 Distribution of attention time and number of physicians per category

Category	Distribution	Mean (min)	Standard deviation (min)	Physicians required
C1	Log normal	108	121	2
C2	Normal	60	20	1
C3	Log normal	10	7	1
C4	Log normal	7	3	1

attention, the simulation will be performed for these patients only. The forecast has an error with a normal distribution. To simulate the different demand scenarios for each month, the forecast was adjusted several times by different values sampled from the normal distribution of the error. Due to the stability of its daily behavior, the demand of each scenario was distributed uniformly across every day of the month. The daily demand was further disaggregated into hourly demand. As a consequence, we were able to generate several scenarios of monthly demand disaggregated per hour. Using the hourly forecasted demand from each of the scenarios generated as described earlier, the average forecasted demand was calculated for each hour of the day. We assumed that the hourly demand arrives according to a Poisson process; then this average corresponds to the mean of the Poisson distribution per hour.

On their arrival at the emergency service, patients are categorized and served according to the time distributions, which are also stochastic. Now that the stochastic behavior of the demand and the medical attention has been incorporated into the problem, we will discuss the construction of the simulation model and its role in the management of hospital capacity. In capacity configuration management, we want to determine how different designs of the hospital facilities, which determine the production process, may affect the quality of service, measured in length of wait (LOW) before the first medical attention. The simulation model allows us to observe how the expected flow of patients will use the different services offered in the facilities of the hospital, and how the available capacity performs when attending such demand. As a consequence, capacity can be redistributed or adjusted with the objective of eliminating bottlenecks

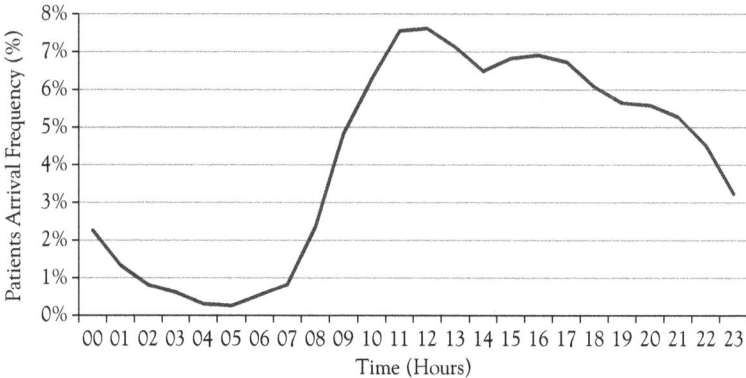

Figure 5.6 Patients' arrival distribution per hour

and reducing idle resources. This provides a powerful decision tool for managing capacity in such a way that a given service level can be guaranteed at minimum cost.

As stated earlier, the average LOW will be used as the main criterion to compare the performance of the system designs. This metric was calculated weighing the demand per category by its respective average LOW. The results for this metric for the Base and Fast-Track simulated configurations are presented in Table 5.4.

On the basis of the scenarios run in the simulation, a 95-percent confidence interval was generated for the LOW of each configuration. The intervals obtained were (55.5, 59.1) and (61.8, 66.6) for the Base Case and Fast-Track with Triage, respectively. To test if the LOW differs significantly between these two configurations, we applied the procedure proposed by Law and Kelton.[4] This comparison is established based on the difference of their respective statistical distributions, as displayed in Table 5.5. Since the confidence interval does not contain the value zero, we confirm that the difference shown is statistically significant.

On the basis of the results presented in Tables 5.4 and 5.5, we observe that:

- The simulation model resembles the actual behavior of the system, since current average LOW is within the confidence interval of the simulated Base Case.

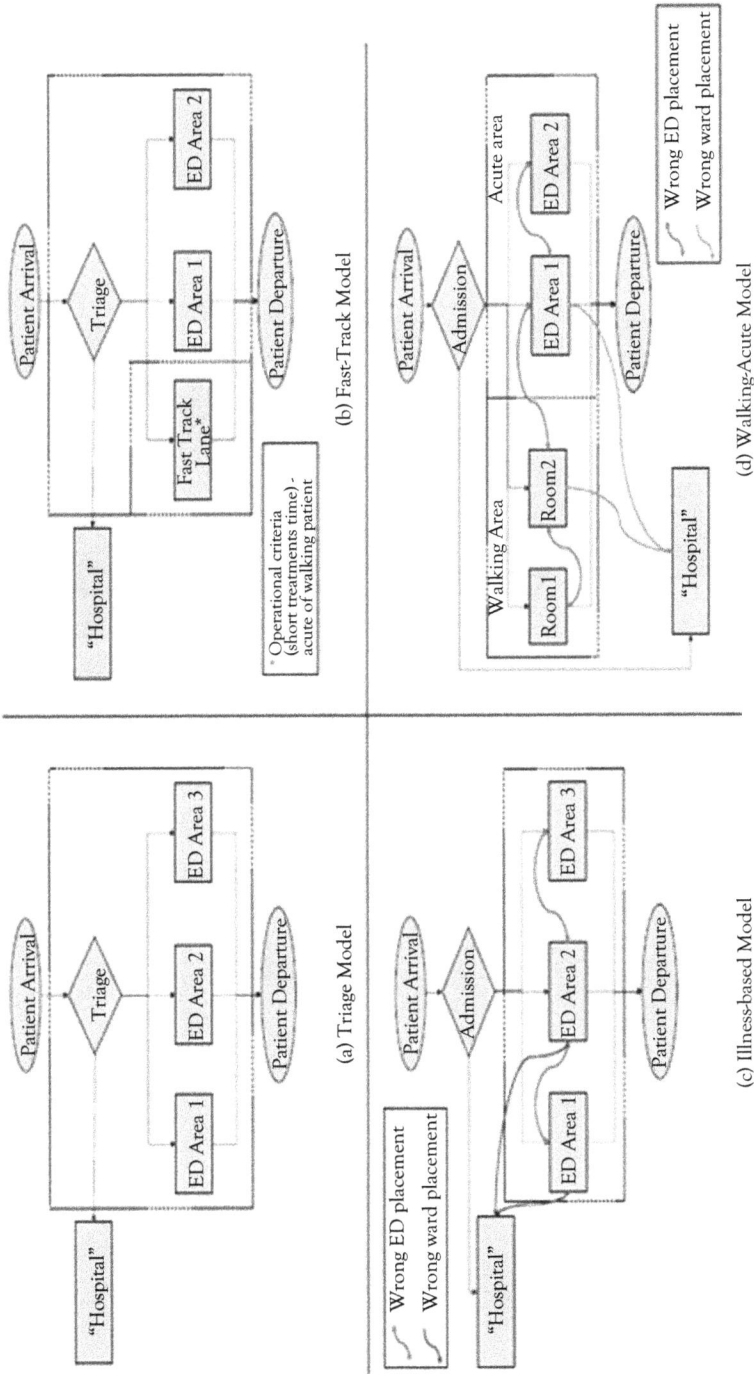

Figure 5.7 *Alternative configurations for emergency services*

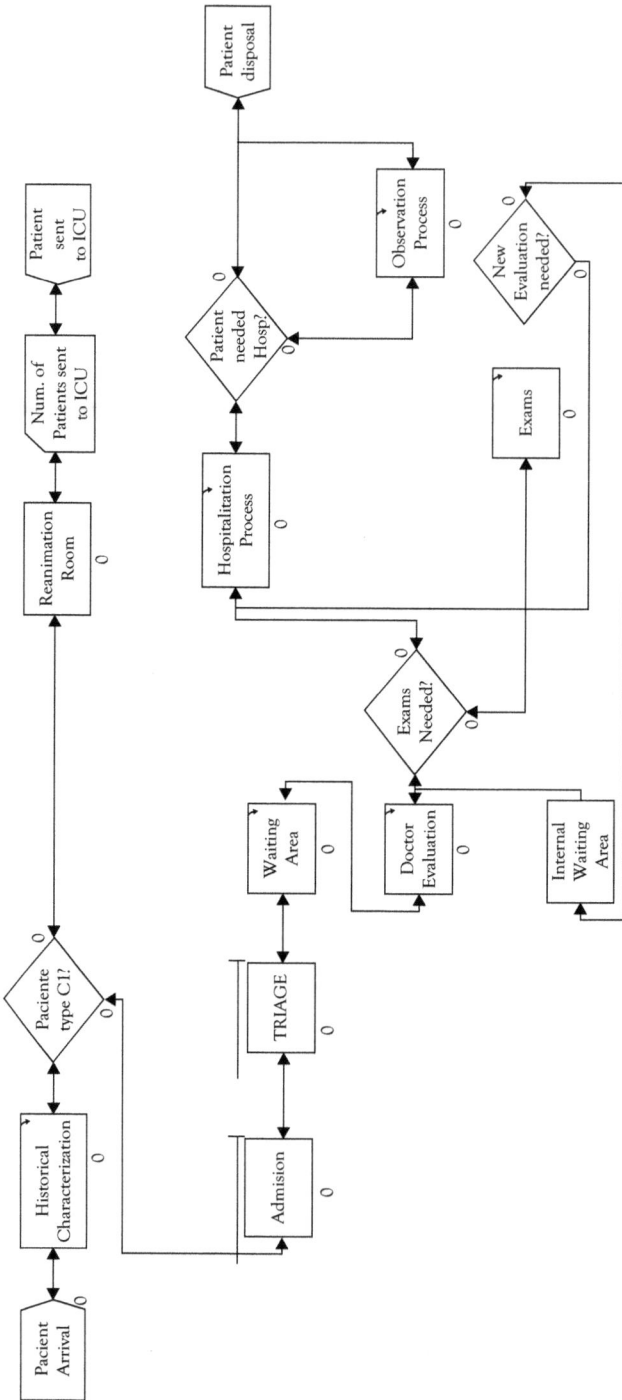

Figure 5.8 Simulation model for Capacity Analysis

Table 5.4 *Simulated LOW of different emergency service configurations*

Configuration	Average (min)	Standard deviation (min)
Base Case	64.2	1.2
Fast-Track with Triage	57.3	0.9

Table 5.5 *Base Case and Fast-Track configurations comparison*

Comparing configurations	Average (min)	Standard deviation (min)	Lower bound 95% (min)	Upper bound 95% (min)
Base Case or Fast-Track with Triage	6.9	1.5	3.9	9.9

- The main bottleneck occurs in the medical consults and during the day shift.
- The Fast-Track with Triage reduces the average LOW in 6.9 minutes, which corresponds to a 10.8-percent reduction of the current average waiting time.
- Hence, it was decided to implement the Fast-Track with Triage configuration and it was the one used in the hospital where work was performed. Another hospital is replicating the forecasting and simulation-based processes, due to the good results obtained in the first hospital.

Then, using the previous models, the resource management process is designed, for which the relevant pattern is also "Demand Analysis and Management" in Figure 5.1, performed at a lower level of detail. In the previous analysis, we considered aggregated demand for configuration (which in this case also implies service production) design, and in resource management we must use disaggregated demand for the resources needed and assign them to process operation.

For forecasting demand in the first subprocess of Figure 5.1, the same models are used as in the previous analysis, but at a more disaggregated level. Then a Capacity Analysis has to be executed. Here the key resource is availability of doctors, since they are the ones who diagnose and provide treatments for emergency patients. Hence, demand has to be converted into medical hours needed of different specialties, which were determined through technical coefficients. Comparison with available resources defines lack or excess of resources, which are the basis for the determination of correcting actions; of course, there may be a feedback among these activities in order to analyze resources for given correcting actions, such as changing number or schedules of doctors. We then evaluate the impact that redistribution, reduction, or addition of medical resources would generate on the performance of the system. The resource management analysis, then, will be performed for the Fast-Track configuration only. The same simulation model of the previous section, shown in Figure 5.8 is then run for several assignments and number of doctors per shift under the Fast-Track configuration with Triage and assuming a stochastic demand.

If the current structure of two 12-hour shifts is maintained, an initial scenario would consider only redistributing the doctors available in a different manner. Given the greater arrival of patients during the day, a possible redistribution could include the reassignment of doctors from the night to the day shift. As a consequence, more doctors would attend during the day shift than at night. The average LOW of this scenario would be 45.1 minutes. Further, resource management considerations may determine the addition or reduction of medical hours for attending the patients. Since these resources are known to be quite expensive, the different scenarios were simulated by changing the existing capacity in 0.5 doctor intervals. The extra half doctor interval was included through the creation of a new shift of 6 hours, from 12:00 to 18:00, which is precisely the period in which most patients arrive at the service. Thus, the number of 6.5 doctors available means that 4 doctors attend on the day shift (8:00 to 20:00), 1 doctor on the half shift (12:00 to 18:00), and 2 doctors at night (20:00 to 8:00). The average LOW obtained with this configuration is 40.5 minutes. The simulation was run using from 5 to 7 doctors within 24 hours, and distributed as explained earlier. The idea behind analyzing the reduction of the current number of doctors is to assess whether the performance of the system is affected in a significant manner when these resources are lacking, either by management decision or by absenteeism.

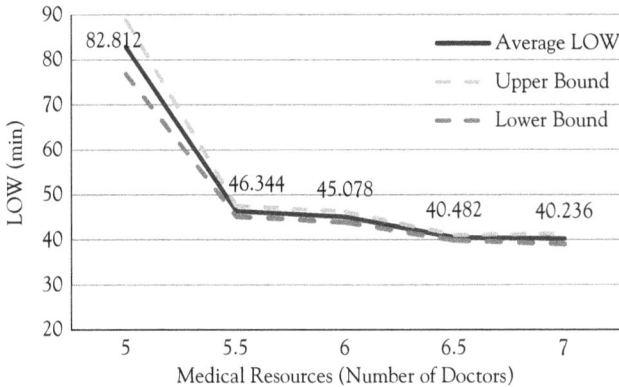

Figure 5.9 Average LOW and confidence intervals for different numbers of doctors

The average LOW for different numbers and assignments of resources are summarized in Figure 5.9, including the 95-percent confidence interval for each of the points.

As expected, the addition of medical resources improves the service quality, measured in average LOW. The interesting result is that the average LOW decreases dramatically when increasing the number of medical resources from 5 to 5.5 doctors, while it decreases more gradually when new resources are added. To test whether the LOW difference between all the scenarios included in Table 5.6 is statistically significant, we applied again the procedure proposed by Law and Kelton. Table 5.6 shows the confidence intervals when comparing the LOW of these scenarios. As it can be observed, increasing from 5 to 5.5 doctors provides a significant improvement to the performance of the system, while the change between 5.5 and 6 doctors does not. Nevertheless, increasing from 5.5 to 6.5 doctors does show statistical significance.

The previous analysis of the system performance provides hospital managers a decision tool for determining the number and distribution of medical resources on the emergency service, based on a cost or benefit analysis of resources and service improvement. The previous results were used to assign doctors to the different kind of boxes and define their work schedules and also to assign additional doctors. Each of the activities of the process "Demand Analysis and Management" in Figure 5.1 has computer system support, as exemplified in the model in Figure 5.10 for "Capacity Analysis," which uses the BPMN notation. Notice that, in

Table 5.6 Confidence intervals for compared scenarios

Comparing scenarios	5.5	6	6.5	7
5	[30.4; 42.6]	[31.6; 43.9]	[36.3; 48.3]	[36.5; 48.7]
5.5	-	[–0.4; 3]	[4.5; 7.2]	[4.4; 7.8]
6		-	[3.3; 5.9]	[3.1; 6.5]
6.5			-	[–1.1; 1.6]

order to use these tools routinely, one has to embed the models and the application logic we have described in the supporting system to the actors of the process as specified in the design of such figure.

It should be remarked that the process designed, with the imbedded Analytics and Information System support, is not a one-time effort. In fact, it is designed for periodically executing the whole process under changing conditions, such as unexpected demand, for example, epidemic episodes and new campaigns, which require adapting capacity.

We also notice that the process design presented includes the relationships to the other components of the Hospital Architecture. Thus, the relationship to the organizational structure is included in the process definitions, such as shared services, which is the case of "Demand Analysis and Management" of Figure 5.1, which was presented for Emergency, but needs to be coordinated with ambulatory and hospitalization and other shared services, such as surgery. We did not go into such coordination, but in a complete design it should be taken into account. If this is done it means that we are redesigning the organization as well as design the processes. Also job definition is included, since the roles in the lanes of Figure 5.10 have been assigned specific tasks in the execution of the process. IT support is specified in a very precise way as data processor and, more importantly, as a container for embedded logic that allows optimizing resource assignment. Finally, the relationships to the systems architecture and IT infrastructure should be taken into account, since the data come from current systems and the process design should be integrated with such systems. Furthermore, new technological tools, such as Analytics packages should also be integrated into the design.

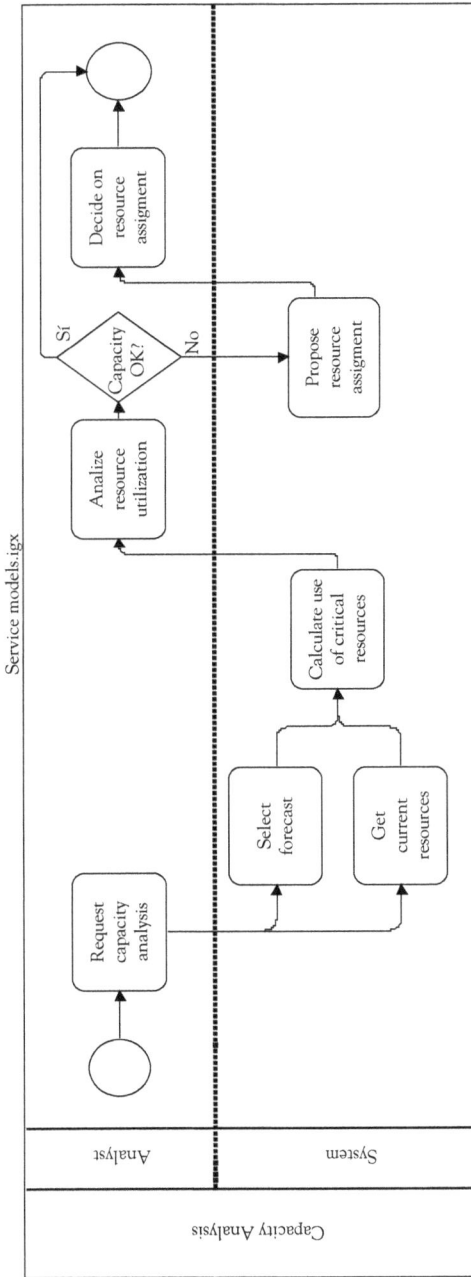

Figure 5.10 BPMN for "Capacity Analysis"

CHAPTER 6

Health Operating Management Process Design

The fourth type of design, Level v, is for the processes that perform the day-to-day management of resources, including their scheduling. This corresponds to the last level of detail of the Hospital Architecture in Figure 2.7 and concerns the procedural detail of the realization of the activities for each of the subprocesses of processes, such as the ones presented in Figures 4.9 to 4.11 of the "Operating Room Capacity and Assignment" case, presented in Chapter 4 for subprocesses that allow demand prediction and capacity analysis. In all these cases the activities of the subprocesses deal with assignment and scheduling of resources, such as resources that are needed to provide a certain capacity.

In the case of hospitals, we start with a given configuration and capacity design, which was possibly determined in the previous design levels, and try to use the available resources in the best possible way to improve service (fairness) and efficiency. In public hospitals, there is usually excess demand, which means that patients have to wait long times before service. Hence, the value that can be generated for patients at this level of detail is to improve the service in terms of waiting time and providing the right service (fairness and quality). So this is an example of the projects that should be promoted by health central authorities for systematically improving hospitals that perform poorly, as proposed in the section "Innovation Resource Assignment in the Public Sector" of Chapter 4. It is also clear that the Business Pattern behind this type of design is BP6, "Optimum resource usage."

The given resources to be managed are, typically, human—doctors, nurses, paramedics, and the like—and facilities and equipment, such as surgical operating rooms (ORs), beads, and attention boxes. Hence, detail processes that perform activities to do such managing are to be designed. Such detail must show the sequence of the activities involved, the logic of the flow, and the Analytics and computer applications supporting each activity. In advanced applications it is also feasible to introduce Analytics-based logic for determining medical actions. At this level, the modeling style changes to full formal Business Process Management Notation (BPMN) models, in order to make possible their simulation and eventually their execution with, for example, a Business Process Management System Suite (BPMS). Two cases are presented to illustrate how to make designs for improving service and optimizing the use of resources and, also, the possibilities of process execution. Other two cases that illustrate innovative logic for supporting medical decisions are summarized.

Operating Room Scheduling

As a first case of operation management we will consider ORs, which are one of the key resources in a hospital. For the process of managing OR the pattern given in Figure 2.11 is proposed; the process starts with "Demand Analysis" that, in this case, corresponds to prioritizing the patients' waiting list in order to decide the order of surgery execution. Then, in "Operating Room Scheduling," selected patients are sequenced on several OR, typically at least for a week ahead, making sure that, for a given patient, the right doctor and other resources are available at the chosen time in the room in which he is to be operated, and, at the same time, trying to make the best possible use of facilities. Finally, in "Surgery Resource Scheduling," given an OR schedule, other resources, such as medical supplies, are determined in order to assure that they are available during the operation time.

Some details of the logic for prioritizing the patients' waiting list are given, since this is the key variable that affects fairness, one of the objectives that are pursued. Currently, patients are, in general, attended according to the time they record in the waiting list and this is how such lists are generated. Obviously, this is very unfair since it does not consider the risk the patient has according to the pathology involved and other factors. Hence, a formal way for prioritizing patients is proposed, which is similar to the logic proposed in the case "Operating Room Capacity and Assignment" of Chapter 4. The priority is defined in terms of the characterization of each surgical specialty based on the maximum wait-ing times (MWTs) for surgery allowed for categories A, B, C, D, and E. These categories are defined in terms of the risk the patient faces if it is not operated: A is maximum risk and E is minimum risk. Certainly, the MWT allowed before surgery should be low for A and high for E. This time is determined based on medical factors by doctors and also depends on aggravating factors such as age and general health of a patient.

In what follows in this case, we assume that the outlined prioritizing logic has been implemented, which is the situation of the hospital where this case was developed. In fact, the team that designed the scheduling process was the one that first put into practice the prioritizing logic as we will present later.

More detail is given for the "Operating Rooms Scheduling" subpro-cess, which is a complex activity; it influences the number of patients operated, their waiting time, and performance of the whole hospital. Hence, there is the need to use good processes supported by powerful Analytics and appropriate computer system support.

Complexity of scheduling relates to the great variety of surgical inter-ventions, the variability of operation time, patient priority, scarce avail-able capacity, doctors' schedule, and many other factors. What is needed is to design a process that reduces cost and manages capacity with efficient use of resources and provides fairness in the access and quality of service for patients, particularly, in opportunity of surgical procedures required. In this case the value is increased by giving timely attention to patients on the basis of medical criteria, resulting in the reduction of waiting time, especially for patients who are unable to wait.

A simplified version of the design of the OR scheduling process is shown in Figure 6.1, where a BPMN diagram is presented. Key ideas of the design are that the scheduling should be based on the current state of resources, priorities based on medical diagnosis and criteria calcu-lated with current patient information, and an algorithm that meets all requirements for surgery and maximizes the number of relevant patients included. The System that manages data and performs the analytical support is explicitly shown in the diagram.

Next we describe the logic used by the key activity of this subprocess: "Calculate patients priority and schedule OR." On the basis of medical criteria, patients' priorities must be determined. This starts, in previous

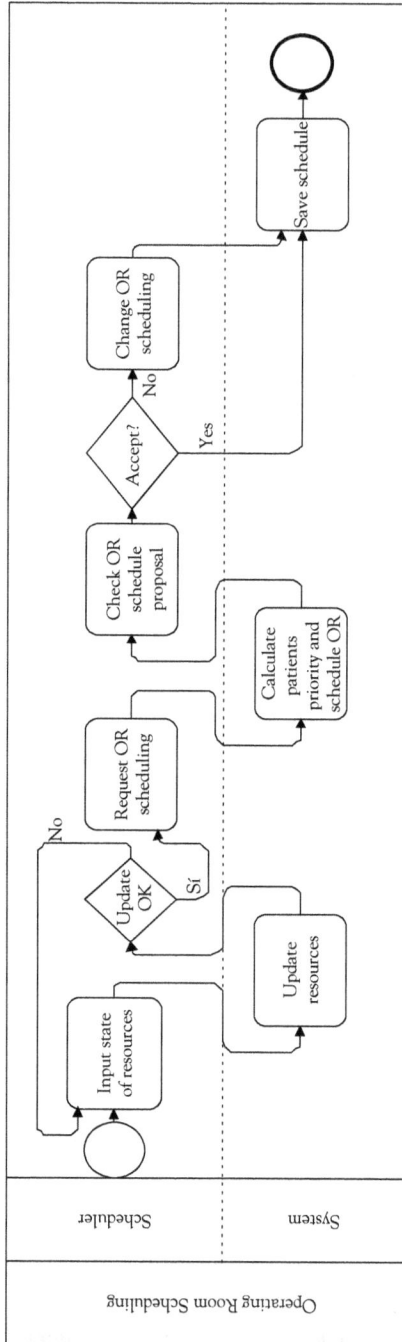

Figure 6.1 "Operating Room Scheduling" design

subprocesses, with a medical examination that determines how acute is the disease that originates the need for surgery, assigning the patient to a class among five alternatives, already described, that go from mild to very acute (A to C), and aggravating factors, such as age and other conditions that make the operation more urgent. Then, based on criteria extracted from medical knowledge and experience, an MWT for surgery is determined according to the classification and aggravating factors, which determines a dynamic priority by comparing the date in which the patient should be operated (date of diagnosis plus MWT) and current date. This is a formal logic that originates an algorithm that is run by the System. Then prioritized patients are scheduled, for a given week, taking into account the following factors:[1]

1. A patient cannot be operated twice in a week.
2. Detailed schedules of personnel availability, in particular, doctors.
3. Load should be balanced among doctors within a week.
4. The programmed times of operation for each OR.
5. Special patients are considered; their condition determines a particular timing for surgery.
6. Priority can be violated because of patient limitations.
7. Two doctors should be assigned for each operation.
8. Specification of the operations a doctor can perform.
9. Patients can be prioritized for certain times within a day for reasons other than type of surgery.
10. OR operating working times can be violated within certain limits to increase utilization.

Two methods have been developed for scheduling. First alternative is an Integer Linear Programming (ILP) model that defines constraints for each of the conditions stated earlier and others for logical consistence, and sets an objective function that establishes the maximization of the number of patients operated and the satisfaction of the order defined by the priorities defined previously;[2] this model was implemented and results of its use are given in the following. Second possibility is a heuristic that first decides the day on which a patient is to be operated and then the sequence within the day.

The heuristic proposed for this problem consists of a backtracking algorithm for a week scheduling of patients selected from a large group of prioritized patients, which executes the following steps, presented in a simplified way:

1. Search for feasible solutions, within lists of all the available time modules (half days), during the week, in which a given surgical operation for a patient can be alternatively performed, taking into account its length, availability of a doctor who can perform the operation, and considering if the operation is "special" or ambulatory.

2. Create combinations of feasible solutions by patient aggregation, taking into account that such combinations do not occupy more time than the one available in each time module, feasibility of aggregation and that no more than two special patients are included in each day; several linked lists are generated with the combinations that contains the maximum numbers of different patients that can be operated, in the order of priority, using all the time modules defined for a week.

3. In general, patients are selected in the priority order, but when it is not feasible to add a given one to a combination, the next patient with highest priority is selected.

4. More than one feasible solution can be generated, due to the large number of patients from which to select, so an evaluation is made to select the best one using additional criteria not included previously, such that more urgent patients should be included at the beginning of the week and that certain patients should be operated earlier during the day.

5. The patients selected for a given day are then ordered setting first the ones that are "special" and then by age, according to criteria given by doctors.

The heuristic and the ILP were tested in two hospitals with the following results. The testing was done for realistic scenarios with real data defined in terms of number of patients, available OR shifts, and surgical intervention times. For each one of these scenarios, an evaluation of the quality of the schedule in terms of priority satisfaction and use of available OR time was made. For one particular representative scenario for 100

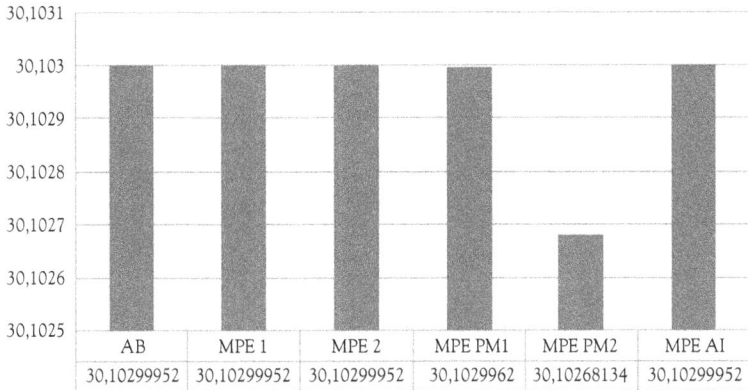

	AB	MPE 1	MPE 2	MPE PM1	MPE PM2	MPE AI
	30,10299952	30,10299952	30,10299952	30,1029962	30,10268134	30,10299952

Figure 6.2 Quality index of priority satisfaction for different scheduling methods

patients in a prioritized waiting list for the Urology specialty, the relative priority satisfaction for the heuristic (AB), and several variations of the ILP (MPE) are given in Figure 6.2.

The quality index indicates that there is a high satisfaction of patients'priorities and the heuristic perform as well as the ILP alternative variations; this was confirmed with several other scenarios. Hence, the heuristic is a good tool for scheduling patients according to priorities. There is no possible comparison with current methods, as they do not use priorities.

Now the use of available capacity is analyzed. The use of an OR is measured as the percentage of time assigned for patients' interventions with respect to the amount of minutes available. One of the objectives that motivate this work is to obtain an improvement in the use of the OR. For the evaluation of this objective, several representative scenarios were considered using the same parameters defined earlier. A large number of situations with variety of patients, duration of patients' interventions and available shifts were evaluated. In summary, the result showed that for most of the normal cases the use of OR is close to 100 percent for the heuristic and the ILP. However, the more interesting comparison is the performance of these models as compared to that of the current schedul-ing. To evaluate this, schedules generated with the heuristic and ILP were compared with the schedules generated with the current procedure. One of the comparisons that were made corresponds to a given week where the schedule generated by a hospital for the Urology specialty is shown in Table 6.1, which details how the OR time is assigned to patients.

Next, the schedules generated with the heuristic and two of the ILPs, which produced the same results, are presented in Table 6.2. The table also lists the doctor who was assigned in the schedule. For the scheduling it was considered that the doctor who operated a patient in the current schedule (Table 6.1) was also assigned in the proposed schedule and that the patients who were first in its day in the current schedule were also assigned first in the proposed schedule. This is to make the comparison more realistic, since in this way feasibility of doctors' assignment is assured and patients with special characteristics are scheduled first.

Table 6.3 presents the schedule for the same week, eliminating the constraints that the first doctor who was scheduled to operate the patient in Table 4.1 is assigned for this patient and that the first patient is maintained. As it should be, the elimination of constraints gives more flexibility for assignment and improves results, as it is clear in Table 6.4, where all the schedules are compared.

Table 6.4 shows that less restrictive rules positively impact the use of the OR and that using the methods proposed in this case can significantly increase the use of the surgical facilities.

Another test of the proposed methods reinforce the conclusions, since doing a similar experience in other hospital, scheduling OR during three weeks, results in Table 6.5 were obtained.

These results are very consistent with the one in Table 6.4, and confirm that there is every possibility of increasing OR utilization, considering that the current use for the specialty is taken into account, which is of the best managed hospital, is 82.6 percent.

In conclusion, use of optimization techniques, according to the results presented, can increase the number of operations significantly, without the need to increase the costs associated with the used resources. Since approximately 40 percent of the costs of the hospital are associated with surgical operations, improvements in OR use can significantly impact the economic results of the hospital (efficiency). Hence, from the patients' point of view, increase in the number of interventions generates a reduction in the waiting times of all the patients in the waiting list (fairness). Besides, use of prioritization policies that consider the severity

Table 6.1 OR scheduling with current method

Pabellon 3

Lunes	Martes	Miércoles	Jueves	Viernes
Paciente 1	305 Paciente 7	270 Paciente 15	270 Paciente 18	230
Paciente 2		Paciente 16	Paciente 19	
		Paciente 17	Paciente 20	
Tarde	Tarde	Tarde	Tarde	Tarde
	Paciente 8	165		
	Paciente 9			
	Paciente 10			

Pabellon 4

Lunes	Martes	Miércoles	Jueves	Viernes
Paciente 3	275 Paciente 11	185	Paciente 21	330
Paciente 4	Paciente 12		Paciente 22	
Paciente 5	Paciente 13			
	Paciente 14			
Tarde	Tarde	Tarde	Tarde	Tarde
95 Paciente 6			Paciente 23 60	

Table 6.2 Schedule generated by heuristic and ILP models

Pabellón 3

	Lunes	Martes	Miércoles	Jueves	Viernes
	Paciente: 1; Doctor1: 1, Doctor2: 4, Paciente: 2; Doctor1: 1, Doctor2: 14	305 Paciente: 7; Doctor1: 3, Doctor2: 10, Paciente: 4; Doctor1: 3, Doctor2: 10	285 Paciente: 15; Doctor1: 7, Doctor2: 8, Paciente: 16; Doctor1: 7, Doctor2: 8, Paciente: 17; Doctor1: 8, Doctor2: 4	270 Paciente: 18; Doctor1: 2, Doctor2: 4, Paciente: 8; Doctor1: 5, Doctor2: 2, Paciente: 53; Doctor1: 5, Doctor2: 2, Paciente: 20; Doctor1: 2, Doctor2: 4	280
Tarde		Paciente: 31; Doctor1: 10, Doctor2: 13, 115 Paciente: 30; Doctor1: 10, Doctor2: 13	Tarde		Tarde

Pabellón 4

	Lunes	Martes	Miércoles	Jueves	Viernes
	Paciente: 3; Doctor1: 3, Doctor2: 5, Paciente: 9; Doctor1: 5, Doctor2: 3, Paciente: 10; Doctor1: 5, Doctor2: 3	320 Paciente: 11; Doctor1: 6, Doctor2: 13, Paciente: 19; Doctor1: 6, Doctor2: 13, Paciente: 13; Doctor1: 6, Doctor2: 13, Paciente: 12; Doctor1: 6, Doctor2: 13, Paciente: 14; Doctor1: 6, Doctor2: 13	265	Paciente: 21; Doctor1: 9, Doctor2: 10, 250 Paciente: 23; Doctor1: 9, Doctor2: 10, Paciente: 34; Doctor1: 10, Doctor2: 9	
Tarde	Paciente: 6; Doctor1: 3, Doctor2: 5, 195 Paciente: 28; Doctor1: 3, Doctor2: 5, Paciente: 5; Doctor1: 3, Doctor2: 5		Tarde	Paciente: 22; Doctor1: 9, Doctor2: 10 170	Tarde

Table 6.3 Alternative schedule generated by heuristic and models

Pabellón 3

	Lunes	Martes	Miércoles	Jueves	Viernes
	Paciente: 2; Doctor1: 1, Doctor2: 14, Paciente: 8; Doctor1: 1, Doctor2: 14, Paciente: 71; Doctor1: 7, Doctor2: 1, Paciente: 24; Doctor1: 1, Doctor2: 14, Paciente: 14; Doctor1: 1, Doctor2: 14	270 Paciente: 3; Doctor1: 3, Doctor2: 10, Paciente: 9; Doctor1: 10, Doctor2: 3, Paciente: 10; Doctor1: 10, Doctor2: 3	320 Paciente: 1; Doctor1: 4, Doctor2: 8, Paciente: 20; Doctor1: 8, Doctor2: 4	310 Paciente: 15; Doctor1: 7, Doctor2: 2, Paciente: 18; Doctor1: 2, Doctor2: 4	285
Tarde		Tarde Paciente: 19; Doctor1: 13, Doctor2: 10, Paciente: 30; Doctor1: 10, Doctor2: 13	205	Tarde	Tarde

Pabellón 4

	Lunes	Martes	Miércoles	Jueves	Viernes
	Paciente: 4; Doctor1: 3, Doctor2: 5, Paciente: 7; Doctor1: 3, Doctor2: 5	285 Paciente: 62; Doctor1: 6, Doctor2: 13, Paciente: 26; Doctor1: 6, Doctor2: 13, Paciente: 11; Doctor1: 6, Doctor2: 13, Paciente: 13; Doctor1: 6, Doctor2: 13, Paciente: 12; Doctor1: 6, Doctor2: 13, Paciente: 16; Doctor1: 6, Doctor2: 13	295	Paciente: 21; Doctor1: 9, Doctor2: 10, Paciente: 23; Doctor1: 9, Doctor2: 10, Paciente: 17; Doctor1: 10, Doctor2: 9	280
Tarde	195 Paciente: 6; Doctor1: 3, Doctor2: 5, Paciente: 28; Doctor1: 3, Doctor2: 5, Paciente: 5; Doctor1: 3, Doctor2: 5			Tarde Paciente: 22; Doctor1: 9, Doctor2: 10	179

Table 6.4 *Results and comparison for different schedules*

	Used minutes	Available minutes	Use percentage	Improvement
Current schedule	2185	2820	77.5%	-
First schedule	2455	2820	87.1%	9.6%
Second schedule	2624	2820	93.0%	15.6%

Table 6.5 *Results for three weeks OR scheduling*

	Total time available (min)	Scheduled time [min]	Use percentage
Week 1	1120	1010	90.2%
Week 2	1120	1045	93.3%
Week 3	810	770	95.1%
Average			92.8%

of the diagnosis and the delay time of the patient allows giving the right treatment at the right time (quality).

Both methods explained earlier generate better schedules than today's practices, since they are: (a) feasible, by doctor's evaluation, (b) of better quality in terms of satisfying all the constraints, which are difficult to assure by nonformal methods, and (c) better in terms of capacity use, increasing occupation by at least 15 percent and up to 20 percent in certain cases.

The method implemented in the System lane activity "Calculate patient priority and schedule OR" of the process in Figure 6.1 is the heuristic, because it furnishes results close to the optimization model and is more stable in terms of always giving results. This is not true for the ILP that sometimes runs long times without getting a solution, due to the particular form of the objective function that includes weights to favor schedules that process priority patients. Then the heuristic is embedded within the System support of the process.

Waiting List Management for Ambulatory Patients

Here we present another case of resource scheduling in hospitals, which has the innovative characteristic that a formal process model is designed that allows its execution with software of the BPMS (Business Process Management Suite) type. Such execution avoids writing most of the code needed for process support. We select "Ambulatory Elective Care Service" of Figure 2.8, and concentrate on managing the incoming patients to such services, with an emphasis on waiting list prioritization to increase fairness and efficiency due to better use of resources. Incoming patients to hospital outpatient service can occur from two sources: referrals of patients from primary care to the hospital, commonly known as interconsultations, or from medical check-ups for patients who have already been previously attended because of certain symptoms.

The case will focus on improving the problem of waiting lists for interconsultations.[3] As shown in Figure 6.3, the number of patients who remained in waiting lists for interconsultations during 2011 fluctuated between 1,000 and 2,500 patients, while in the first half of 2012 registered an increase to 3,500 patients.

Figure 6.3 reveals interesting information. First, it provides evidence of the number of patients who remain without service, which is not less than 1,000 patients and that tends to remain around 2,500. Second, certain behaviors of the hospital, which are highlighted in the preceding graph, are clear. As it can be seen, the hospital attends to a larger number of patients on certain days, with the purpose of meeting the goal of importantly reducing the number of patients in the waiting list, but it is a reactive action, possibly motivated by authorities' pressure, and with no apparent periodicity. Furthermore, the behavior of the waiting lists for the different specialties is not encouraging. Indeed, the indicator number of incoming over outcoming patients shows that they cannot eliminate their waiting lists; on the contrary, they will remain constant or growing. By way of example, for every 3.4 patients that joined the Neurology waiting list during the first half of 2011, only 1 patient was attended. This concludes that there are medical specialties that keep a constant number of patients on the waiting list, others that grow moderately, and, finally, some medical specialties that have serious capacity problems, as is in the case of Neurology and Dermatology. Thus, all this indicates the need of a formal process for the management of waiting lists.

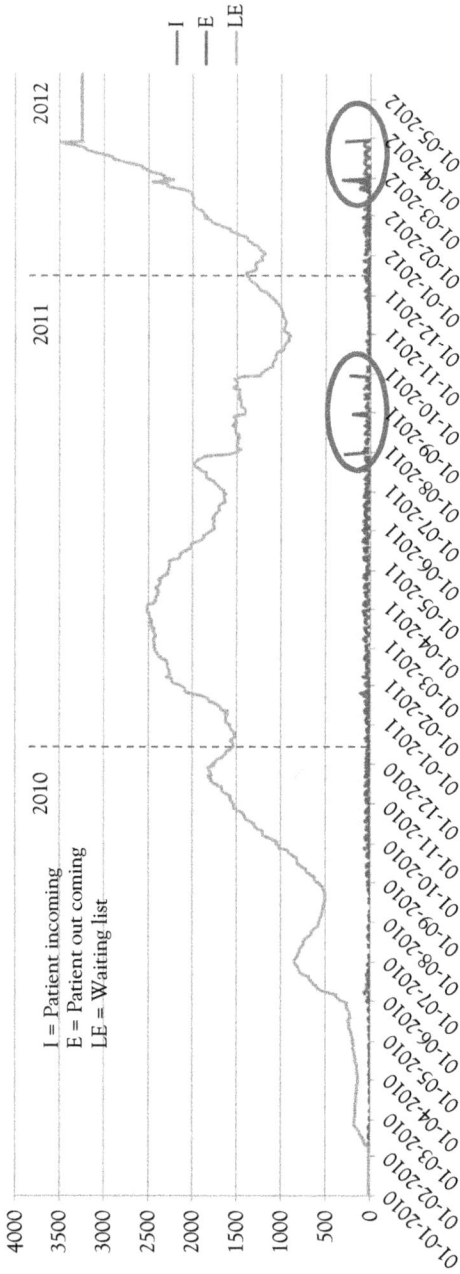

Figure 6.3 *Number of patients waiting for interconsultations*

The problem of waiting lists can be handled by three different strategies:

1. **Increase capacity** adds to the medical resources in terms of hiring more staff, and possible increases in enabling infrastructure.
2. **Improve productivity** serves a larger number of patients subject to current capacity constraints (efficiency) in terms of the objectives established in Chapter 2.
3. **Opportunity of attention**: Use available medical resources for meeting the opportunity care criteria related to each patient's illness (fairness).

Considering these facts, the question is how to address the problem of outpatient waiting lists. In this regard, the international experience shows that increasing capacity is not an effective strategy; in effect, countries such as Canada and Denmark have concluded that the resolution of the waiting lists crisis in health through increased resources has not proven to be an effective strategy. Likewise, countries such as Australia, United States, and the United Kingdom provide more international experience on the initiatives of increasing resources, which have failed to reduce the number of patients on waiting lists.[4]

Canada is one of the countries with greater advances in waiting lists in the health system. Canadian experts have concluded that one of the central aspects in this quest to better manage them and assure patients timely access is to focus on optimizing installed capacity, by improving the quality of the management of the available resources. Enhanced coordination and teamwork inside the organization of health care providers, assisted by improvements in information technologies, makes possible avoiding unnecessary delays between the different stages of treatment of patients.

Western Canada Waiting List Project is one of the best examples of multidimensional approach to improve the management of timeouts in Canada. This project that began in 1998, with the agreement of several regions as well as medical associations and health authorities, seeks to improve justice and fairness in the delivery of medical services, prioritizing treatments, including concepts of emergency care, and improving the management of waiting lists.

On the basis of the international experience reported, the approach used in this case is to manage the opportunity of attention. This means securing an MWT to attend a patient, subject to its medical complexity. In this sense, patient's attention is opportune when MWT is not exceeded. This is similar to what it was proposed in the previous case of priority determination for OR scheduling and also in OR capacity assignment.

The current situation is that, for example, in the Neurology specialty, the one with more unsatisfied demand, patients with reduced complexity tend to be served first than others with more priority. This situation is the product of the first-in first-out (FIFO) approach that underlies the medical hours booking process, which originates disparity in waiting time between patients and that evidently does not consider the opportunity for care. This is not the only specialty with problems, since Traumatology has also similar behavior.

Given the aforementioned findings, it is concluded that the care of patients waiting for interconsultation is not governed by an approach based on opportunity, but rather on access. The enforcement of health indicators is privileged, such as the number of patients waiting, instead of ensuring the fulfillment of individualized MWT for each patient. In this sense, the motivation of this work is to develop criteria to categorize and prioritize patients in outpatient waiting list to deliver a timely health care according to the current hospital capacity restrictions. In designing a service process to accomplish this, first "Ambulatory Elective Care Services" of Figure 2.8 is decomposed in Figure 6.4, following the same pattern as in Figure 2.11, but specialized to ambulatory services.

The "Demand Analysis" process studies the behavior of ambulatory patients. One variable that can be analyzed is absenteeism of the patients, which currently varies between 20 and 30 percent of the medical hours reserved, situation that has a negative impact on the capacity of public hospitals. The idea behind a behavior analysis of absenteeism is to detect patients who are usually absent from their medical hours, with well-differentiated characteristics. With this information, categories (clusters) of patients could be defined and differentiated by absenteeism rate, which could feed a process to control such patients and possibly define an over-citation rate to use the capacity that such absent patients would not use, which obviously generates a better use of resources. We did not include

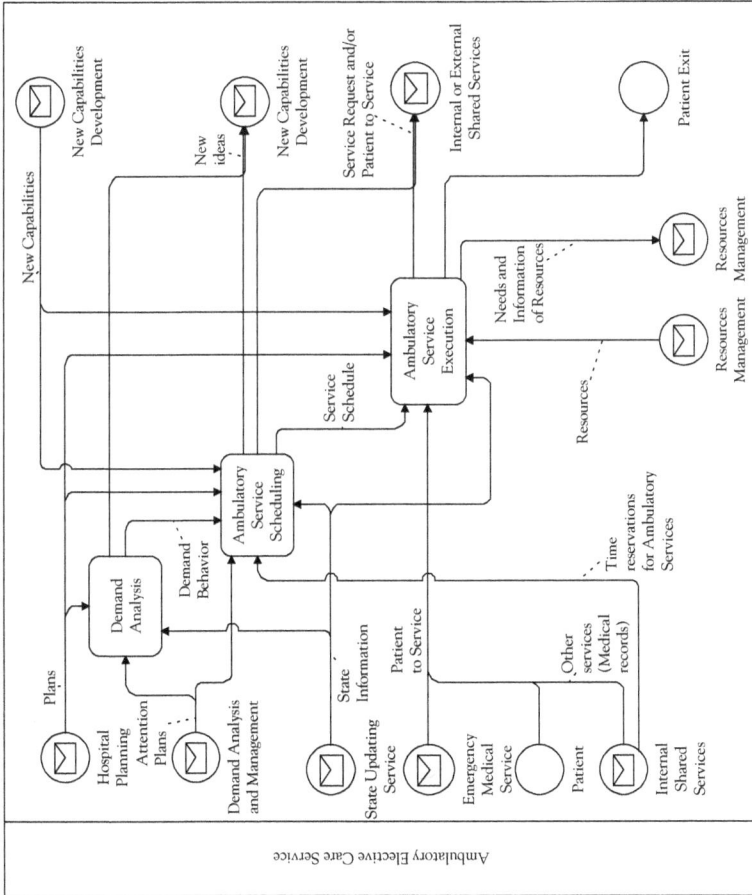

Figure 6.4 "Ambulatory Elective Care Service" decomposition

this option in our design because of lack of information, but it could be easily added to the process to be detailed later.

Next "Ambulatory Service Scheduling" of Figure 6.4 is decomposed in Figure 6.5, which relates to waiting patients. There are two types of patients admitted to the hospital: new and current patients. Patients are considered new when they request a medical evaluation for a particular medical condition, where the diagnosis of the patient is determined. On the other hand they are considered "in course" when it is required that the patient comes again to the hospital for a second time or more occasions to controls in order to observe the evolution of his or her disease. Note that a new patient may change to "in course," and when in this condition he or she may have several interactions with the hospital until the patient is discharged.

New patients are admitted to the hospital through consultations from primary care (interconsultations). The hospital is currently facing a high demand for interconsultations, which generates waiting lists for new patients. This situation is the main problem to be solved by the service process design we have developed. In terms of current patients, the hospital also manages waiting lists; however, they are much smaller than those of new patients. Indeed, reservations of medical controls have an inherent waiting time, determined by the attending physician. Such time is needed to let the health condition of the patient evolve, to be subsequently evaluated in a medical control. As a consequence, the controls' waiting lists are relatively low and do not pose a problem for the hospital. Given the types of patients, new and controls, the planning of services for waiting patients should be treated differently, as shown in Figure 6.6.

The aim of the "New patient scheduling" process in Figure 6.6 is to generate a single prioritized hospital waiting list, which will serve to make reservations of medical hours for patients.

As shown in Figure 6.6, the first subprocess generates a waiting list with interconsultations and applies a logic, that will be presented later, to categorize and prioritize new patients, whose product is a waiting list of patients sorted in descending order according to severity and priority. In the second subprocess, medical hours are programmed, according to priorities determined in the first subprocess, for patients awaiting reserves;

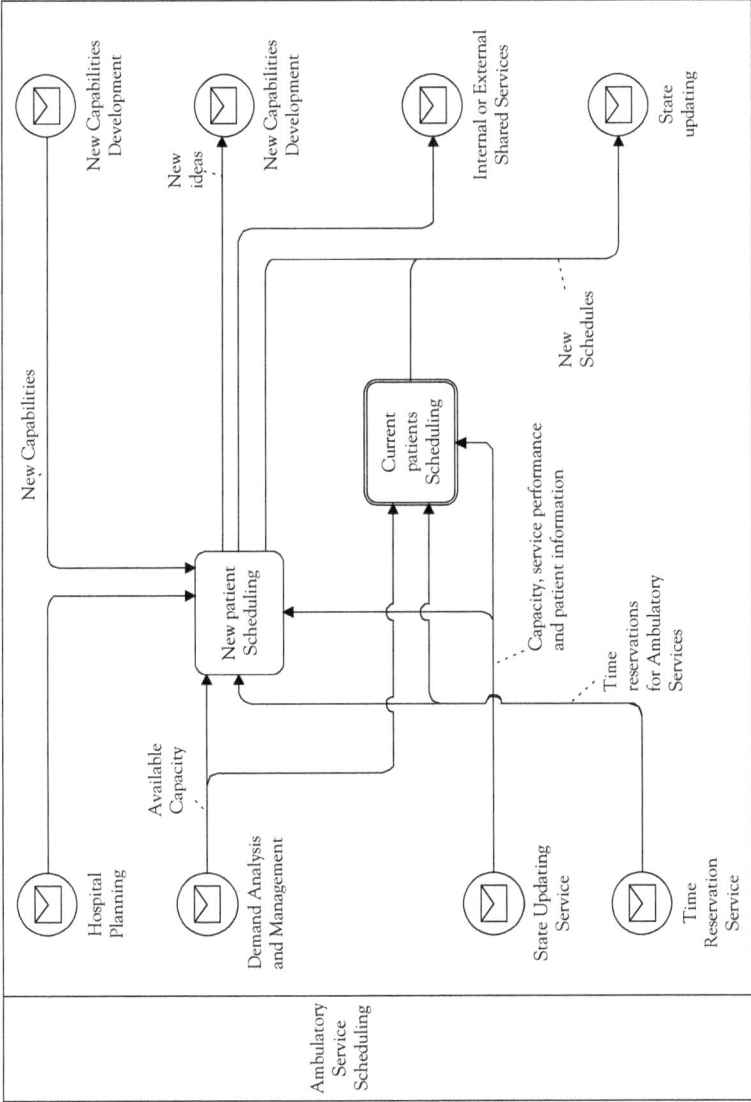

Figure 6.5 "Ambulatory Service Scheduling" decomposition

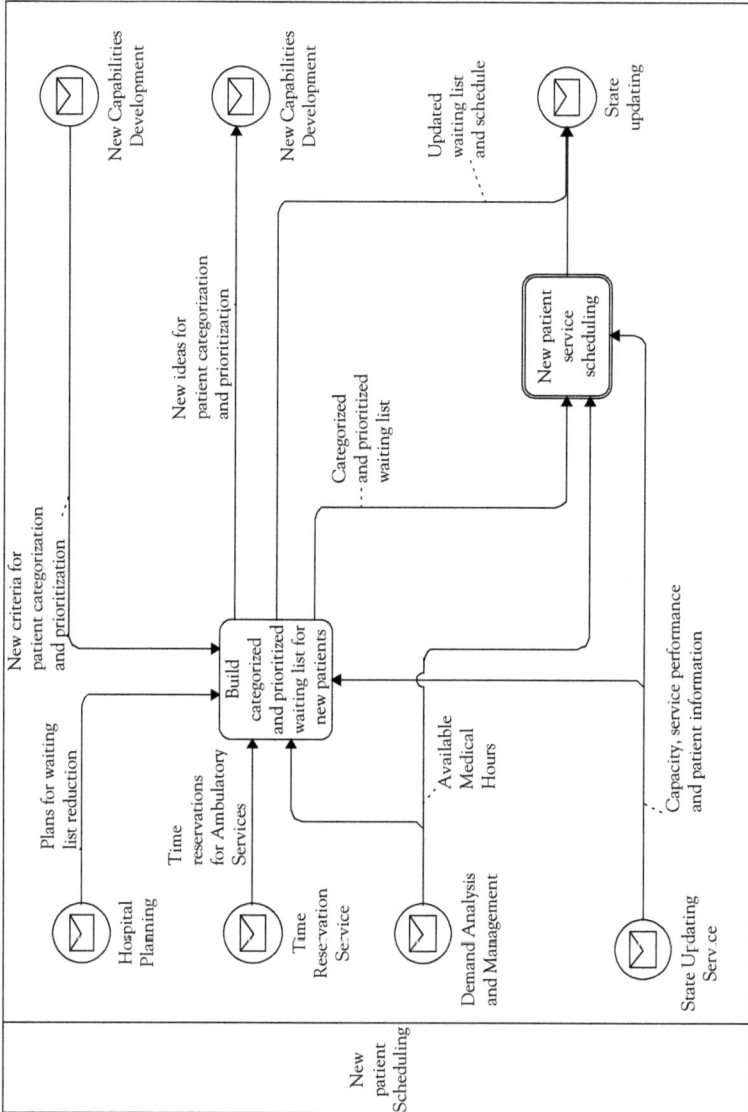

Figure 6.6 "New patient scheduling" decomposition

for this the design specifies that hospital administrative personnel routinely contact the waiting patients to notify the medical time assigned to them.

Information of patients on waiting lists is provided to hospitals by a centralized information system of the health care network. Each primary attention unit directs their patients to the hospitals in the public sector; while doing this it registers the interconsultation in the system. The total number of interconsultations make up the waiting list for new patients. While the system provides a platform for the entry of the interconsultations, they are usually not well recorded, that is, they do not follow the technical standard of registration of waiting lists, using, for example, medical specialties that are not declared in the technical standard. It is therefore required to debug the waiting lists so that the information is adequate for prioritization.

Figure 6.7 shows the process to determine new patients' waiting lists. This activity is performed by the "Head Patient Management," for which he has access to the waiting list that is exported from the previously described system. The waiting list must be loaded to the "System" developed for this case, which is responsible for performing the debugging explained earlier. In some cases, manual cleaning is made by the "Head Patient Management," since the "System" does not recognize some fields. When performing a manual cleaning of the waiting list, the "System" saves the criteria that were used, with the purpose to include them in the automatic debugging later. Prolonged use of the process should eventually eliminate the manual debugging. Once the waiting list is corrected, it is saved in the database of the "System," which records the interconsultations that are not already registered in the database. This process that replaces the existing one, mostly done manually, will reduce updating of waiting lists from at least two weeks to daily.

Now the logic used to categorize and prioritize interconsultation patients in the design in Figure 6.7 is detailed. First, some ideas proposed in the literature are reviewed.

The linear formulation of Edwards[5] is one of the well-known and currently used methods for prioritization. It proposes a score for the patient given by

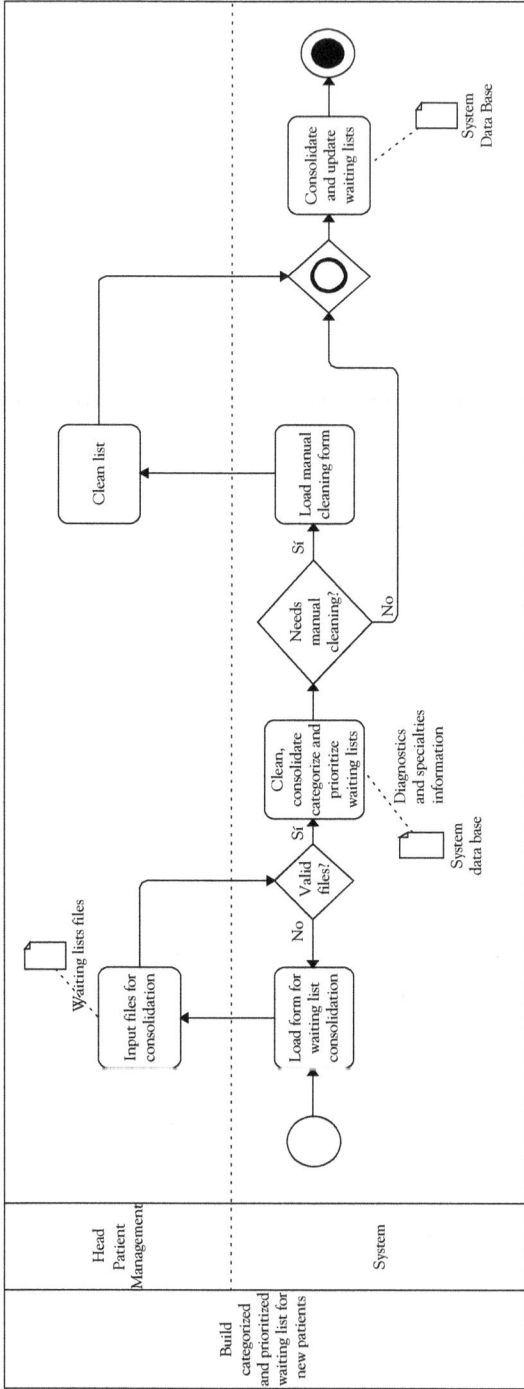

Figure 6.7 "Build categorized and prioritized waiting lists for new patients" design

$$P = \sum_{i=1}^{5} S_i^2 * w_i$$

where P is the priority score and S_i is the score for factor i, and

$i = 1$ rate of progression of the disease, valued 1–4,

$i = 2$ pain (1–4),

$i = 3$ disability or dependency (1–4),

$i = 4$ occupation lost (1–4),

$i = 5$ parameterized waiting time (0–4),

w_i is the relative weight of the S_i factor.

The age-old formulation of Edwards is still used widely today. It is the case of the prioritization of patients system on waiting list for cataract surgery and hip replacement used in Spain since 2004.[6]

Other weighted scoring methods correspond to those presented by Lack,[7] which is a variation of the one by Edwards and Dennett,[8] whose formulations are the following:

$$\text{Lack: } P = \sum_{i=1}^{4} S_i^2 * w_i + (\frac{5t}{m} - 1)^2$$

$$\text{Dennett: } P = \sum_{i=1}^{3} A_i * \sum_{j=1}^{2} B_j$$

Where t is the patient's waiting time and m is the largest waiting time a patient has; A_i and B_j are clinical and social attributes, respectively.

In this case, a method that categorizes patients according to the diagnosed sickness gravity is proposed, which results in a category and an MWT, as it was presented in a case in the section "Operating Room Capacity Assignment" in this chapter. Once all patients are categorized, they are sorted according to priority in the waiting list. This is done by a simple rule that considers the waiting time the patient has suffered with respect to his maximum allotted time. From this, two scenarios are possible: that the patient stays in normal wait, because he has not attained the MWT, or that the patient is overdue, given that he has exceeded the MWT. Then the proposed ordering is based on the calculation of the number of days remaining to reach MWT for patients not yet overdue. For patients that are overdue, the days since the expiration of the MWT is the relevant figure and the larger it is for a patient, he should go higher on the waiting list; and, of course, before people who are not overdue. Furthermore, it is proposed that a patient with expired MWT should leverage (multiply by a factor) his waiting time, in order to reflect that the waiting days after maximum allotted time have greater impact on the perception of the patient. Indeed, if the hospital failed to deliver the service at the agreed time, it is considered that the patient's health will be significantly worse for each additional day of waiting post expiration.

Then the situation of patients waiting is described by means of the function $E(t)$, where t is defined as the chronological days of waiting since attention was requested for him by means of interconsultation. Then the days of waiting leveraged is defined as:

$$E(t) = \begin{cases} t, & \text{if } t < T_{max} \\ T_{max} + a * (t - T_{max}), & \text{if } t \geq T_{max} \end{cases}$$

where T_{max} corresponds to the MWT associated with the medical diagnosis, and α is a leverage factor.

Another way to describe the waiting function is through the attribute "waiting days remaining to T_{max}," $E(d_r)$:

$$E(d_r) = \begin{cases} T_{max} - d_r, & si\ d_r > 0 \\ T_{max} - a * d_r, & si\ d_r \leq 0 \end{cases}$$

$$d_r = T_{max} - t$$

It remains to specify the calculation of the leverage factors. Notice that there is a direct relationship between the days of waiting for each category; for example, if the highest category has an MWT of 5 days, and the lower-priority 90 days, then a waiting day for patients of high category is equivalent to 18 days of waiting for low category patients (90/5 = 18 days). Similarly, another category can have a maximum time of waiting for 60 days, so every waiting day equals 1.5 days of the low category (90/60 = 1.5 days). These examples suggest a way to calculate the leverage factors, which consists of measuring how much each waiting day for a category weights in relation to the lowest category. Thus, it is concluded that the leverage of the category of priority factor p is obtained as:

$$a_p = \frac{\max_i T_{max,i}}{T_{max,p}}$$

where $T_{max,i}$ is the MWT of the category i. With this, the category p waiting function $E(d_r, p)$ is summarized as:

$$E(d_r, p) = \begin{cases} T_{max,p} - d_r, & \text{if } 0 < d_r \\ T_{max,p} + \dfrac{\max_i T_{max,i}}{T_{max,p}} * d_r, & \text{if } 0 \geq d_r \end{cases}$$

The priority rule proposed is that patients are placed in the ascending order of $E(d_r, p)$. Thus, Figure 6.8 shows the waiting function for each category; where it is clear that the higher categories increase their priority faster than lower ones.

Now a particular feature of this case is presented, which is the implementation approach of the proposed design, including the development of the "System" support specified in Figure 6.7. For this, a process execution approach is used, which will be illustrated with the model in such figure. In doing this, a tool of the BPMS type is needed, which in this case was integrated with several open components. This was done to minimize cost, since public hospitals in Chile cannot pay the cost of commercial high-end technology of this type. So the idea was to show that the advantages of process execution—fast development, minimum code, flexibility for changes in the process, and the code and reuse of services—can be obtained at a reasonable cost.

In particular, after testing several low-cost alternatives, Activiti was chosen as the core of the execution. Activiti is an open framework for the implementation of a business process modeled in BPMN 2.0, developed in Java, and owned by the company Alfresco.[9]

Activiti is not really a BPMS, because there are some missing components in the framework to be considered as such. The main component of the Activiti framework is a Process Engine, which has the necessary

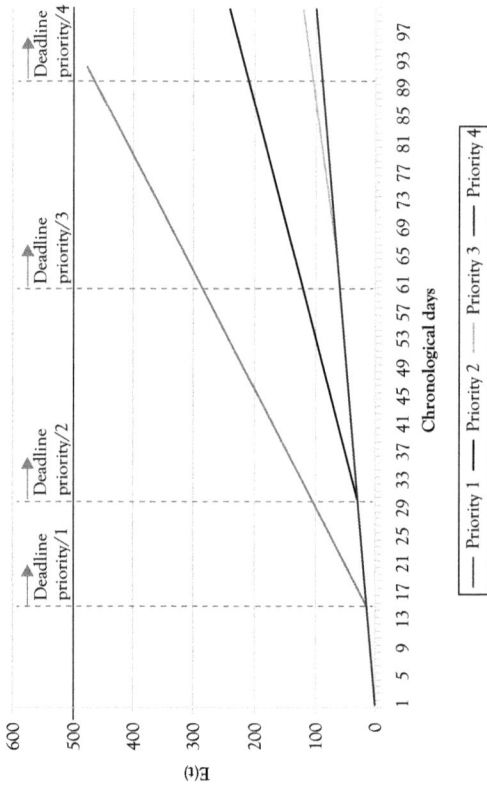

Figure 6.8 Waiting function

features to execute business process designed with BPMN 2.0, standard that it fully incorporated. This obviously favors portability of the designs to other eventual alternatives.

Activiti has a number of components that allow managing business processes, which are classified in Design Tools, Process Engine, and Support Tools. Unlike the Process Engine, the rest of the components of activities are considered Add-ons (accessory) to the framework. Some of the components are:

1. **Activiti Engine**: Main component of the framework, which provides all the functionality of execution to the Process Engine.
2. **Activiti Modeler**: Web application that allows business-oriented BPMN 2.0 process modeling.
3. **Activiti Designer**: Corresponds to a plugin for the Eclipse development environment. Activities Designer is currently the only functional process modeler of the framework and is purely focused on process execution.
4. **Activiti Explorer**: Web application that allows running and visualizing the graphical user interfaces involved in business processes. Activities Explorer is a solution for the design of simple displays and does not support dynamic web interfaces. So, in order to build system support for complex activities, an interface designer component is needed.
5. **Activiti REST**: Web application that allows to remotely executing business processes through web services (alternative of the well-known SOA protocol).

This set of components enables to build a BPMS solution, with the Activiti Engine being the most robust solution of the framework. The rest still lacks sufficient maturity to adopt them as a final solution. Given this, only the Activiti Engine was used in this case and for other requirements, available open tools were integrated with the engine.

One of the basic features a BPMS must have is the ability to run processes, which in terms of design corresponds to link the graphical display environment with the process engine. That is, from an action in the graphic environment, the execution of an activity of the process should be triggered. Activiti process engine has an API of seven interfaces developed to control it from an external application. In particular, there is the Run time Service interface that allows initiating processes. This interface can be used from a controller class, which receives instructions to run specific processes. For the purposes of design, such controller class will be called Instance Service, since its work is to instantiate processes. The Instance Service class should be invoked from the graphical display environment. When a user interacts with a graphical interface, he specifies a requirement for process execution. The graphical interface captures the process identifier, invokes the class Instance Service and this initiates the process through the Run time Service interface. This simple dynamics is nothing more than a specification of the model view. For simplicity, the graphical display is described as a generic package of classes, since each developer could design a GUI according to his preferences.

We examine now how the facilities provided by Activiti just described relate to BPMN.

BPMN 2.0 UserTask activities, by the standard definition, do not support any programming code. The only activities in BPMN 2.0 that support code are ScriptTask and ServiceTask explained in Table 6.6. In connection to our BPMN design models, as in Figure 6.7, the first activity of such a table is in a user lane, as the "Head Patient Management" in such a figure, and the last two in a "System" Lane.

A very important aspect of the Activiti Engine is that ServiceTask activities execution can be delegated to classes outside Java classes, in order to process complex logic.

So, in summary, we have the Activiti Engine that has interfaces for integrating with tools that allow building complex graphical user interfaces, as the ones needed by the "UserTask" of Table 6.6, and with tools to program complex logic as the ones that may be required by "ServiceTask" of the same table. So, open tools do these jobs and integration with Activiti is required, as described later.

For the development of the graphical interfaces, Google Web Toolkit (GWT) was selected. Google has defined a mechanism for using object-oriented applications for graphic interfaces in web applications. They released an open framework called the GWT in 2006, allowing to

Table 6.6 Elements of BPMN 2.0 Activiti

Activity BPMN 2.0	Technical characteristics
User task	**UserTask:** It does not support programming code; therefore, forms or views assigned to this activity must be provided by the environment BPMS as one particular solution of each one. UserTask activity is technically only a pause in the process assigned to a specified user, which must be terminated when the activity is completed.
Script task	**ScriptTask:** System activity that allows validating data or performing low complexity arithmetic. It supports programming in Groovy and JavaScript code, both adopted by the Object Management Group (OMG) as languages for BPMN 2.0 standard.
Service task	**ServiceTask:** System activity that supports complex programming logic. Used to consume web services or execute code in Groovy or JavaScript language.

design object-oriented web Java interfaces, which the web browser interprets as traditional web interfaces, that is, as programmed in HTML, CSS, JavaScript, AJAX, among other techniques. GWT is a tool that has been widely adopted and most of the applications developed by Google are programmed in GWT.

Although the graphical interfaces of the BPMS system developed in this work were programmed in GWT, we used a particular framework called Vaadin. Examples of interfaces follow:

1. **Interface to determine new patient waiting list:** Figure 6.9 shows how the interface supports the activities that are performed in this process to determine the new patient waiting list, such as files validation, automatic debugging of waiting list, manual debugging of lists and consolidation, and updating of database. It also shows the status of the activity and also the elapsed time. This interface is the one used by the first activity of "Head Patient Management" in Figure 6.7.

2. **Interface to see the new patient prioritized waiting list:** Figure 6.10 shows the result of cleaning and prioritization of patients, which is evaluated by the "Head Patient Management."

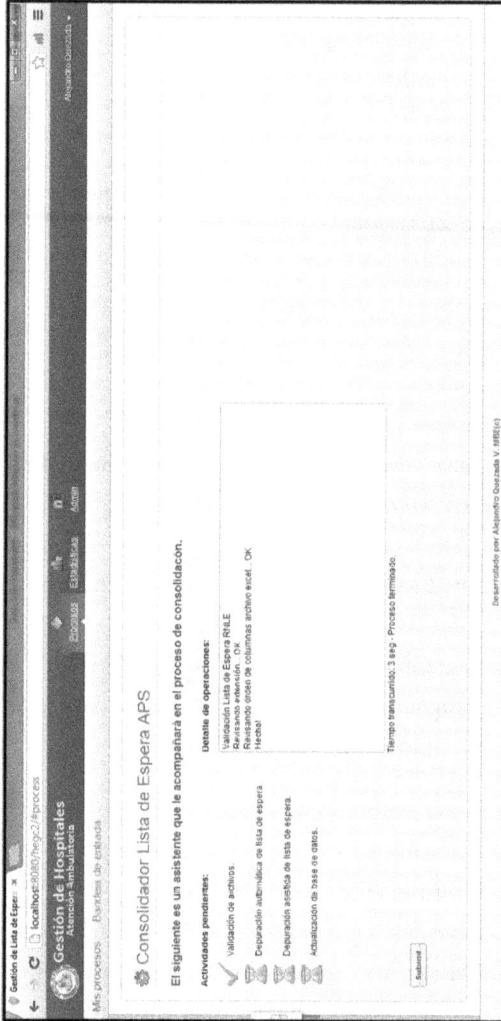

Figure 6.9 Interface to determine new patient waiting list

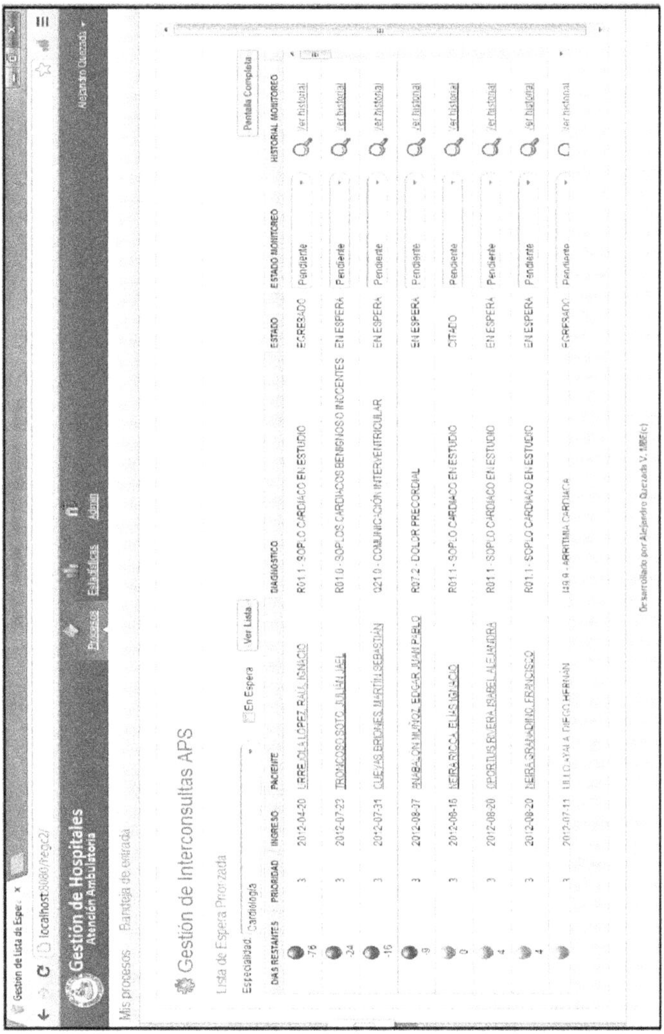

Figure 6.10 Interface to see prioritized waiting list

Then, as explained earlier, there is the need to program and insert in the execution of the process the logic for waiting list prioritization. For this task another tool was used, which is the Spring framework. Spring is an open-source framework for developing web applications in Java. The advantages of using the Spring framework are that it proposes the concept of container objects (factory objects). This means that there is a repository that instances and keeps the objects used in an application. The developer must set the object container in a single file, which specifies classes (objects) and their relationships. The advantage of having an object's container is that future changes to the software are only made in one file, without compromising excessive code. Then all the logic imbedded in the activities in the "System" of Figure 6.6 was coded using Spring.

The physical layer of the "System" corresponds to the communication with databases and, in particular, with the Activiti database and the database that store hospital's information. Typically, under an object-oriented programming approach, communication with databases is performed by means of class entities, which have SQL queries inside to be processed in the databases. Such an approach has been widely questioned by developers; in fact, class entities have inside SQL code and Java code (or another programming language). This duplicity of languages generates problems of system's maintenance; hence, SQL code should be separated of the Java code, in such a way that entities classes only maintain the information and do not process SQL queries.

Then, operations carried out by the entity classes, such as setting or capturing information (methods, Setters, and Getters) materialize directly on the databases, without programming SQL code inside such classes. This is called the "Principle of Data Persistence."

There are multiple frameworks that implement data persistence in Java. One of them is Java Persistence API (JPA), as also Hibernate[10] and Ibatis.[11] For the purposes of the BPMS of this work, Hibernate and Ibatis were used as follows.

Ibatis is an open source framework developed by the Apache Foundation, the same organization that developed the well-known Apache Tomcat application server. Ibatis uses an XML file in which SQL queries should be programmed; each inquiry must be registered with a logical name. As a result, Ibatis delivers a repository of SQL queries that are used by entities classes when necessary. Then, Ibatis allows separating programming in Java code of programming in SQL code, so cleaner and more maintainable applications are obtained.

Moreover, the Hibernate framework was also used to manage databases. This is owned by the JBoss organization that is also known for its application server that receives the same name (JBoss Application Server). The communication that Hibernate establishes with databases is more direct that the one made by the Ibatis Framework. Hibernate is a pure data persistence framework, that is, entities classes are directly related to the database tables, so the operations that are performed with the entity classes automatically materialize on the databases. Unlike Ibatis, Hibernate does not use intermediate files and also does not require that the SQL queries are scheduled. Indeed, Hibernate performs the operations carried out in entity classes as SQL queries later reflected on transactional operations on databases. Using Ibatis Framework in the BPMS environment is because the database management of Activiti's processes is originally made with this framework. As the project added more functionality to the process engine, which are reflected in operations on the Activiti database, Ibatis Framework was needed. On the other hand, Hibernate was used to operate on the database of the hospital, which keeps information required by the processes that are performed in the BPMS environment.

The prototype was developed in a few weeks with the tools just described and implements the process "Build categorized waiting lists for new patients" specified in Figure 6.6. We show some results for this application next.

The prototype enables the "Manager Patient Service" to determine a single, consolidated, and refined waiting list, incurring a computing time of one to two minutes. Today, the same process in its manual version, performed by a clerk, takes between one and three days. The process current version is performed every two weeks, so patients have a further two-weeks' wait only by administrative considerations. In this line, the prototype allows to determine the waiting list every day and, in consequence, eliminate unnecessary waiting time. Finally, the process is supported by a database, which stores information refined and structured according to a formal data model. Thus, the prototype leaves the hospital a source of useful information for upcoming projects, which is a plus, given that the majority of technological projects requires a structured data layer, and that was nonexistent for this project.

The prototype uses a well-defined and medically supported logic to categorize and prioritize patients. Such logic requires that the prototype has the equivalences between the diagnostics used by the primary attention units and the ones used for the hospital, work that was done for the specialties of Nutrition and Neurology to test the results.

The process and system developed can be easily adapted to other hospitals. In particular, the integration of primary attention and hospitals in a given zone can be done by means of the approach to waiting-list integration and prioritization proposed and tested in this work, since today the implicit rule for attending patients is FIFO, which is absolutely in contradiction with the fairness objective proposed at the beginning of this chapter.

Other Cases

We summarize other cases emphasizing novel features of health service design.

Diabetes Management in a Private Hospital

We present a real case of this type developed in a large private hospital,[12] which centers on preventive health services for diabetes patients.

The Strategy that motivates this case is integral services to users, changing from a reactive approach, where a patient has to request a health service, to one where the hospital continuously monitors patient's data to discover possible health problems and discover crisis before they occur, advising the patient on preventive treatments. So the Business Model is to provide value to the patient by avoiding the consequences of such crisis, which in diabetes' patients can go from member amputation to death. Also value is provided to society by increasing useful life for patients.

Then Capabilities needed are to have useful medical historical data to be able to develop diabetes predictive models; to have practices that allow for continuous patient health monitoring; and a good process to proactively act on patient to prevent crisis. So an Intelligent Structure II is needed for model development and action taking and as a consequence a Business Pattern 1, "Client's Knowledge-Based Selling," is needed. Selling can be a little offensive in health services, so one may use "Offering" instead.

In this case we are in "Ambulatory Elective Care Service" of the architecture in Figure 2.8, from which a decomposition, similar to the one in Figure 6.4, tells us the subprocceses to be designed. We concentrate on "Ambulatory Services Scheduling" but do not give detail by decomposing it. Instead we emphasize the logic that it executes based on a predictive model that is detailed in the following.

The predictive model is based on Data Mining, by analyzing historical data for chronic diabetes patients; first, variables that are statistically correlated to risk for diabetes patients were determined based on such data. The ones that are relevant, with data from 1,487 cases, are the ones in Table 6.7. With selected variables a Classification, as explained in section "Analytics" of Chapter 2, is done, from which the binary tree in Figure 6.11 is generated.

Table 6.7 Selected variables for Classification

```
═══ Run information ═══


Scheme:      weka.classifiers.trees.J48 -C 0.25 -M 2
Relation:    riesgo_final_SinLDL_binario_1HDL
Instances:   1487
Attributes:  10
             hba1c_bin      Hemoglobina glicosilicada
             hdl-single     High density lipoprotein
             sexo
             colTot_bin     Colesterol total
             tg_bin         Triglicéridos
             edad_bin
             tabaco
             hta            Hipertensión, si o no
             ec             Enfermedad coronaria, sí o no
             riesgo
Test mode:   10-fold cross-validation
```

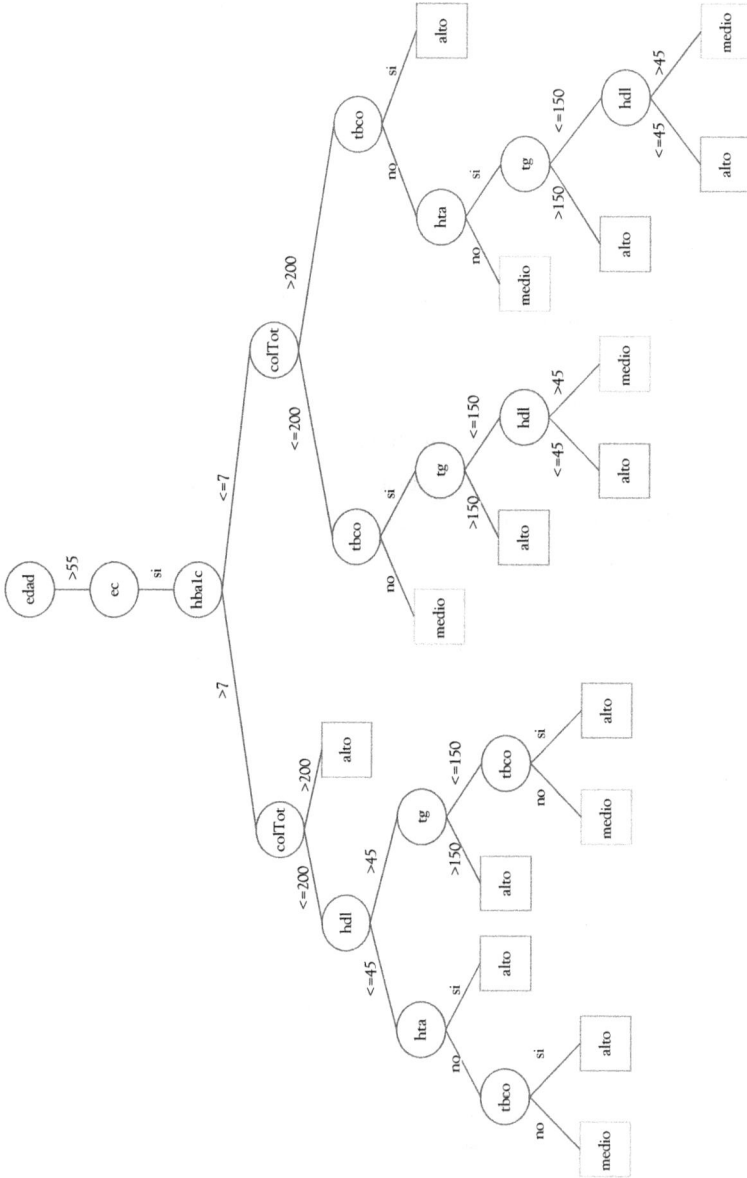

Figure 6.11 Decision tree for diabetes data

The tree clearly shows which combinations of variables with what values define cases with medium (medio) and high (alto) risk. Then patients which fit the values that define a case can be classified in a risk level and action defined for them accordingly. So, for example, patients which values that mean high risk can be subjected to preventive treatments.

Operation of Services for Patients at Home

The Strategy analysis and Business Model for this case was presented in Chapter 3; also Intelligent Structure IV and Business Pattern 2, "Creation of New Streams of Service," were determined as the proper ones; the main idea being to proactively provide customized services for patients at home using large amounts of data about medical variables monitored online. It was concluded that this solution needs a new Value Stream. Then what is done here is to provide a design for the operation of such stream. We start by locating the new stream as contained in the process "Hospitalization Service" in the architecture of Figure 2.8. Then the pattern that defines this stream is based on Macro1's processes for service management and execution, which is presented in Barros;[13] it is the same used to model "Ambulatory Elective Care Service" in Figure 6.4 and the specialization for this case is in Figure 6.12. The mapping of the Business Design in Figure 3.5 to this process design is as follows:

1. Besides the Macro1 structure emphasized in Figure 6.12, there is the need of a Macro2 that takes care of the continuous development of "Design criteria for at home services" and "Design of improved or new Value Stream "of Figure 3.5, since the dynamics of the situation, in particular new historical data, requires the revision of the models and related criteria and, also, of the Value Stream for its adaptation to such revision. Macro2 is present providing inputs to the structure in Figure 6.12 and requires other processes that are not given here.

2. "Predictive model processing and crisis detection" relates to "Definition of patients with access to service" and the model application part of "Service operation management" of Figure 3.5.

3. The other subprocesses in Figure 6.12 are part of the Value Stream that operates the service.

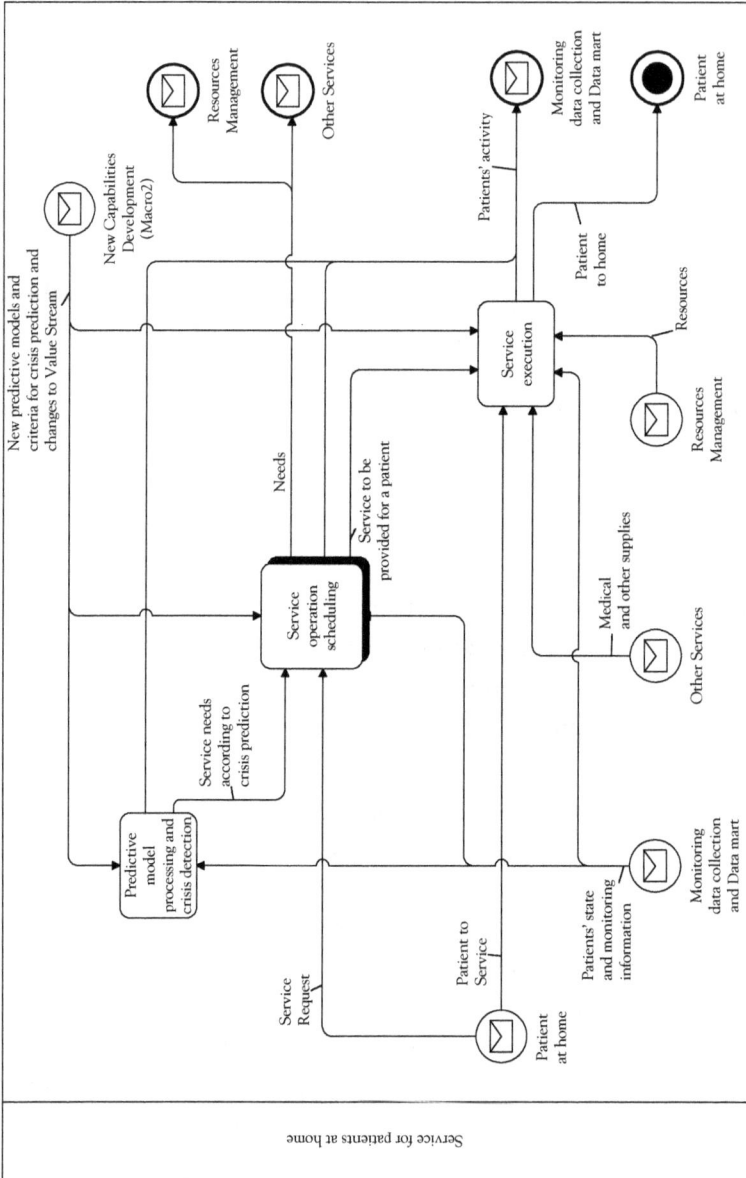

Figure 6.12 Service for patients at home

In what follows we concentrate on the logic that is executed in "Predictive model processing and crisis detection." Such logic is based on predictive models that permit criteria generation for crisis detection, which we now explain.[14]

Logic stars with patients clustering that, due to lack of historical information previous to this project, is made using age groups based on medical expert opinion: 0 to 1 month; 1 to 6 months; 6 to 24 months; and more than 24 months. Then the possibility that key variables that define the situation of a patient, such as oxygen saturation, temperature, cardiac frequency, and respiratory frequency, may have a distinct behavior for different pathologies in each group is considered, in order to refine segmentation.

For the predictive model for each preceding segment, the possible variables to be considered are evaluated by means of correlation; variables are the ones already considered in the segmentation plus the period of a day-day or night-in which they are taken. The conclusion of the correlation analysis is that cardiac frequency appears to be the best predictor, besides oxygen saturation and time of the day. For such variables, fuzzy membership functions are applied; for example, oxygen saturation was modeled with a Gaussian function in diffuse intervals for low saturation and normal saturation.

The static risk in the model is determined using the following groups of input variables:

- Group A: Vital signs
  - Temperature
  - Cardiac frequency
  - Respiratory frequency
  - Arterial pressure
- Group B: Oxygenation
  - FIO2
  - Oxygen saturation
- Group C: Visual
  - Secretions color
  - Secretions quality
  - State of awareness

Last group of variables are categorical and informed by patients' relatives; rules for the normality of such variables are given by doctors.

Then the rules to determine static risk, from Level 1 (stable) to Level 4 (abnormal), take, topically, the following form:

1. Assign Level 1 if any of the following conditions apply:
   i. All indicators are in normal ranges.
   ii. Only one indicator, different from the ones in Group B, present a moderate deviation from normal.
2. Assign Level 2 if any of the following conditions apply:
   i. Temperature and cardiac or respiratory frequency are in abnormal levels.
   ii. If visual variables are not at normal level.
3. Assign Level 3 if any of the following conditions apply:
   i. Visual variables present a clear deviation from normality.
   ii. Vital sign are as a whole far from normal.
4. Assign Level 4 if any of the following conditions apply:
   i. Oxygenation presents alteration.
   ii. Vital signs and visual signs are clearly abnormal.

There is also a dynamic risk that is determined by the temporal behavior of the previous variables.

These rules are preliminary and should be refined, using the Macro2 in Figure 6.12, by their experimental application that permits validation. The ongoing pilot implementation of the hardware and software that allows monitoring will generate the data to do this.[15]

CHAPTER 7

Conclusions

General

As proposed by Spohrer and Demirkan,[1] the idea of "integrating scientific, engineering, and management disciplines to innovate in the services that organizations perform to create value for customers and shareholders that could not be achieved through disciplines in isolation" produces impressive results when there is an approach that orchestrates innovation and value generation. Our version for this integration is what we call Business Engineering, which is a hierarchical top-down approach allowing systemic design of a complete enterprise, or part of it, starting from Strategy and Business Model, putting them into practice by determining needed Capabilities and Business Design, and finishing with processes and IT support design that make the whole innovation operative. The proof that this approach works is empirical, with its application to many real cases, successfully implemented, in very different situations in manufacturing, distribution, financial services, government services, and health, both private and public.

Another important conclusion is that it is possible to continuously formalize and structure design experience in patterns—business, architecture, and processes—that provide innovation design ideas at different levels of the proposed design hierarchy. We have shown in all the cases presented that innovations are accelerated when a design pattern is used, specializing it to the particular situation, which is much more efficient and effective than to start design from a scratch or from so-called as-is models.

The use of a hierarchical design approach based on patterns has also the advantage of allowing to position at the right place the integration of Spohrer and Demirkan's disciplines when performing service innovations. Thus, for example, as we have presented in this book, quantitative marketing—with the tools of Data Mining—is used to model customers needs and options; Management Science allows characterizing providers' logistic; Economics theory permit to model competitors' behavior; knowledge management and change management define people's roles in service change; Industrial Engineering and Information Sciences provide the tools for information analysis and supporting IT tools definition; and all these disciplines as well as Strategic Planning, Analytics—as Optimization Models and Business Analytics—process modeling and design, project management and others serve as a basis to generate ideas to produce and implement a design that realizes and innovation that generates value for the customers and stakeholders.

Students at the Master in Business Engineering (MBE) at the University of Chile develop projects as part of their thesis; then all the knowledge and experience gathered from the cases, some of which have been reported in this book, are being continuously incorporated into existing patterns as well as new specialized ones for domains such as health. This means that reuse of knowledge incorporated into the patterns is increasingly used in areas of new applications and this produces a virtuous circle: knowledge generated enrich the patterns and permit generating new ones. Additionally, this creates the possibility that, when very detailed patterns exist in a domain, general software solutions can be developed to support the detailed process patterns. Subsequently, general flexible solutions—including business, processes, and software design—can be developed for a domain, which can be specialized to particular cases. The advantage of this approach, as compared to ERP, is in the feasibility of customizing the whole design, from business to software, with reasonable effort, especially when this is combined with process execution, using BPMN models and a Business Process Management Suites (BPMS). We have already shown that this approach is feasible in the health domain; a detailed conclusion of the same is stated in the next section of this chapter.

One last general conclusion concerns the power of a well-defined design approach as the one we propose, with appropriate tool support, to make possible that students with little or no experience generate solutions in complex cases in a short period of time. This has been the situation in all the cases in the health sector as reported, with results that will be elaborated later.

Health Care Cases

The case of the private hospital, reported in Chapters 3 and 4, reinforces the conclusions of the previous section that there is a large potential for service innovation in all kinds of businesses. In fact, the hospital, in this case, which is recognized as one of the best in Latin America, completely reformulated its Strategy and investment initiatives generation and evaluation by means of a design that assures developing new services that maximize value for the stakeholders. Thus, the hospital maintains its competiveness by the continuous services innovation that is generated by well-designed processes and supporting systems.

In the public hospital cases, presented in Chapter 3 to 6, value has been generated in several dimensions: quality, efficiency, and fairness. These objectives, defined in detail in Chapter 2, are related to ideas proposed by Porter and Teisberg and Christensen et al.[2] The important result here proves that very significant improvements can be obtained in all these objectives by using the approach we propose for service design. In particular, we have stressed the increase in quality and fairness that can be generated in public hospitals, with no additional resources, by designing service to patients taking into account all the relevant variables, as opposed to current emphasis on the reduction of waiting lists ordered by time of first medical service request. We have proved that this is basically a wrong approach, in which government has wasted tens and possibly hundreds of millions of dollars to reduce such lists, by giving extra resources, which can be spent in private hospitals, to eliminate the patients who have waited a longer time since they entered the lists, in a first-in-first-out (FIFO) rule. The solution we have designed and implemented in various hospitals is to prioritize patients according to type of pathology and aggravating factors, which means, as proposed by Porter and Teisberg and Christensen et al., to provide the right service at the right time. We have actually proved that many patients with severe risk for their lives have been overlooked with current waiting list management and that our solution gives the correct ordering of patients. This has been publicly acknowledged by doctors, who have actively participated in the determination of the rules that define priorities, and also by several hospitals' directors. Other cases that have provided more quality and fairness are the ones that have allowed designing hospital's right configuration of services and capacity to insure a predetermined service level for patients. This was done for emergency services and for surgical services. Behind these cases, the idea is also of optimizing the level of resources by providing what is strictly necessary to give the desired service level.

The results on the efficiency objective are extremely important, since we have been able to show that there is a high potential for productivity improvements in public hospitals. We executed work on two fronts to prove this. First, the hospitals' efficiency was compared with analytical techniques that allowed determining what is called "efficiency frontier," which defines hospitals that perform better than the rest. Then, for hospitals that perform poorly, typically 20 to 30 percent below, as compared to those on the frontier, investment initiatives can be defined to "move" these hospitals up to better efficiency levels. The important factor here is that the health sector investments can be optimized by acting over hospitals where there is sure return in better productivity. To facilitate this we designed processes that can pinpoint those hospitals and determine the specific performance variables that should be acted upon to ensure results. The second way in which we contributed to increase hospitals' efficiency was to select key resources and show that they can be used more efficiently. We proved this for surgical facilities or operating rooms, for which we showed that their use can be increased up to 20 percent more than today, under similar conditions and, possibly, up to 50 percent, if resources are better planned and monitoring and control are exerted over them. As a matter of fact, this is one of the key projects on which we are working currently. Also in the line of efficiency we have shown, in Chapter 3, how to manage innovation and change in networks of public health facilities oriented to define projects that improve use of resources and, possibly, increase quality at the same time. Finally, we have presented cases for emergency services, in Chapters 3 and 4, which are also important in terms of efficiency improvements and also quality. These cases show that configuration and capacity can be designed, using Analytics, to assure a desired quality level and, at the same time, use the right amount of resources; also that the chaotic flow of emergency services can be improved by using predictive models to forecast problems and try to prevent them, and flow monitoring to detect situations that require actions to speed up patients or to avoid wasting of resources.

Another important line of work presented in this book is a preventive approach in chronic diseases. Thus we have shown that it is possible to develop analytical models for crisis' prediction for this type of disease, allowing preventive actions to avoid health risks. Two cases were presented in Chapter 6: one related to diabetes patients in a private hospital and another for children with respiratory problems in a public hospital, which are treated at their homes; this last case is particularly impressive, since it allowed the possibility of optimizing a solution that is not only good for patients, but also liberates beds at the hospital, which is very scarce resource. Such solution is now routinely working at the hospital.

A complementary factor to the preceding objective has been relevant, which is the speed with which solutions can be developed. For example, we have been able to generate proposed designs for key parts of health service in a couple of months and implemented solutions in less than six months. Among others, solutions already working routinely in at least three hospitals are the design of emergency service configuration implemented with the introduction of a Triage, which has been automated in one case, and a fast-track line; emergency monitoring and capacity planning, resulting in a reduction of patient waiting time; demand analysis for surgery waiting list prioritization, which has reduced the list by about 50 percent and greatly improved the decisions on who is to be operated first, including the identification of many cases of patients who have been overlooked with a risk for their lives. But the most important result is that all the designs we have done so far for hospitals services, which are based on general patterns, are common and can be easily applied to other hospitals with small adaptations, which is facilitated by the fact that they are based on formal BPMN models and can be easily edited in specializing them to particular situations at a given hospital. As a matter of fact, we are already replicating the solutions in hospitals not involved in the initial development.

An extension of the work that we are developing is the execution of BPMN models by using Business Process Management SuitsService Oriented Architecture (BPMS-SOA) technology. We have implemented the patient prioritization in ambulatory services and operating room scheduling using open BPMS technology, described in a case in Chapter 6, and proved that it is feasible to execute the complete pattern workflow, including forms for people interaction with the system, using web services for the implementation of the analytical support and invocations to databases that contain the data needed for execution. The key result expected with these extensions is the capability of incrementing flexibility and rapidity in implementing our general design patterns for services design.

The pattern-based design approach supported by BPMS modeling and execution makes possible that the solutions developed would be eventually used in all Chilean public hospitals.

Finally, the cases for Enterprise Architecture design for public health in Chapters 2, 3, and 4 show that it is feasible to do formal design for very complex health structures. Such designs provide a well-founded and economically sound solution for very acute problems, such as innovation to improve quality of service and improve efficiency. This is in the line of several proposals that have been made in the literature to improve health, among others the one presented by a group of experts to President Obama,[3] recommendations by Porter and Teisberg[4] and findings at the University of Pennsylvania.[5] We feel we are contributing with solutions related to such proposals.

Notes

Prologue

1. Information about the Master in Business Engineering can be obtained at its website MBE (2016), where there are links to Facebook, Linkedin, and Twitter; also the blog Barros (2016b) contains books, papers, and theses related to the MBE.
2. Brocke and Rosemann (2010).
3. Alexander (1964).
4. Gamma, Helm, Johnson, and Vlissides (1995).

Chapter 1

1. IBM Research (2004).
2. Chesbrough and Spohrer (2006); Spohrer, Maglio, Bailey, and Gruh (2007); Spohrer and Maglio (2008); Maglio, Kieliszewski, and Spohrer (2010).
3. Barros (2004).
4. Barros (2004, 2007, 2016a); Barros and Julio (2010a, 2010b, 2011); Barros et al. (2015); Barros, Seguel, and Quezada (2011); Barros and Aguilera (2015).
5. Porter (1996).
6. Hax and Wilde (2001); Hax (2010).
7. Johnson, Christensen, and Kageman (2008).
8. Osterwalder and Pigneur (2009).
9. Nagji and Tuf (2012).
10. Barros (1998, 2000, 2004, 2005, 2007, 2016a); Barros and Julio (2011).
11. Many real application cases developed at the Master in Business Engineering, mentioned in the Prolog, are documented in Barros (2004, 2007, 2016a, 2016b) and the site MBE (2016).
12. White and Miers (2009).
13. Pant and Juric (2008); Barros and Julio (2011).

Chapter 2

1. Porter (1996).
2. Hax and Wilde (2001).
3. Rohwedder and Johnson (2008).

4. Farhoomand, Ng, and Cowley (2003).
5. Johnson, Christensen, and Kageman (2008); Osterwalder and Pigneur (2009).
6. Farhoomand, Ng, and Cowley (2003).
7. Johnson, Christensen, and Kageman (2008).
8. Farhoomand, Ng, and Cowley (2003).
9. Johnson, Christensen, and Kageman (2008).
10. Osterwalder and Pigneur (2009).
11. Davenport, Cohen, and Jacobson (2005).
12. Davenport (2006); Davenport and Harris (2007).
13. Rud (2009).
14. Der Aalst (2011); Liu (2007); Witten, Frank, and Hall (2011).
15. Davenport (2013).
16. McKinsey (2011a).
17. McAffe and Brynjollfson (2012).
18. Dell (2014).
19. Barros (2016a).
20. Davenport (2013).
21. Lloyd (1982).
22. Alsabti, Ranka, and Singh (1997).
23. This topic is covered in detail in Tsiptsis and Choriannopoulos (2009).
24. SPSS (2016).
25. Rapid Miner (2016).
26. Pentaho (2016).
27. Castellanos et al. (2009).
28. Pant and Juric (2008).
29. Der Aalst (2011).
30. There has been important developments in Machine Learning the last 10 years which are summarized in LeCun, Bengio, and Hinton (2015).
31. McAffe and Brynjollfson (2012).
32. LeCun, Bengio, and Hinton (2015).
33. Sherman and Zhu (2006, 2013).
34. Barros and Aguilera (2015).
35. This section on forecasting is based on the paper by Barros et al. (2015).
36. See Adya and Collopy (1998) for a discussion of over fitting on this type of models.
37. Chen, Lin, and Schölkopf (2005); Smola and Schölkopf (2004).
38. Vapnik (1995).
39. Smola and Schölkopf (2004).
40. Vapnik (1998).

41. Cherkassky and Ma (2004).
42. Kuhn (1955).
43. Burkard, Dell'Amico, and Martello (2009).
44. Applegate and Cook (1991).
45. White and Miers (2009).
46. OMG (2013).
47. IDEF0 (1993).
48. Barros and Julio (2011).
49. Barros et al. (2015).
50. Barros and Quezada (2015).
51. The problem of different levels of design and appropriate representation by using BPMN constructs is discussed in Barros and Julio (2009) and Barros and Julio (2011).
52. This section is based on Porter and Teisberg (2006, 2007).
53. This was the result of the thesis of E. Quiroz for the Master in Business Engineering.
54. Defined by Hax and Wilde (2001).
55. Christensen, Grossman, and Hwang (2009).
56. White House Executive Office (2014).
57. Moses (2010).
58. McKinsey (2011a).
59. Knowledge@Wharton (2016).
60. DRG (*Diagnosis-related Group*) is a methodology to standardize the production of multiple different outputs of a hospital, for which a weighted measure has been proposed. In the literature, the use of DRG as an adjustment of hospital's production is common since it has been empirically observed that the relative weights are related to hospital's costs as proposed by Fetter (1991).
61. The strategic concepts come from Porter (1996), Hax and Wilde (2001) and Hax (2010), which were summarized in the Strategy section of this chapter.
62. Based on the definition of Johnson, Christensen, and Kageman (2008). Porter (1996); Hax and Wilde (2001).
    Based on the definition Business Model in this chapter.
63. Pant and Juric (2008).
64. Barros (2004, 2016a).
65. Kaplan and Norton (2001).
66. Barros (2016a).
67. Barros et al. (2015).
68. Cito Research (2015).
69. Abu-Mostafa (2012).
70. Davenport, Dalle Mule, and Lucker (2011).

71. Asthmapolis (2016).
72. McKenna (2013).
73. This data on the Asthmapolis experience is taken from www.atelier.net/en/trends/articles/asthmapolis-tracks-asthma-symptoms-attaching-sensors-inhalers_418579
74. Barros (1998, 2000, 2004, 2005, 2007); Barros and Julio (2010a, 2010b, 2011).
75. Porter (1996).
76. Ross, Weill, and Robertson (2006).
77. These economic concepts and their relevance to business design are given in Barros (2000, 2004, 2016a); many references to papers in English on the subjects covered are given in these publications; they are summarized in the first volume of this book.
78. This presentation of hospitals architecture is based on Barros and Julio (2010b, 2011).
79. Barros and Julio (2011).
80. Barros and Aguilera (2015).
81. Hax (2010).

Chapter 3

1. This case is a summary of the thesis of Patricio Anguita for the Master in Business Engineering; it is available in MBE (2016).
2. Porter and Teisberg (2006).
3. Christensen, Grossman, and Hwang (2009).
4. Agency theory is summarized in previous volume; classical reference is Arrow (1985).
5. Moses (2010).

Chapter 4

1. The pattern for "New Capabilities Development" is included in the previous volume "Business Engineering and Service Design" of this editorial and also documented in Barros (2000, 2004, 2005, 2007, 2016a).
2. PMBOK (2016).
3. Barros (2016a).
4. A summary of agency theory is presented in the previous volume "Business Engineering and Service Design" of this editorial. Classical reference is Arrow (1985).
5. Farrell (1959).

6. All the economics summary of DEA and its application to hospitals is based on the thesis of Ismael Aguilera for the Master in Business Engineering; the thesis is available in MBE (2013) and a paper summarizing its findings is Barros and Aguilera (2015).

7. Charnes, Cooper, and Rhodes (1978).

8. Banker, Charnes, and Cooper (1984).

9. Jacobs (2000).

10. Charnes et al. (1994).

11. Valdmanis (1992).

12. Dyson, Thanassoulis, and Boussofiane (1990).

13. Hollingsworth (2008).

14. Andersen and Petersen (1993).

15. Xue and Harker (2002).

16. O'Neill and Dexter (2004).

17. O'Neill (1998).

18. GAMS (2013).

19. Hollingsworth (2008).

20. Pettengill and Vertrees (1982); Health Information Systems (2006); Wynn and Scott (2008).

21. Fetter (1991).

22. Fetter et al. (1980).

23. Wynn and Scott (2008).

24. Health Information Systems (2006).

25. Charnes, Cooper, and Rhodes (1978).

26. O'Neill and Dexter (2004).

27. This case is based on work done by Maria Jose Gorigoitia for the Master in Business Engineering; the thesis is available at MBE (2016).

28. These techniques are summarized in the previous volume "Business Engineering and Service Design" of this editorial and detailed in Barros et al. (2015).

29. Zhang et al. (2009).

30. ProModel Tutorial (2011).

Chapter 5

1. See for example, Armstrong (2001).

2. A summary of these methods is presented in previous volume "Business Engineering and Service Design" of this editorial.

3. Barros et al. (2015).

4. Law and Kelton (2001).

Chapter 6

1. This case is based on the thesis of Patricio Wolff for the Master in Business Engineering; the thesis is available at www.tesis.uchile.cl/
2. The ILP model and an alternative heuristic are detailed in Wolff, Duran, and Rey (2012).
3. This case is based on work done by Alejandro Quezada for the Master in Business Engineering; it is available at www.tesis.uchile.cl/
4. This is the conclusion of a study made by Health Authorities reported in MINSAL (2010).
5. Edwards (1994).
6. Espallargues and Commas (2004).
7. Lack (2000).
8. Dennet (1998).
9. Activiti (2013).
10. Hibernate Framework (2016).
11. Ibatis Framework (2013).
12. This case is based on the MBE thesis of E. Quiroz; see in www.tesis.uchile.cl/
13. Barros (2007); Barros and Julio (2011).
14. This presentation is based on the MBE thesis of M. Echeverría; see in www.tesis.uchile.cl/
15. This project was started by the author, based on the experience of Asthmapolis reported by McKenna (2013); the implementation of the physical monitoring hardware and software was done by another group and the hospital has reported, as this book goes into printing, that the whole design was successful and it is routinely working.

Chapter 7

1. See the Systems-Discipline Matrix in the Prolog of this book.
2. Porter and Teisberg (2006, 2007); Christensen, Grossman, and Hwang (2009).
3. White House Executive Office (2014).
4. Porter and Teisberg (2006).
5. Knowledge@Wharton (2016).

References

Abu-Mustafa, Y.S. 2012. "Machines that Think for Themselves." *Scientific American* 289, no. 7, pp. 78–81.

Activiti. 2013. "Activity Tutorial." Retrieved August 10, 2016 from www.activiti. org/

Adya, M., and F. Collopy. 1998. "How Effective are Neural Nets at Forecasting and Prediction? A Review and Evaluation." *Journal of Forecasting* 17, pp. 451–61.

Alexander, C. 1964. *Notes on the Synthesis of Form*. Cambridge, MA: Harvard University Press.

Alsabti, K., S. Ranka, and V. Singh. 1997. *An Efficient k-means Clustering Algorithm* (Paper 43). Syracuse, NY: Electrical Engineering and Computer Science, Syracuse University.

Andersen, P., and N.C. Petersen. 1993. "A Procedure for Ranking Efficient Units in Data Envelopment Analysis." *Management Science* 39, no. 10, pp. 1261–64.

Applegate, D., and W. Cook. 1991. "A Computational Study of the Job-Shop Scheduling Problem." *INFORMS Journal on Computing* 3, no. 2, pp. 149–56.

Armstrong, J.S. ed. 2001. *Principles of Forecasting*. Norwell, MA: Kluwer Academic Publishers.

Arrow, K. 1985. "Principals and Agents: The Structure of Business." In *The Economics of Agency*, eds. J.W. Pratt and R.J. Zeckhauser. Cambridge, Mass: Harvard Business School Press.

Asthmapolis. 2016. Last Retrieved August 30 from www.propellerhealth. com/2012/07/10/asthmapolis-receives-fda-clearance-asthma-inhaler-sensor-technology-accompanying-software-system/

Banker, R.D., R.F. Charnes, and W.W. Cooper. 1984. "Some Models for Estimating Technical and Scale Inefficiencies in Data Envelopment Analysis." *Management Science* 30, no. 9, pp. 1078–92.

Barros, O. 1998. *Modelamiento Unificado de Negocios y TI: Ingeniería de Negocios*. (Paper CEGES 5). Santiago: Industrial Engineering Department, University of Chile. Retrieved October 10, 2016 from www.researchgate. net/publication/289377779_INGENIERIA_DE_NEGOCIOS_DISENO_ INTEGRADO_DE_SERVICIOS_SUS_PROCESOS_Y_APOYO_TI_-_ DISENO_DE_LOS_SISTEMAS_DE_APOYO_A_LOS_PROCESOS

Barros, O. 2000. *Rediseño de Procesos de Negocios Mediante el Uso de Patrones*. Santiago: Dolmen Ediciones.

Barros, O. 2004. *Ingeniería e-Business: Ingeniería de Negocios para la Economía Digital*. ed. J.C. Sáez. Chile: Press Santiago.

Barros, O. 2005. "A Novel Approach to Joint Business and Information System Design." *Journal of Computer Information Systems XLV* 45, no. 3, pp. 96–106.

Barros, O. 2007. "Business Process Patterns and Frameworks: Reusing Knowledge in Process Innovation." *Business Process Management Journal* 13, no. 1, pp. 47–69.

Barros, O. 2016a. "Ingeniería de Negocios: Diseño Integrado de Negocios, Procesos y Aplicaciones TI." Amazon Kindle e Books www.amazon.com/Kindle-eBooks/

Barros, O. 2016b. "Master in Business Engineering." Retrieved October 10, 2016 from blog.obarros.cl

Barros, O., and C. Julio. 2009. *Integrating Modeling at Several Abstraction Levels in Architecture and Process Design.* BPTrends. www.bptrends.com

Barros, O., and C. Julio. 2010a. *Enterprise and Process Architecture Patterns.* BPTrends. www.bptrends.com

Barros, O., and C. Julio. 2010b. *Application of Enterprise and Process Architecture Patterns in Hospitals.* BPTrends. www.bptrends.com

Barros, O., and C. Julio. 2011. "Enterprise and Process Architecture Patterns." *Business Process Management Journal* 17, no. 4, pp. 598–618.

Barros, O., R. Seguel, and A. Quezada. 2011. "A Lightweight Approach for Designing Enterprise Architectures Using BPMN: An Application in Hospitals: 3rd International Workshop on BPMN, Lucerne, Business Process and Notation (BPMN)." *Lecture Notes in Business Information Processing* 95, no. 2, pp. 118–23.

Barros, O., and A. Quezada. 2015. "Integrated Modeling of Business Architecture and Process Design with BPMN: Application to Hospitals." *Journal of Enterprise Architecture* 10, no. 1, p. 7.

Barros, O., and I. Aguilera. 2015. "Planning Resource Assignment in Public Hospitals: Promoting Innovation and Efficiency." Retrieved August 10, 2016 from www.researchgate.net/publication/273258652_PLANNING_RESOURCE_ASSIGNMENT_IN_PUBLIC_HOSPITALS_PROMOTING_INNOVATION_AND_EFFICIENCY_Oscar_Barros_and_Ismael_Aguilera

Barros, O., R. Weber, C. Reveco, E. Ferro, and C. Julio. 2015. "Demand Forecasting and Capacity Planning for Hospitals." Research Gate. Retrieved August 10, 2016 from www.researchgate.net/publication/274390870_Demand_Forecasting_and_Capacity_Management_for_Hospitals

Brocke, J.V., and M. Rosemann. eds. 2010. *International Handbook on Information Systems.* Berlin, Germany: Springer.

Burkard, R., M. Dell'Amico, and S. Martello. 2009. *Assignment Problems.* Philadelphia, PA: SIAM.

Castellanos, M., K.J. Alves de Medeiros, J. Mendling, B. Weber, and J.M.M. Weijters. 2009. "Business Process Intelligence." In *Handbook of Research on*

Business Process Modeling, eds. J. Cardoso and W.M.P. van der Aalst. New York: Information Science Reference.

Charnes, A., W.W. Cooper, and E. Rhodes. 1978. "Measuring the Efficiency of Decision Making Units." *European Journal of Operational Research* 2, no. 6, pp. 429–44.

Charnes, A., W.W. Cooper, A.Y. Lewin, and L.M. Seiford. 1994. *Data Envelopment Analysis: Theory, Methodology and Applications.* Boston, MA: Kluwer Academic Publishers.

Chen, P.H., C.J. Lin, and B. Schölkopf. 2005. "A Tutorial on V-Support Vector Machines." *Applied Stochastic Models in Business and Industry* 21, no. 2, pp. 111–36.

Cherkassky, V., and Y.Q. Ma. 2004. "Practical Selection of SVM Parameters and Noise Estimation of SVM Regression." *Neural Networks* 17, no. 1, pp. 113–26.

Chesbrough, H., and J. Spohrer. 2006. "A Research Manifesto for Services Science." *Communications of the ACM* 49, no. 7, pp. 35–40.

Christensen, C.M., J.H. Grossman, and J. Hwang. 2009. *The Innovator's Prescription: A Disruptive Solution for Health Care.* New York: McGraw-Hill.

Cito Research. 2015. "End Small Thinking about Big Data." Retrieved August 10, 2016 from www.citoresearch.com/data-science

Davenport, T.H., D. Cohen, and A. Jacobson. 2005. *Competing on Analytics.* (Working Knowledge Research Report). Babson Park, MA: Babson Executive Education.

Davenport, T.M. January 2006. Competing on Analytics. *Harvard Business Review* 84, no. 1, pp. 98–107.

Davenport, T.M., and J.G. Harris. 2007. *Competing on Analytics: The New Science of Winning.* Cambridge, MA: Harvard Business Press.

Davenport, T.H., L. Dalle Mule, and J. Lucker. December 2011. "Know What Your Customers Want Before They Do." *Harvard Business Review* 89, no. 12, pp. 84–92.

Davenport, T.H. December 2013. "Analytics 3.0." *Harvard Business Review* 91, no. 12, pp. 64.

Dell. 2014. *Seeing the Big Picture.* Dell Software Solutions and Services, Case Study 10013464.

Dennet, E. 1998. "Generic Surgical Priority Criteria Scoring System: The Clinical Reality." *New Zealand Medical Journal* 111, no. 1065, pp. 163–66.

Der Aalst, W.M.P. 2011. *Process Mining Discovery, Conformance and Enhancement of Business Processes.* Berlin, Germany: Springer.

Dyson, R.G., E. Thanassoulis, and A. Boussofiane. 1990. *Data Envelopment Analysis. Tutorial Papers in Operational Research.* Birmingham, England: Operational Research Society.

Edwards, R. 1994. "An Economic Perspective of the Salisbury Waiting List for Coronary Bypass Surgery." *New Zealand Medical Journal* 110, no. 1037, pp. 26–30.

Espallargues, M., and M. Comas. 2004. "Elaboración de un sistema de priorización de pacientes en lista de espera para cirugía de catarata, artroplastia de cadera y artroplastia de rodilla: Resumen de los resultados principales." *Breus AATRM Septiembre*, pp. 1–11.

Farhoomand, A.F., P.S. Ng, and W. Cowley. 2003. "Building a Successful E-Business: The FedEx story." *Communications of the ACM* 48, no. 4, pp. 84–89.

Farrell, M.J. 1957. "The Measurement of Productive Efficiency." *Journal of the Royal Statistical Society Series* 120, no. 3, pp. 253–78.

Fetter, R.B., Y. Shin, J.L. Freeman, R.F. Averill, and J.D. Thompson. 1980. "Case Mix Definition by Diagnosis-Related Groups." *Medical Care* 18, no. 2, pp. 1–53.

Fetter R.B. 1991. "Diagnosis Related Groups: Understanding Hospital Performance." *Interfaces* 21, no. 1, pp. 6–26.

Gamma, E., R. Helm, R. Johnson, and J. Vlissides. 1995. *Design Patterns: Elements of Reusable Object-Oriented Software*. Reading, MA: Addison-Wesley.

GAMS (General Algebraic Modeling System). 2013. Retrieved August 10, 2016, from www.gams.com/

Hax, C., and D.L. Wilde. 2001. *The Delta Project*. New York: Palgrave Macmillan.

Hax, C. 2010. *The Delta Model: Reinventing Your Business Strategy*. Berlin, Germany: Springer Verlag.

Health Information Systems. 2006. *International Refined Diagnosis Related Groups v2.1. Definitions Manual 2006*. Vol 1. Salt Lake City, UT: 3M Health Information Systems.

Hibernate Framework. 2016. Retrieved August, 2016 from www.hibernate.org/

Hollingsworth, B. 2008. "The Measurement of Efficiency and Productivity of Health Care Delivery." *Health Economics* 17, no. 10, pp. 1107–28.

Ibatis Framework. 2013. Retrieved August 10, 2016 from http://ibatis.apache.org/

IBM Research. 2004. "Service Science: A New Academic Discipline?" Retrieved August 10, 2016 from www.almaden.ibm.com/asr/resources/facsummit.pdf

IDEF0 (Integrated Computer Aided Manufacturing). 1993. *FIPS Release of IDEFØ* (Publication 183). Gaithersburg, MD: Computer Systems Laboratory of the National Institute of Standards and Technology (NIST).

Jacobs, R. 2000. *Alternative Methods to Examine Hospital Efficiency: Data Envelopment Analysis and Stochastic Frontier Analysis*. Centre for Health Economics (Discussion Paper 177). York, England: The University of York.

Johnson, M.W., C.M. Christensen, and H. Kageman. December 2008. "Reinventing Your Business Model." *Harvard Business Review* 86, no. 12, pp. 57–68.

Kaplan, R.S., and D.P. Norton. 2001. *The Strategy-Focused Organization: How Balanced Scorecard Companies Thrive in the New Business Environment.* Cambridge, MA: Harvard Business Press.

Knowledge@Wharton. 2016. "Medical Waste: Why American Health Care Is So Expensive." Last Retrieved August 30 from http://knowledge.wharton.upenn.edu/

Kuhn, H.W. 1955. "The Hungarian Method for the Assignment Problem." *Naval Research Logistics Quarterly* 2, nos. 1–2, pp. 83–97.

Lack, A. 2000. "Weights for Waits: Lessons from Salisbury." *Journal of Health Services Research and Policy* 5, no. 2, pp. 83–88.

Law, A.M., and W.D. Kelton. 2001. *Simulation Modeling and Analysis.* New York: McGraw-Hill.

LeCun, Y., Y. Bengio, and G. Hinton. 2015. "Deep Learning." *Nature* 521, no. 7553, pp. 436–44.

Liu, L. 2007. *Web Data Mining: Exploring Hyperlinks, Contents and Usage Data.* Berlin, Germany: Springer.

Lloyd, S.P. 1982. "Least Squares Quantization in PCM." *IEEE Transactions on Information Theory* 28, no. 2, pp. 129–37.

Maglio, P.P., C. Kieliszewski, and J. Spohrer. 2010. *Handbook of Service Science: Research & Innovations in the Service Economy.* France: Lavoisier.

MBE (Master of Business Engineering). 2016. Retrieved August 10, 2016 from www.mbe.cl

McAffe, A., and E. Brynjollfson. October 2012. *Big Data: The Management Revolution.* Boston: Harvard Business Publishing.

McKenna, M. March 2013. "The New Age of Medical Monitoring." *Scientific American* 308, no. 3, pp. 33–34.

McKinsey. May 2011a. *Big Data: The Next Frontier on Innovation, Competition and Productivity.* McKinsey Quarterly.

Moses, J. Springer 2010. "Flexibility and Its Relation to Complexity and Architecture." *Complex Systems Design & Management*, pp. 197–206.

Nagji, N., and G. Tuf. May 2012. "Managing Your Innovation Portfolio." *Harvard Business Review* 90, no. 5, pp. 66–74.

OMG (Object Management Group). 2016. "Object Management Group BPMN Specifications." Retrieved August, 2016, from www.omg.org/spec/BPMN/2.0.2/PDF/

O'Neill, L. 1998. "Multifactor Efficiency in Data Envelopment Analysis with An Application To Urban Hospitals." *Health Care Management Science* 1, no. 1, pp. 19–27.

O'Neill, L., and F. Dexter. 2004. "Evaluating the Efficiency of Hospitals Perioperative Services Using DEA." *Operations Research and Health Care,* pp. 147–68.

Osterwalder, A., and Y. Pigneur. 2009. *Business Model Generation.* Hoboken, NJ: Hoboken Publications.

Pant, J., and M.B. Juric. 2008. *Business Process Driven SOA Using BPMN and BPEL: From Business Process Modeling to Orchestration and Service Oriented Architecture.* London, England: PACKT Publishing.

Pentaho. 2016. "Weka." Retrieved August 2016 from http://weka.pentaho.com/

Pettengill, J., and J. Vertrees. 1982. "Reliability and Validity in Hospital Case-Mix Measurement." *HCFR* 4, no. 2, p. 101.

PMBOK (Project Management Body of Knowledge). 2016. "Guide and Standards. Project Management Institute." Retrieved August 10, 2016 from www.pmi.org/pmbok-guide-standards

Porter, M.E. November–December 1996. *What is Strategy?* Harvard: Harvard Business College.

Porter, M.E., and E.O. Teisberg. 2006. *Redefining Health Care: Creating Value-Based Competition on Results.* Cambridge, MA: Harvard Business School Press.

Porter, M.E., and E.O. Teisberg. 2007. "How Physicians Can Change The Future of Health Care." *Journal of the American Medical Association* 297, no. 10, pp. 1103–11.

ProModel Tutorial. 2003. "Modeling and Simulation software Products." Retrieved August 10, 2013 from www.promodel.com/products/

Rapid Miner. 2016. "Rapid Miner Studio." Retrieved August 10, 2016 from https://rapidminer.com/

Rohwedder, C., and K. Johnson. 2008. "Pace-Setting Zara Seeks More Speed to Fight its Rising Cheap-Chic Rivals." *The Wall Street Journal,* February 20, p. 20.

Ross, J.W., P. Weill, and D.C. Robertson. 2006. *Enterprise Architecture as Strategy.* Cambridge, MA: Harvard Business School Press.

Rud, O. 2009. *Business Intelligence Success Factors: Tools for Aligning Your Business in the Global Economy.* Hoboken, NJ: Wiley & Sons.

Sherman, H.D., and J. Zhu. 2013. "Analyzing Performance in Service Organizations." *MIT Sloan Management Review* 54, no. 4, p. 37.

Smola, A.J., and B. Schölkopf. 2004. "A Tutorial on Support Vector Regression." *Statistics and Computing* 14, no. 3, p. 19.

Spohrer, J., P.P. Maglio, J. Bailey, and D. Gruh. 2007. "Steps Toward a Science of Service Systems." *Computer* 40, pp. 71–77.

Spohrer, J., and P.P. Maglio. 2008. "The Emergence of Service Science: Toward Systematic Service Innovations to Accelerate Co-Creation of Value." *Production and Operations Management* 17, no. 3, pp. 238–46.

SPSS (Statistical Package for the Social Sciences). 2006. "Predictive Analytics Enterprise." Retrieved August 10, 2016 from www-03.ibm.com/software/products/es/spss-predictive-analytics-enterprise

Tsiptsis, K., and A. Choriannopoulos. 2009. *Data Mining Techniques in CRM: Inside Customer Segmentation*. Hoboken, NJ: Wiley & Sons.

Valdmanis, V. 1992. "Sensitivity Analysis for DEA Models: An Empirical Example Using Public Versus NFP Hospitals." *Journal of Public Economics* 48, no. 2, pp. 185–205.

Vapnik, V. 1995. *The Nature of Statistical Learning*. Berlin, Germany: Theory Springer-Verlag.

Vapnik, V. 1998. *Statistical Learning Theory*. Hoboken, NJ: Wiley & Sons.

White House Executive Office. 2014. "Report to the President, Better Health and Lower Costs: Accelerating Improvement Through Systems Engineering." Council of Advisors on Science and Technology. Retrieved August 10, 2016 from www.whitehouse.gov/sites/default/files/microsites/ostp/PCAST/pcast_systems_engineering_in_healthcare_-_may_2014.pdf

White, S.A., and D. Miers. 2009. *BPMN Modeling and Reference Guide*. Lighthouse Pt, FL: Future Strategies Inc.

Witten, I., E. Frank, and E.M. Hall. 2011. *Data Mining: Practical Machine Learning Tools and Techniques*. 3rd ed. Burlington, MA: Morgan Kaufmann.

Wolff, P., G. Durán, and P. Rey. 2012. "Modelos de Programación Matemática para Asignación de Pabellones Quirúrgicos en Hospitales Públicos." *Revista Ingeniería de Sistemas* 26.

Wynn, B.O., and M. Scott. 2008. *Evaluation of Alternative Methods to Establish DRG Relative Weights*. RAND Working paper. Santa Monica, CA: RAND.

Xue, M., and P. Harker. 2002. "Ranking DMUs with Infeasible Super-Efficiency DEA." *Management Science* 48, no. 5, pp. 705–10.

Zhang, B., P. Murali, M. Dessouky, and D. Belson. 2009. *A Mixed Integer Programming Approach for Allocating Operating Room Capacity*. Los Angeles, CA: Department of Industrial and Systems Engineering, University of Southern California.

Index

OTHER TITLES IN OUR SERVICE SYSTEMS AND INNOVATIONS IN BUSINESS AND SOCIETY COLLECTION

Jim Spohrer, IBM and Haluk Demirkan, Arizona State University, Editors

- *Modeling Service Systems* by Ralph Badinelli
- *Sustainable Service* by Adi Wolfson
- *People, Processes, Services, and Things: Using Services Innovation to Enable the Internet of Everything* by Hazim Dahir, Bil Dry, and Carlos Pignataro
- *Service Design and Delivery: How Design Thinking Can Innovate Business and Add Value to Society* by Toshiaki Kurokawa
- *All Services, All the Time: How Business Services Serve Your Business* by Doug McDavid
- *Obtaining Value from Big Data for Service Delivery* by Stephen H. Kaisler, Frank Armour, and William Money
- *Service Innovation* by Anders Gustafsson, Per Kristensson, Gary R. Schirr, and Lars Witell
- *Matching Services to Markets: The Role of the Human Sensorium in Shaping Service-Intensive Markets* by H.B. Casanova
- *Business Engineering and Service Design, Second Edition, Volume I* by Óscar Barros

Announcing the Business Expert Press Digital Library

Concise e-books business students need for classroom and research

This book can also be purchased in an e-book collection by your library as

- a one-time purchase,
- that is owned forever,
- allows for simultaneous readers,
- has no restrictions on printing, and
- can be downloaded as PDFs from within the library community.

Our digital library collections are a great solution to beat the rising cost of textbooks. E-books can be loaded into their course management systems or onto students' e-book readers.
The **Business Expert Press** digital libraries are very affordable, with no obligation to buy in future years. For more information, please visit **www.businessexpertpress.com/librarians**. To set up a trial in the United States, please email **sales@businessexpertpress.com**.